White Hip Hoppers, Language and Identity in Post-Modern America

This book examines language and identity among White American middle and upper-middle class youth who affiliate with Hip Hop culture. Hip Hop youth engage in practices that range from the consumption of rap music and fashion to practices like MCing (writing and performing raps or "rhymes"), DJing (mixing records to produce a beat for the MC), graffiti tagging, and break-dancing. Cutler explores the way in which these young people stylize their speech using linguistic resources drawn from African American English and Hip Hop slang terms. She also looks at the way they construct their identities in discussions with their friends, and how they talk about and use language to construct themselves as authentic within Hip-Hop. Cutler considers the possibility that young people experimenting with AAVE-styled speech may improve the status of AAVE in the broader society. She also addresses the need for educators to be aware of the linguistic patterns found in AAVE and Hip Hop language, and on ways to build on Hip Hop skills like rhyming and rapping in order to motivate students and promote literacy.

Cecelia A. Cutler received her Ph.D. from New York University in 2002. She is currently an associate professor at Lehman College. Her research explores the speech practices of white Hip Hoppers and how they construct their authenticity linguistically and discursively. She has published pieces in the *International Journal of Bilingualism, Journal of Sociolinguistics, Language and Linguistics Compass, Journal of Linguistic Anthropology, Language Variation and Change,* and *Language and Education.*

Routledge Studies in Sociolinguistics

White Hip Hoppers, Language and Identity in Post-Modern America

By Cecelia A. Cutler

Routledge
Taylor & Francis Group

NEW YORK AND LONDON

First published 2014
by Routledge
711 Third Avenue, New York, NY 10017

and by Routledge
2 Park Square, Milton Park, Abingdon, Oxon OX14 4RN

Routledge is an imprint of the Taylor & Francis Group,
an informa business

© 2014 Taylor & Francis

Library of Congress Cataloging-in-Publication Data

Cutler, Cecilia A.
  White hip-hoppers, language and identity in post-modern America /
Cecelia A. Cutler.
     pages cm. — (Routledge studies in sociolinguistics ; 8)
    Includes bibliographical references and index.
  1. Hip-hop—Influence—United States.   2. Hip-hop—Social aspects—
United States.   3. Language and culture—United States.   4. Group
identity—United States.   5. Sociolinguistics—United States.   I. Title.
    P40.5.H552U55   2014
    306.44089'09073—dc23
    2013036701

ISBN: 978-0-415-89004-5 (hbk)
ISBN: 978-1-315-85816-6 (ebk)

Typeset in Sabon
by Apex CoVantage, LLC

This book is dedicated to my parents, Joanie and Garr Cutler, who taught me to be curious about the world, and to my two grandmothers, Dr. Coral Gordon Bolin and Dr. Virginia Farrar Cutler, who showed me by example what women with much greater challenges than I could accomplish.

Contents

Figures

Tables

Abbreviations

AAE (African American English)
HHN (Hip Hop Nation)
HHNL (Hip Hop Nation Language)
MTV (Music Television)
NYU (New York University)
r-Ø (post-vocalic /r/-lessness)
US (United States)

Transcription Conventions

[ ]	IPA phonetic transcription
[	overlapping with previous turn
=	latching (one turn immediately followed by another)
–	false start
ALL CAPS	loud or emphatic enunciation
(( ))	non-verbal utterances; prosody; speech inaudible; plausible utterance
// //	stage directions
Bold	instance usage or content relevant to discussion.
Italics	ironic or emphatic tone
[-AGR]	lack of subject-verb agreement (They is going).
[POSS]	possessive pronoun
[-INVERSION]	negative inversion; when a negated auxiliary or modal precedes a quantificational (or indefinite; e.g., Ain't nobody who can beat him)
[-CONCORD]	negative concord or "multiple negation"; when more than one negative element appears in a clause (e.g., He **don't** know **nothin'**)
[-AUX]	omission of auxiliary do/does
Ø	zero copula (absence of *is/are*)
(r-Ø)	post-vocalic /r/-lessness ("car" pronounced "kah")
(r-1)	post-vocalic /r/-fulness ("car" pronounced "kar")
(rr)	emphatic or hyper-rhotic realization of post-vocalic /r/
(light /l/)	apical realization of /l/; articulated with the tip rather than the blade of the tongue

Preface

I began my journey into sociolinguistics while training to be a high school social studies teacher at New York University. I was assigned by Phil Hosay to write a term paper for a course about cultural socialization which gave me the chance to explore the work of William Labov, particularly his groundbreaking work on the rule-governed nature of African American Vernacular English. When I eventually entered the classroom, I was baffled by the difference between the way I spoke as a native of the Pacific Northwest and the speech of my students in the New York City public schools, most of whom were from immigrant or ethnic minority backgrounds and who spoke varieties of English that I often found difficult to understand. Later, after enrolling in the M.A. program in Linguistics at New York University in 1994, I became curious about Hip Hop culture and how young people who affiliated with it, regardless of their ethnic background, appeared to be adopting African American English features in their speech as part of their personal identity display. I have been exploring the various dimensions of this phenomenon and the broader topic of people who adopt language varieties and styles other than the ones they grew up with ever since, in an attempt to arrive to a better understanding of how and to what extent "outgroup" language use is bound up with personal identity versus fleeting alignments and stances in interaction.

I am not, nor do I claim to be, a scholar of Hip Hop (unlike many of my colleagues who write about similar themes, H. Samy Alim, Marcy Morgan, Awad Ibrahim, Geneva Smitherman, and Alastair Pennycook among others). However, the direction of my research has taken me quite a ways out of linguistics and into the realm of Hip Hop culture, critical race studies, whiteness studies, and cultural studies. These diversions have been enormously informative to me as a sociolinguist and have, I hope, made my work more accessible to a general readership.

In 2007, I was asked to present some of my work at the Language and Hip Hop Culture in a Globalizing World workshop at the University of Illinois, Urbana-Champaign. One of the participants who was not a linguist threw up her arms during the discussion period, asking why any of this mattered, and what difference it makes whether a speaker has a 25% rate of copula absence or is almost entirely non-rhotic. Her challenge to me and to the field of sociolinguistics as a whole is to answer these "real world" sorts of questions: What is the social meaning of sociolinguistic variation? What can it tell us about the relationship of different groups of people to one another in society and the broader structure of society? And can it tell us anything about ongoing social changes? This book endeavors to situate the phenomenon of white hip hop youth and their language practices within the cultural context of a still quite racialized US social order. Among other questions, this research leads us to ask whether attitudes towards African American English might be shifting in a more positive direction because of the enormous popularity of Hip Hop culture in the US and globally, and because white youth use features of it to style their speech. Most of us who follow language in society are aware of how negative language attitudes are closely bound up with attitudes towards groups of people and that without changing the status of those groups, changing attitudes towards their language can be very challenging. While harboring no illusions about how negatively the speech patterns of African Americans continue to be viewed, as the 1996 Ebonics controversy following the actions of the Oakland School Board so painfully showed us, it also suggests that people are becoming more aware of linguistic diversity.

Acknowledgements

I feel very relieved to have arrived at this point in the writing process. Acknowledging the wonderful individuals who have shaped my thinking, supported me, tolerated my weaknesses, and shown me how to be a better scholar. First I must thank a group of wonderful professors and mentors at New York University including John Singler, Renee Blake, Bambi Schieffelin, Gregory Guy, and Anna Szabolsci. I particularly want to acknowledge John Singler, Renee Blake, and Bambi Schieffelin for all of the fabulous speakers they invited to the Sociolinguistics Working Group and Linguistics Symposia over the years and for ongoing support throughout the writing of my dissertation and beyond. I want to acknowledge my fellow students at New York University who made me feel like my work mattered—Anna Trester, Meredith Josey, Zvjezdana Vrzic, Philipp Angermeyer, Sonya Fix, Ken Lacy, Aria Adli, Erika Solyom, Maryam Bakht, and Keith Fernandes. I am particularly indebted to a group of scholars who invited me to present my data at NWAV 1996, encouraged me to publish it, and who ultimately steered me towards new ways to think about my data—Ben Rampton, Mary Bucholtz, and Miriam Meyerhoff. I will always be grateful to another group of scholars for their foundational work in sociolinguistics and Hip Hop linguistics including Samy Alim, Geneva Smitherman, Awad Ibrahim, and Marcy Morgan. Most recently, I have received enormous support from a group of colleagues in Europe who invited me to present at the Sociolinguistics Symposium 16 in Limerick and the Sociolinguistics Symposium 19 in Berlin, including Jacomine Nortier, Margreet Dorleijn, and Bente Svendsen. I am particularly thankful for the opportunity to present my work at the University of Oslo in 2011 given me by Bente Svendsen and Unn Røyneland, and to Unn Røyneland in particular for inviting me to the University of Chicago in 2012. Each of these invitations helped me to develop my work further and to see the connections with similar phenomena in Norway and other parts of Europe. At my home university, the City University of New York, I have been given wonderful opportunities to teach, present, invite speakers, and collaborate by and with my colleagues Ricardo Otheguy, Gita Martohardjono, Michael Newman, Miki Makihara, Joye Smith-Munson,

Margo DelliCarpini, Nikki Fayne, Gaoyin Qian, Nancy Dubetz, and Imm-aculée Harushimana.

I will always remember my first opportunity to publish the material in Chapter 2, which came from Miriam Meyerhoff and which appeared in the *University of Pennsylvania Working Papers* in 1997, and later in the *Journal of Sociolinguistics* in 1999. I would be remiss not to express my gratitude to Mary Bucholtz for inviting me to contribute an article to the *Journal of Linguistic Anthropology* which became Chapter 3. I would also like to extend special thanks to Malcah Yaeger-Dror and Tom Purnell for suggestions on improving the analysis, to Greg Guy whose model I employed, and to the anonymous reviewers for help with the content of Chapter 4. I am indebted to Jacomine Nortier and to Margreet Dorleijn and Jacomine Nortier for putting together a Special Issue of the *International Journal of Bilingualism* in 2008 in which the material for Chapter 5 first appeared. I am enormously grateful to Awad Ibrahim, Samy Alim, and Alistair Pennycook for inviting me to contribute the material that appears here in Chapter 6. Lastly, I owe a debt of gratitude to Jacquelyn Rahman and to Marina Terkourafi for inviting me to present the material that went into Chapter 7 and to Marian Terkourafi for her careful editing of the volume in which it appeared: *The language(s) of global hip-hop*.

I would also like to acknowledge Marlene Hennessey who told me about the "writing oasis" that is also known as the Wertheim Room at the New York Public Library and to Jay Barksdale for granting me access to this incredible place.

I am enormously thankful to Lehman College for granting me release time and to PSC-CUNY for grant money that assisted me in the initial stages of writing the book in 2008–2009, to the CUNY Faculty Fellowship Publication Program (2010), and to my mentor and fellow colleagues there who gave me enormous confidence in the development of the proposal for this book.

I also wish to express special thanks to New York University for supporting my research through graduate and teaching assistanceships from 1997–2000 and the Dean's Dissertation Fellowship from 2000–2001. I must also acknowledge the enormous help I got from Ms. Beth Malchiodi's social science research students at Brooklyn Technical High School in conducting interviews including Lien Ly, Andrew Marshall, Julia Bonsignore, Eugene Babenko, Oswald Espinoza, and "Kitoko." Sara Siebold, Melissa Manousis, and other members of Project 5 at New York University were enormously helpful in gathering interviews and allowing me to be a "participant observer" at their meetings and events, and also for providing me with insider information about Hip Hop and rap music.

This work would not have been possible without the moral support of my husband Adam Snyder and my father, Garr, who dutifully waded through thickets of sociolinguistic jargon to make the final product more readable to non-linguists. Finally, I owe an enormous debt to all of the young people who participated in my project as interview subjects, and without whose goodwill and cooperation this book would not have been possible.

Permissions

The author and publishers would like to thank the following for permission to reproduce copyright material:

John Wiley and Sons for reprinting an excerpt from "Yorkville Crossing: A case study of hip hop and the language of a white middle class teenager in New York City," which appeared originally in the *Journal of Sociolinguistics* 3(4), 428–42, which is available at: http://onlinelibrary.wiley.com/journal/10.1111/%28ISSN%291467–9841

The American Anthropological Association for permission to reprint " 'Keepin' It Real': White Hip-Hoppers' Discourses of Language, Race, and Authenticity," from the *Journal of Linguistic Anthropology* 13(2), 1–23, which is available at: http://onlinelibrary.wiley.com/journal/10.1111/%28ISSN%291548–1395

To Sage for allowing me to reprint "Hip-Hop, White Immigrant Youth, and African American Vernacular English: Accommodation as an Identity Choice," and "Brooklyn Style: Hip Hop markers and racial affiliation among European immigrants." The final, definitive versions of these papers have been published in the *Journal of English Linguistics* 38(3), 248–69 and the *International Journal of Bilingualism*, 12(1–2), 2008 by SAGE Publications Ltd./SAGE Publications, Inc., All rights reserved. © 2010 and © 2008 respectively. These articles are available online at: http://ijb.sagepub.com/

To Taylor and Francis, LLC for permission to reprint "You shouldn't be rappin', you should be skateboardin' the X-games: The co-construction of whiteness in an MC Battle," which appeared in *Global linguistic flows: hip hop cultures, youth identities, and the politics of language*, edited by H. Samy Alim, Awad Ibrahim, and Alistair Pennycook, 2008.

To Bloomsbury (Continuum) for permission to reprint "She's so hood: ghetto authenticity on the White Rapper Show," which appeared in *The language(s) of global hip-hop*, edited by Marina Terkourafi, 2010. The original version is available at: www.bloomsbury.com/uk/the-languages-of-global-hip-hop-9780826431608/

1   Introduction
White Youth and the Appeal of Hip Hop Culture in the 1990s

INTRODUCTION: WHITE KIDS AND HIP HOP CULTURE

Since the mid-1990s, there has been a surge of academic manuscripts and books about Hip Hop coming out of cultural studies, musicology, urban studies, and sociology. The focus of most of this work is on Hip Hop as a form of cultural practice with implications for understanding popular music, subcultures, social change, and identity formation. The focus of this book, by contrast, is upon the language and identity practices of white American youth who affiliate with Hip Hop culture—a group that has not received a great deal of attention in studies of US Hip Hop or in the field of sociolinguistics in the US. As such, it provides a uniquely American perspective into the role of language in the construction of adolescent identity. Understanding the complicated role of language and its use among white Hip Hop youth in the US can provide insights for meaningful comparisons with similar processes in numerous countries and localities now that Hip Hop culture has gone global and is becoming indigenized and adapted to the needs of young people in local communities around the world.

My introduction to the language of white Hip Hop youth came back in the early 1990s when I overheard a friend's adolescent son, "Mike" (a pseudonym), engaging in a self-repair so as to use a linguistic form that I associated with African American English (AAE).[1]

Responding to his friend on the phone, Mike said, "I gotta ask—I mean *aks* my mom." That same year, he had begun dressing in the baggy style that characterized Hip Hop fashion in the 1990s. He would scrawl his "tag" (graffiti name) on the buildings around his affluent Manhattan neighborhood and began to change the way he spoke, adopting many patterns found in the speech of young African Americans in New York City. During his early teenage years, he continued to expand his verbal repertoire, adopting a wide range of Hip Hop expressions and structural patterns found in AAE. But Mike was not the only white kid who was drawn to Hip Hop during the 1990s and 2000s; young people in the US from every conceivable background were becoming fans of rap music, teaching themselves how to rhyme, and sporting Hip Hop fashions. In my subsequent research, I encountered a range of white teenagers from elite private high schools as well as more middle class public high schools in New York City, immigrant youth from Eastern Europe, and white college students at New York University who were drawn to the symbolic capital of urban African American Hip Hop culture and language and the rhetorical power of rap music.

The book explores the stories of these young people by focusing on how they stylize their speech using linguistic resources drawn from AAE (e.g., /ay/ glide reduction and the use of uninflected "be" as in "We *be* trippin") and Hip Hop lexis such as *bling* for "showy jewelry," and *bougie* meaning "upscale." It also examines how they construct their identities in discussions with their friends, and how they talk about and use language to construct themselves as authentic within Hip Hop. White Hip Hop youth are engaged in a complex identity project that may signal new trends in how young people construct and project their personae. Adopting ways of talking, dressing, walking, and dancing from other social groups (i.e., urban African American youth) is increasingly part of how young people shape their identities in late modernity (Rampton 2006). Furthermore, the normative status of African American youth within US Hip Hop (judging by the preponderance of African American rappers in US music charts and Hip Hop-oriented magazines) challenges white youth to establish themselves as legitimate participants in what is widely perceived to be a "black" space. This book explores the ways in which they go about this at the linguistic level, and the complications associated with using features of an ethnic style that is not one's "own" (Rampton 1995).

Indeed, Rampton (1995), Coupland (2007), and others have noted a shift that has been taking place in the developed world since World War II, in which the hierarchical class and ethnic structures that characterized previous periods began to give way to greater social and geographical mobility, resulting in a greater degree of social fragmentation, instability, and risk. Socially, people in these "post-modern" times are thought to have greater options in terms of lifestyle and a wider range of choices in terms of how they define themselves, which has, in turn, complicated social identities, social relationships, and social institutions. Coupland (2007) also observes that wider choices in terms of consumption allow people to take on the social attributes of different social classes, which changes the meaning of social class (30). Language, as a key resource for constructing social identity, functions alongside other stylistic markers such as clothing and other forms of behavior to give individuals a greater degree of agency in how they construct their identities. This book is directly concerned with these processes as they pertain to post-modern youth who, because of the spread of global media and access to digital images and music, have an ever-increasing array of ethnic and subcultural style choices in terms of how they wish to project their identities. The youth I describe, like generations of white American teenagers before them, are drawn to the music and culture of urban African American youth. This was reflected symbolically in the clothing they wore, how they walked, their gestures, and also in their language style, which draws on stylistic features of AAE and Hip Hop lexis, dubbed Hip Hop Nation Language (HHNL) by Alim (2004a).

Throughout the book, I use the term HHNL as a way to signal the subjectivity of white youth who see their language practices as a symbol of their affiliation with Hip Hop. However, because many of the features associated with HHNL derive from AAE, I often refer to them together as "HHNL/ AAE." I employ the racial identifiers "white" and "black" throughout the book, but recognize them as social constructs that have particular meanings in the US rather than biologically meaningful categories. So-called "white" Americans are thought to have European origins in addition to having white or fair skin even though in the past, the Irish, Jews, and Italians were not always included in this group. "Black" Americans in the US are narrowly defined as individuals who have any observable physical qualities that suggest sub-Saharan African ancestry (the so-called "one-drop" rule). In recognizing the essentialism of biological categories, some institutions and individuals use the more politically correct ethnic terms "African American" or "European American" rather than "black" and "white." But in practice racial and ethnic terms are used almost interchangeably in everyday discourse. The ethnic term "European American" is used much less often than "African American" due to the normative status of whiteness in American culture. Thus it is common to read about an "African American historian" or a "Latino activist" but not a "white historian" or a "white activist." In using the term "white" to describe the young people in this book, I hope to expose and challenge the normativity of whiteness by naming it, and making it more visible.

Some explanation is also needed for the term "African American English." Over the past fifty years, American sociolinguists have used a variety of terms to describe the language patterns and dialectal features associated with African Americans in the US. In the 1960s and 1970s, Labov (1966, 1972), Wolfram (1969), and others used terms such as Black English, Black English Vernacular, and Negro Dialect. These terms were replaced in the 1980s by African American Vernacular English (AAVE). But concerns about the inadequacy of the term "vernacular," particularly with regard to the speech of middle class, educated African Americans, led some to use the term African American English, or AAE, as a way to distinguish it from AAVE. Labeling the speech of all African Americans a "vernacular" has overtones of racism and essentialism and fails to describe the range of standard forms spoken by some (Morgan 1994). For that reason, some sociolinguists use the term African American English as a way to capture the full range of standard and non-standard, or "vernacular," varieties or dialects used by people of African American descent in the US (e.g., Morgan 1998; Spears 1998). A very similar term is African American Language (AAL), which Smitherman (1997) defines as a communication system that functions both as a resistance language and as a linguistic bond of racial and cultural solidarity for African Americans. The evolution of terminology among sociolinguists and dialectologists reflects an ongoing effort to legitimize the speech of African Americans by defining the rules that characterize its phonological and morphosyntactic patterns. By extension, these efforts have attempted to show that the speech of African Americans is both inherently logical and systematic and merits the status of a dialect or variety of English (Labov 1969).

In the wake of the controversy that followed the Oakland California School Board's Resolution to recognize the speech of its African American students as a separate language in late 1996, the term "Ebonics" (originally coined in the 1970s) gained widespread currency among members of the general American public. Sociolinguists like John Rickford and others made valiant efforts at the time to help the Oakland School Board draft a more informed resolution and to get prominent African American leaders to understand the nature of African American varieties of speech and the nature of the effort that the Oakland School Board was trying to make.

Despite these efforts, the public outrage that swept the country following the Ebonics controversy left little doubt as to the low status still accorded to the language of African Americans in the US, both among educated, liberal-minded journalists and public figures, as well as the general public (Rickford 1999). Yet during the same period, rap music, Hip Hop culture, and the language styles emerging from New York's urban African American youth were becoming ever more popular among white youth. Part of the draw for some white youth may have been the off-limits status of this speech variety and the fear and anger it arouses among adult authority figures. But for many others, including youth from most other ethnic backgrounds, it is just as much or more about signaling one's status as a fan of rap music and orientation towards Hip Hop culture. In other cases, and/or simultaneously, it may be a way to signal stances that draw on the indexical meanings of AAE (e.g., masculinity, hardness, street smarts, etc.).

THEORIZING LANGUAGE AND STYLE IN HIP HOP

The centrality of African American culture within Hip Hop culture is undisputed, as is the connection between AAE and the speech style associated with Hip Hop (Alim 2004a, Rose 1994, Morgan 2001, Pennycook 2007, Smitherman 1997). Scholars have used terms such as "Hip Hop Nation Language" (Alim 2004a) and "urban youth language" to describe the language of Hip Hop-affiliated youth (Morgan 2001), but no consensus has emerged about what to call it and what its status as a variety is. Nor has its relationship to AAE been investigated empirically in a comprehensive way.[2]

This is not to say that AAE is identical to the speech style associated with Hip Hop. There is a wide range of social and regional variation among speakers of AAE which is in part reflected in the linguistic differences among rappers who come from different parts of the country and from different social backgrounds. African American rap artists are generally speakers of some regionally and socially defined variety of AAE, but may also participate in some degree of lexical and morphosyntactic innovation and variation when they rhyme and freestyle. Hip Hop youth who are not AAE speakers must engage in a process of conscious learning of the speech patterns they associate with Hip Hop, but which often originally come from AAE, and their linguistic repertoire typically includes styles they grew up with as well as HHNL/AAE-styled speech.

Given the degree of overlap with AAE in terms of phonology, morphosyntax, and lexis, one possible approach is to call the language style associated with Hip Hop a register, or a special kind of language produced in particular social situations by speakers to index a common affiliation. Ferguson (1994), in describing registers, writes, "People participating in recurrent communication situations tend to develop similar vocabularies, similar features of intonation, and characteristic bits of syntax and phonology that they use in those situations" (20; e.g., sports announcer talk, news, sermons, legalese, etc.). Yet, the notion of register fails to describe the more quotidien and identity-laden linguistic displays that I have observed among Hip Hop youth.

An alternative approach is to draw on various theoretical conceptions of "speech style," "styling," and "stylization" (Coupland 2001, 2007; Eckert 2003, 2008; Rampton 1995, 2006). Departing from the Labovian conception of style as attention paid to speech, styling involves the use of variables linked to identity categories for constructing social meanings, social categories, and identity discursively (Eckert 2008). "To style dialect is to construct a social image or persona that inter-connects with other facets of a speaker's communicative design (ideational, relational, pragmatic, nonverbal) in a particular event or act" (Coupland 2001: 348). In other words, speakers agentively control and manipulate aspects of their speech to shape the way they wish to be seen by others. Coupland (2007) describes social styles as the language and clothing resources people use to make personal and interpersonal meaning and styling as the activation of this stylistic meaning (2–3). Stylization, in contrast entails the performative deployment of culturally familiar styles in sometimes playful and fleeting ways that deviate from the expected forms for a given speaking context (Coupland 2001; Rampton 2006). Stylizing speakers speak in "altera persona," or "as if this were me" (Coupland 2001: 349). This contrasts with a great deal of traditional sociolinguistic/variationist research that generally assumes that individuals speak in their own voices or in "propria persona" (Coupland 2001: 349).

Speakers often style aspects of their social identities such as place of origin, gender, ethnicity, sexuality, and class in ways that often involve making new meanings out of "old" social categories in discourse (Coupland 2007: 138). Describing the relationship between stylistic practice and the creation of social meaning, Ochs (1991), writes that

[S]tandard language is associated with education, institutional affiliation, homogeneity, and conservatism; vernaculars, by contrast, are associated with an anti-institutional stance, local orientation, diversity of contact, and local innovation. Standard and vernacular language features manifest themselves in stylistic practice not simply as elements of ready-made ways of speaking but as resources for the construction of more complex styles. Particular linguistic features may on occasion directly index social categories, but more commonly they index particular stances (such as toughness or intellectual superiority) that are constitutive of those categories (cited in Eckert 2003: 113).

Thus, stylistic practice involves the use of particular enregistered or culturally noticed styles (Agha 2007) in order to signal temporary stances, alignments, and personae (Eckert 2008). Such an understanding of style suggests that it works both as a fundamental tool in the projection of identity, but also in the more ephemeral projection of temporary alignments and stances that typify everyday interactions among speakers. Styles are also clearly rooted in local understandings of the valence of local varieties of language because of the associations between locally recognized groups and ways of talking (i.e., language ideologies). This is illustrated by Ben Rampton's work on British adolescents in which the strategic/playful and ritualized use of West Indian Creole forms symbolized assertiveness, verbal resourcefulness, and opposition to authority, whereas Asian English stood for a surfeit of deference and dysfluency (Rampton 2010).

Adopting the concept of style to describe the speech of white Hip Hop youth allows for an interpretation of their language practices that encompasses the expression of identity as well as more ephemeral alignments that emerge in interaction. Drawing on a range of stylistic markers including phonological, morphological, and syntactic features, lexical items, expressions, and paralinguistic markers such as teeth sucking from HHNL, allows Hip Hop youth to project their participation in and affiliation with Hip Hop culture. As noted, many of these stylistic markers are found in AAE, including phonological features like the reduction of the /ɑy/ glide in words like *time* and *style,* and the variable use of morphosyntactic markers such as the Ø-copula (We __ bad) and Ø subject-verb agreement (They _was_ messed up).[3] By using the style to describe the language practices of my informants, I am attempting to distinguish their speech from those who were socialized as speakers of AAE from childhood. For white Hip Hop youth to adopt a speech style reflects the idea that language is part of a semiotic system that contributes to the construction of identities and stances in interaction.

One nagging question pertaining to this kind of data (i.e., styling that involves features of ethnic varieties) is precisely what meanings speakers wish to convey in deploying such style markers (cf. Nortier 2008; Eckert 2008; Jaspers 2008). However, unlike the more systematic distribution of speech markers that one would tend to find in social interactions between two speakers of AAE, styling involves a more symbolic or emblematic use of such features in ways that index stereotypical qualities or traits associated with certain speakers of AAE (e.g., urban, often male, Hip Hop-affiliated African American youth). Coupland (2007) asserts that there is a limit to which the kind of styling demonstrated by white teens such as "Mike" (referred to above) can be called "ethnic styling," because the African Americanness of this way of talking, while indexing coolness and hardness, is incidental, reflecting "the historical origins of Hip Hop rather that its current values for young people" (128). And indeed, it would be simplistic to conclude that white Hip Hop youth are drawn primarily to AAE rather than to Hip Hop.

Yet, the instrumental role of language use in the projection of social identity is a widely held belief in sociolinguistics and in society at large. Indeed, as Hall (1995) writes, "the ideological link between language and ethnicity is so potent that the use of linguistic practices associated with a given ethnic group may be sufficient for an individual to pass as a group member" (cited in Bucholtz 1995: 355). The following example (1) illustrates how Hip Hop outsiders assume that white Hip Hop youth are trying to "talk black" or even to project a black identity. When PJ, a 16-year-old young man of Russian-Jewish heritage, was asked if anyone had ever told him that he was trying to sound black, he replies that this happens repeatedly (as indicated by the habitual marker BE in line 1), but says that he doesn't let it bother him. His use of AAE syntactic markers such as the absence of the copula in the first line, multiple negation ("ain't nobody's business") in the second line, and discourse markers such as "you know what I'm saying" in the last line, give some indication as to why people might assume he's trying to sound black.

> PJ: People—people **BE** callin' me a wannabe, but I don't know what they Ø talking about, you know. I'm just doin' my thing. I'm just handlin' my business. What I do **ain't nobody's** business, **you know what I'm saying**, except for mine.

PJ's comment illustrates that there is an important distinction to be drawn between the stylistic use of HHNL/AAE features and the desire to project membership in the AAE speech community. Hip Hop youth, in employing features of HHNL (along with other forms of semiotic display such as clothing, gestures, and styles of walking), signal their preference for rap music and participation in various forms of Hip Hop practice such as writing rap lyrics ("rhyming"), break dancing, graffiti art, battling, DJ-ing, and freestyling ("ciphers"), and certain traits associated with urban African American youth.

As Eckert (2008) observes, material style (clothing and other forms of adornment) provides important clues to the study of linguistic style. Before oversized clothes became the norm in the mid-1990s, Hip Hop youth ("homeboys") simply wore their regular-sized jeans lower down at hip-level, which forced them to walk with their feet in a wide stance to keep the pants from falling down.[4] This style is said to have derived from the way prisoners walk, because they are not allowed belts. Thus, for the wearers, this style may have symbolic ties to the culture of prisons, criminality, and gang culture. In the early 1990s, African American and Latino male Hip Hop youth began wearing pants size several sizes larger than their waist and low on the hips, revealing brightly colored boxer shorts or designer briefs. They also often wore some form of head covering such as a knitted cap pulled down low to obscure the eyes, a baseball cap worn backwards, a "doo rag" (a thin, nylon wrap tied at the back of the head), and even ski masks in winter. These styles were quickly adopted by white youth who identified with Hip Hop culture in the mid to late 1990s.

Morgan (1996) interprets the oversized clothing and closely shorn hair as a way for non-African American young men to project ambiguous racial identities—something particularly important for white male Hip Hop youth who often want to play down their racial origins. Although few of the white Hip Hop youth I observed wore doo-rags, many did wear bandannas, which appeared to be a less racially marked imitation of the doo-rag look. In the 1990s, Hip Hop style for "homegirls" consisted of tight-fitting jeans or slacks and tops revealing some midriff and the hair was often worn long and pulled back in a very tight ponytail. However, some Hip Hop girls opted for the same baggy style as the boys, particularly girls who participated in Hip Hop performance genres such as MC battling. This may have been a way for them to liberate themselves from tight, revealing clothing as much as a way for them to free themselves from mainstream definitions of femininity, something Mendoza-Denton (1997) has written about in her ethnographic work on Chicana girl gangs in California.

The next two sections provide a brief overview of the history of Hip Hop culture and place white participation in Hip Hop within the context of other examples of white cultural appropriation in the United States.

HISTORY OF HIP HOP IN THE US AND GLOBALIZATION OF HIP HOP CULTURE

The term "Hip Hop" emerged in the mid-1970s during the early development of rap music. Dalzall (1996) writes that "without doubt, the most vigorous youth culture to arise since the demise of the hippie movement in the early 1970s has been the Hip Hop movement" (198). According to most accounts, Hip Hop was born in the South Bronx amidst rampant poverty, joblessness, and the controversial efforts to replace traditional "slum" neighborhoods with housing projects (Chang 2005). Rose (1994) writes that it was against this "bleak urban landscape" that black and Puerto Rican teenagers were able to forge "alternative local identities" through fashions, language, street names, and the establishment of neighborhood *crews* or *posses* (34). Kool DJ Herc is credited with creating the Hip Hop DJ style. Herc was born in Kingston, Jamaica, and moved to New York in 1967. Building on the connections between reggae and rap, Herc began to bring his sound system to block parties in the Bronx from 1969 onwards. By 1975, he was using the brief rhythmic sections of records to create beats at venues like the Hevalo in the Bronx (www.zulunation.com/).

There are a few different etymologies for the term Hip Hop. Some say it was created by DJ Hollywood, who would get up as he was playing records for the crowd and shout:

> To the Hip Hop the hippy hippy hippy hippy hop and you don't stop. This caught on and other pioneering DJs and JCs in Harlem and the Bronx picked up on it. It became the one expression used by everyone involved. Fans, when explaining the previous night's party experiences, would use the word Hip Hop to describe what type of party it was (Dalzall 1996: 213).

Afrika Bambaataa, founder of Zulu Nation and so-called "father of Hip Hop," has argued that it came from a Bronx MC named "Loveburg Starski" who used to always say, "Hip Hop, you don't stop" when he was performing (Dalzall 1996: 214).[5] " 'Before that, people used to call us ditty boppers or b-boppers,' says Bambaataa" (quoted in Dalzall 1996: 214).

Occasionally, people who write about Hip Hop use the terms "rap" and "Hip Hop" interchangeably. Walcott (1995) writes:

> Hip Hop as a cultural form encompasses everything from music, to clothing choices, attitudes, language and an approach to culture and cultural artifacts positing and collaging them in an unsentimental fashion (cited in Ibrahim 1998: 66).

Hip Hop is not synonymous with rap music. Rap music is the product of Hip Hop culture, specifically the artistic form resulting from DJ-ing and MC-ing. Rap is an important part of Hip Hop culture and constitutes one of its most commercially successful elements, but it is only one element. When asked to describe their culture, Hip Hop "heads" or aficionados (also written "headz" in Hip Hop orthography) almost uniformly say it is composed of "four pillars": writing (graffiti art or "graffing"), b-boying (break dancing), DJ-ing, and MC-ing. DJ-ing is the art of mixing records, especially the practice of "scratching" or manually reversing the direction of the record on the turntable with the needle in place to achieve a rhythmic backdrop for the MC (master of ceremonies). The MC, in turn, raps to the rhythm supplied by the DJ. The art of MC-ing is often called "rhyming," which may involve the performance of pre-scripted lyrics or the spontaneous creation of rhymes, called "freestyling." DJ-ing was the predominant form in the 1980s, but the 1990s witnessed the rise in prominence of MCs, e.g., Sean "Puffy" Combs, Snoop Doggy Dog, Nas, Nelly, Raekwon, and more recently white MCs like Eminem. MC "battles" now proliferate where DJ battles once did.[6]

In some cases, the term Hip Hop is used to denote music that has more of an inclusive, progressive message and rap is reserved for the radical, Afro-centrist genre. The term rap is also applied to the gangster or "gangsta" rap genre much more frequently than it is to the R & B-influenced style of female rappers like Lil' Kim. In the present study, however, I follow the widespread practice of using the term "rap" to refer specifically to music and "Hip Hop" to refer to the culture more generally.

The words "rap" and "rapping" predate the emergence of rap music and Hip Hop culture. According to Smitherman (1997), these words once had connotations among African Americans of "romantic, sexualized interaction," usually initiated by a man "for purposes of winning the affection and sexual favors of a woman," but by the late 1960s, rapping came to mean "any kind of strong, aggressive, highly fluent, powerful talk" (Smitherman 1997: 4; cf. Kochman 1972).[7] Smitherman (1997) writes that rap music is "rooted in the black oral tradition of tonal semantics, narrativizing, significa-tion/ signifyin', the dozens/playin' the dozens, Africanized syntax, and other communicative practices" (4).

Although the media frequently talk about genres like "gangsta rap" and "booty music," Hip Hop youth say that they tend to think of rap in geographical terms. Unlike rock music that is classified on the basis of genres like "alternative," "nu metal," or "adult contemporary," terms like "East Coast," "West Coast," and "Southern" help to distinguish styles of rap. As I was gathering my data in the late 1990s, I interviewed Melissa Manousis of Project Five, an undergraduate Hip Hop club I was following at New York University, and she listed the following categories: West Coast rap, which is characterized by slow, grinding rhythms that are thought to evoke the car culture and slow-moving traffic of Los Angeles and Oakland; East Coast rap, which is usually more traditional and is what people think of when they think of Hip Hop; and Southern rap, which she described as "more bouncy." The term "alternative" refers to the kind of rap one does not typically hear on mainstream commercial radio, according to Manousis. Gangster rap is a salient category for Hip Hop youth as well, but they are more likely to see it as a subvariety of a particular regional type of rap (i.e., East Coast gangster rap vs. West Coast gangster rap). In recent years, Hip Hop scenes have emerged in other US cities including Minneapolis-St. Paul, Chicago, Detroit, St. Louis, Cleveland, Philadelphia, Memphis, Atlanta, New Orleans, Miami, and Houston.

The culture surrounding Hip Hop and the body of its "members" are referred to as "The Hip Hop Nation." Smitherman (1997) writes that rap music and African American rappers such as Treach of Naughty by Nature, Ice Cube, formerly of NWA (Niggas Wit Attitude), Chuck D of Public

Enemy, Ice-T, Queen Latifah, Snoop Doggy Dogg, Dr. Dre, Yo-Yo, Kam, Tupac Shakur and others are the artistic representatives of the Hip Hop Nation (4). But it is important to differentiate Hip Hop culture from black youth culture. Kitwana (1994) warns that

> although some elements of Hip Hop culture are indeed expressions of black culture, Hip Hop culture . . . cannot be defined or discussed as a carbon copy of black culture . . . Just as there are African retentions present in the African American experience, various aspects of Black American culture permeate and influence both Hip Hop culture and commercial popular culture (12).

Back (1996) describes the Hip Hop Nation as a multiracial group of young people with a unique worldview. He writes that Hip Hop was designated a "culture for the kids" that effectively makes "Black symbols and emblems equally accessible" to young people from different ethnic groups and nationalities (Back 1996: 215). According to Back, the Hip Hop nation has a "black culture" but its citizens are "multiracial" (1996: 215). As such, the Hip Hop Nation appears to be open to all and the criteria for membership would appear to have more to with a commitment to one's ideals (e.g., a commitment to racial acceptance and the economic fairness) than one's ethnic or even economic background (Wimsatt 1994).

White Youth and Hip Hop

In the view of many writers who have addressed the topic, white consumption of Hip Hop often plays on the most exaggerated stereotypes about black Americans. Samuels (1991) writes, "the ways in which rap has been consumed and popularized speak not of cross-cultural understanding, musical or otherwise, but of a voyeurism and tolerance of racism in which Black and White are both complicit" (251). Henry Louis Gates, Jr. blames black American rappers and their white American fans alike, saying they "both . . . affect and commodify their own visions of street culture" (cited in Samuels 1991: 251). But the most exaggerated depictions of "street culture" come out of the gangster rap style, heavily promoted by the music industry in the mid to late 1990s. Originally, gangster rap was an explicitly political genre, but by the mid-1990s, "materialism, licentiousness, dumb misogyny, and black-on-black violence had become the main themes of the genre" (Seabrook 2000: 74).

In a 2000 *Newsweek* interview, Chuck D of the rap group Public Enemy, by then in his early 40s, insisted that he didn't want to sound like "some bitter old man," but went on to say that Hip Hop's "verbal and video images of young black men strutting, rutting, and shooting only feeds racist stereotypes" (quoted in Samuel et al. 2000: 62). In the same interview, Chuck D laments that, "The endorsement of thugs is white people's fantasy of what they want us to be. It's minstrelsy because that's what white people want to believe about us—that' it's about 'money, cars, hos' [sic] for all of us" (Samuel et al. 2000: 62). Despite its problematic subject matter (or perhaps because of it), so-called "gangsta rap" was the salvation of the record business in the late 1990s. According to Seabrook (2000), gangsta rap rescued the music industry from stagnant rock music sales in the mid-1990s. By 1998, 81 million rap records had been sold, 70% by rough estimates to white fans, and the genre surpassed country as the most popular category in all pop music (Seabrook 2000: 76).

Many white male adolescents during this time were attracted to the very narrow definition of Hip Hop culture as synonymous with the gangster lifestyle. During the mid to late 1990s, at the height of this trend, some white teens formed "posses" in large urban centers and tried to live out their interpretation of gang-style activities. Sales (1996) documents one such group of very wealthy white teens in Manhattan who took to selling drugs to their prep school friends from hired limos.

But there were obvious limits to which affluent white youth could adopt the Hip Hop and particularly the gangster lifestyle. Dalzall (1996) notes that,

> Unlike [during] the hippie movement where anyone could don a tie-dye shirt and become a weekend hippie, the Hip Hop culture did not provide a lifestyle that most American young people could completely embrace. Simply put, white teenagers could not, as much as they might wish to, become black. They could and did, however, listen to the music, dress the dress (emphasis on high-cost sneakers, sagging pants, hooded baggy sweat-shirts, and baseball caps), mirror the haircuts, adopt the rap vocabulary suitable for their daily lives, mimic the cadence of street speech, and admire from a safe distance the lives of prominent black rappers and athletes (200).

Paradoxically for Samuels (1991), where the assimilation of black street culture by Whites once required a degree of human contact, "the street is now available at the flick of a cable channel– to black and white middle class alike" (251). Hank Shocklee of Public Enemy decries this sort of "safe" participation as an extension of consumer culture to the creation of identity:

> People want to consume and they want to consume easy. If you're a suburban white kid and you want to find out what life is like for a black city teenager, you buy a record by N.W.A. It's like going on an amusement park and getting on a roller-coaster ride—records are safe, they're controlled fear, and you always have the choice of turning it off. That's why nobody ever takes a train up to 125th Street and gets out and starts walking around because then you're not in control anymore: it's a whole other ball game (cited in Samuels 1991: 251–52).

The rootedness of Hip Hop and rap music in African American cultural traditions and contemporary urban socioeconomic conditions calls for a measure of scrutiny when it comes to white participation (particularly that of suburban and upper middle class Whites). Indeed, the cultural distance between middle class white kids and their urban black and Latino counterparts led some white youth to romanticize the "ghetto" and fetishize urban, economically marginalized black youth. At its worst, the white appropriation of black cultural symbols smacks of long-standing and competing sentiments of hatred, fear, and desire that have characterized the relationship of Whites to Blacks in the US since the times of slavery. Samuels (1991) writes "'Rap's appeal to Whites rest[s] in its evocation of an age-old image of blackness: a foreign, sexually charged, and criminal underworld against which the norms of white society are defined, and by extension, through which they may be defied" (242).

Images of guns and gangsters are certainly not the only points of reference that Hip Hop has for young Americans. It is also possible for white youth to be mobilized by Hip Hop's social and political message, even if that message is not directed at them. Ironically, writes Potter (1995), "the more [Hip Hop] turns inward, [and] the more it addresses itself (as Tupac says in his second album, '*Strictly 4 my N.I.G.G.A.Z*'), the more certain white listeners want to hear it" (94). Nevertheless, Hip Hop serves to unite many young people who agree with its message.

> Hip Hop's gangsta revolutionary narratives bear with them a powerful political and emotional punch—provided that one actually gives them a listen. Not surprisingly, alliances have been formed via Hip Hop primarily among the younger generation of listeners, who are looking for (sub)cultural modes of identification, and finding them in Hip Hop messages and style (Potter 1995: 88–9).

These narratives soon began to resonate outside of the US, particularly among urban youth in Europe and Asia.

Global Hip Hop Culture

Early accounts of Hip Hop culture questioned the view that Hip Hop's only authentic cultural resonance is with the experience of urban African Americans (Bennett 1999; Gilroy 1993). Gilroy (1993) suggests that Black American Atlantic culture can and ought to be localized or reinterpreted to suit local needs. "The transnational structures which brought the black Atlantic world into being have themselves developed and now articulate its myriad forms into a system of global communications constituted by flows" (Gilroy 1993: 80; cited in Bennett 1999: 4).

Bennett (1999) writes (following Gilroy) that black culture thus becomes global culture, "its styles, musics and images crossing with a range of

different national and regional sensibilities throughout the world and initi-
ating a plurality of 'localized' responses" (4). Accordingly, Bennett (1999)
sees Hip Hop as a global form that gets "localized" or taken up and adapted
in ways that engage with local circumstances. He discusses the response to
Hip Hop in Newcastle (UK) and cites several early studies that examine
the uses of rap and aspects of Hip Hop style in Italy, France, Japan, and
Sweden (Bjürstrom 1997; Condry 1999; Mitchell 1996). In these studies,
young people identify with the struggles of African Americans and see Hip
Hop as a medium for expressing their own experiences with marginalization. Thus, as Potter (1995) observes, just as biblical images of the Hebrews
gave strength to American Blacks from slavery up until the Civil Rights
movement in the US, the black struggle has, in turn, become iconic of the
struggles of many other groups.

> However much a group would like to own its histories, they are inevi-
> tably going to have unexpected lines of influence; if the Jewish captivity
> in Egypt becomes a metaphor for slaves in the US, why shouldn't the
> alienation of young urban blacks strike a chord in the minds of other
> alienated groups, or individuals? . . . It is a mark of postmodernity that,
> even as the full 'ownership' of one's own oppression becomes impos-
> sible, its appropriation becomes a site of struggle (Potter 1995: 141).

For young people in Italy and France, Hip Hop was a vehicle for the discussion of subjects such as racism and police harassment (Androutsopoulos
and Georgakopoulou 2003; Mitchell 1996). Similarly, youth in Japan "take
the idiom of oppression common in American rap, and transform [it] into
an idiom of oppression against youth" (Condry 1999: 232). In Sweden,
ethnic minorities affiliated with Hip Hop as a form of resistance to white
skinhead style (Bjurström 1997), and for white youth in Newcastle, a community notable for the lack of an established black population, Hip Hop is a
celebration of blackness in the absence of black people. Furthermore, there
is a common perception among white Hip Hop enthusiasts in Newcastle
that "the essence of Hip Hop culture . . . directly bespeaks the white British
working class experience" (Bennett 1999: 16). Hip Hop is further localized
by performers in Newcastle who rap in the local Geordie dialect about local
problems like the excessive drinking and violence that characterize the city
center pub and club scene.

   Comparative work on Hip Hop in Japan suggests that for Japanese males
"Hip Hop style . . . is interwoven with the phallus as a signifier of a subtext
of masculine, heterosexual body power" (Cornyetz 1994: 115). Young men
seek to incorporate this power by remodeling themselves in Hip Hop style
and young Japanese women by procuring male African American lovers.
This, according to Cornyetz (1994), is bound to the same subtext of phallic
empowerment that inspires young men, but is "transgressive of assumed

(racially exclusive) Japanese male access to their sexual bodies and belittling of Japanese masculine identity" (115). Other studies of the response to Hip Hop around the world abound. Young people in many other countries, often from oppressed ethnic minorities, seem to identify in a profound way with the political messages they hear articulated by African American Hip Hop artists. Tupuola (2000) describes the significance of Hip Hop among Maori young people in New Zealand who are reformulating it to fit their own issues and frustrations.

The role of rap among the large numbers of disenfranchised North African youth in the ethnically ghettoized suburbs of Paris was the subject of a number of studies during the 1990s (Boucher 1998; Bazin 1995; Wacquant 1993; and others).[8] These young people adopted the dress, gestures, and even voice quality of the African American rappers they see on television. According to Boucher (1998), rap provides young people of African and North African heritage living in depressed urban centers the opportunity to express themselves and find an identity. But the *banlieues* are not the only places one can find Hip Hop fans in France. Much like some of the young people interviewed in this book, some wealthy young Parisians are attracted to the range of consumables offered by Hip Hop. Leland and Mabry (1996) observe:

> Rich kids from the 16th Arrondissement were returning from trips to New York, laden with the latest flavors: not just rap records but Air Jordan sneakers, break-dance steps, the slang, the attitudes. They came back with this music that was talking about life on the street. Though it started as simple appropriation, the French Hip Hop scene—rap, break-dancing and graffiti—soon developed its own voice. It is now less derivative of the United States than contiguous (42).

Yet another response to Hip Hop can be found among continental African immigrants and refugees from several African countries in Canada.[9] Ibrahim (1998) documents the role of Hip Hop in helping African immigrant youth to come to terms with being labeled "black" with all of its negative connotations in Canada—a category they were never faced with in their homelands.

"In their processes of translating the 'new' Canadian context, African students discovered that, given their blackness, they were already imagined, constructed, and thereafter treated as 'blacks'—with the historical memory and representation of blackness in North America which is mostly, if not all, negative. As a result of this construction and treatment, African students enter social processes of 'becoming' Blacks which were reflected in the way they dressed, the way they talked and the way they walked" (Ibrahim 1998: 282). The prestige of Hip Hop and African American youth culture was a way for them to assert agency over the ways they are perceived and labeled within Canadian society.

A study from the mid-1990s of the ways Hip Hop was taken up in Kenya found that this process was mediated by the kinds of images young people saw in rap videos and the prohibitive cost of rap music and Hip Hop fashions. Rebensdorf (1996) found that rap music CDs, magazines, and Hip Hop fashions were so expensive in Kenya that they were only available to the rich.[10] Furthermore, the prevalence of gangster rap videos on television programs and "the glamorization of material goods seemed to have the effect of disassociating many of the lyrical messages about poverty from parallel oppression in Nairobi's social system" (Rebensdorf 1996: 11). As a result, economically deprived young Nairobians were much more interested in reggae because it talked about the ghettos and because its performers were "ruff" and did not "dress up" (Rebensdorf 1996: 11). The fact that many of the American rappers were indeed speaking from ghettos about the oppression associated with such a marginalized position was lost on the vast majority of young people in Kenya.

More recent work on Hip Hop youth and the globalization of Hip Hop culture shows that its spread and influence have continued unabated since the late 1990s. Rap released in France, Italy and Spain spiked in 1995 as rap was becoming indigenized in those markets (Androutsopolous and Scholz 1998). American Hip Hop was ubiquitous in Brazil by the late 1990s, disrupting national discourses of racial unity by Hip Hop's emphasis on the black-white dichotomy (Roth-Gordon 2008). Hip Hop in Britain, also known as Brithop, was originally influenced by the Hip Hop scene in New York City and British rappers often adopted American accents in the early years before they gained the confidence to develop their own linguistic styles.

During the same period, France witnessed the proliferation of local rap groups such as MC Solaar, F. F. F., and Crew Assassin, particularly among North African and sub-Saharan African youth living in the *banlieues* of Paris and Marseille. Although English expressions like "get down" and "dealer" do show up in French rap, most artists rap entirely in French, in contrast to the rock music produced in France, which is mainly sung in English (cf. Cutler 2003b).

By the early 2000s, Hip Hop had gained a foothold across the globe and was rapidly in the process of being indigenized or "glocalized" (Alim 2009; Pennycook 2007). Recent work on Hip Hop in Germany, Hungary, and France shows that it is a tool for minority and immigrant youth to resist and challenge racial and societal injustice, to establish solidarity with fellow community members, and to strengthen their position in society (Androutsopoulos 2010; Hassa 2010; Simeziane 2010). Language is also an important part of this symbolic stance and in countries with large migrant populations such as Germany, France, the Netherlands, Denmark, Norway, and Sweden, it is quite typical to find elements of immigrant languages in the speech and lyrics of Hip Hop-affiliated youth in urban settings (Androutsopoulos 2010; Androutsopolous and Scholz 2003; Hassa 2010; Madsen 2009; Nortier and Dorleijn 2008; Opsahl and Røyneland 2008; Quist 2008).

Work on language and identity among urban youth in Oslo, Norway suggests that Hip Hop plays a decisive role in the creation and formation of a new multiethnolectal speech style, also dubbed "kebabnorsk" (Opsahl and Røyneland 2008). In Norway, immigrants as well as native-born youth are drawn to Hip Hop's oppositional symbolism and use language in ways that challenge standard language ideologies, which insist on the need for immigrants to use the standard language for their own benefit (Jaspers 2008). Urban rappers in Norway employ a multiethnic speech style characterized by a faster-paced, more staccato-sounding Norwegian, laced with a mix of English, Kurdish, Berber, and Arabic loans (Opsahl and Røyneland 2008). This speech style indexes speakers' identities as urban and multi-cultural, as well as their street-orientation, and the solidarity they feel towards other young people like them.

The Emergence of White Hip Hop Culture

Hip Hop has also undergone an internal transculturation, hybridization, and indigenization within the US among diverse groups of young people who are not African American. For some youth from immigrant backgrounds, Hip Hop is a kind of entrée into American culture, giving them a way to be American without having to embrace white identities, as will be discussed further in Chapter 5. Latino, Asian, North African, and other immigrant youth from economically marginalized groups identify with African Americans in much the same way as their counterparts in the suburbs of Paris and in the urban centers of many large European cities. Regardless of where they are living, Hip Hop gives immigrant youth a voice for expressing the frustration they feel when confronted with the racism, poor schools, and lack of opportunity that characterize their experiences (cf. Cutler and Royneland In Press).

In the US, Hip Hop represents one of many possible consumption-based subcultures that young people can identify with (i.e., Metal, Punk, Goth, etc.; Slomanson and Newman 2004). Some white American youth are drawn to the more essentialized, and arguably minstrelized, aspects of Hip Hop culture embodied by gangster rap, and reflect this orientation in their unabashed appropriation of African American symbols and language. For others, Hip Hop seems to be a way to mark their difference from the cultural mainstream, particularly from other subcultures like pop and rock. As discussed earlier, rap music also seems to fuel the escapist dreams of many white suburban youth who romanticize the urban black gangster lifestyle. Writing about the late 1990s, Strauss (1999) observed that "White kids are walking around calling each other 'nigga,' wearing T-shirts that say 'pimpin' ain't easy' and flashing gang signs they don't understand," concluding that white kids are "intrinsically attracted to Hip Hop because it is the only popular music genre that their rockist-music savvy baby-boomer parents just don't get" (28).

Some white middle class youth in the US use Hip Hop and HHNL as a way to express their own personal rebellion against parental or institutional authority or as a vehicle for expressing solidarity with the political struggles of oppressed groups. Still others seem to participate in Hip Hop with a sense of expiation for the historical and ongoing oppression of black people in the US and guilt for the privileges they enjoy as white, middle class Americans (cf. Wimsatt 1994). McRobbie (1996) attributes some of the same sentiments to British working-class youth:

> Black cultural forms reach out and touch many, often socially subordinate white young people who disidentify with racism through strongly identifying with aspects of black culture. Music, fashion and style thus make available a symbolic language for popular anti-racism (43).

Still others got involved in Hip Hop because of their political convictions, such as the members of an undergraduate club I followed at New York University from 1999–2001 called "Zulu Nation" and later "Project Five."[11] The members of this club came from all over the US, tended to be white, and shared a common interest in Hip Hop practices (rapping, DJ-ing, and break-dancing) as well as causes like the "No More Prisons" and the "Free Mumia" campaigns.[12] Communities of practice like "Project Five" are identifiable by common patterns of consumption and style and are strengthened through electronic forms of communication (Eckert and McConnell-Ginet 1995). Giroux (1996) views this tendency as a complex repositioning in the way many young people construct their identities today. "No longer associated with any one place or location, youth increasingly inhabit shifting cultural and social spheres marked by a plurality of languages, ideologies, and cultures" (Giroux 1996: 32; cf. Coupland 2001; Rampton 1995).

In the US, the popularity of Hip Hop among white youth since the mid-1990s has continued unabated. Many critics assumed that white rappers would eventually take over the genre much in the same way that white artists like Elvis Presley, the Beatles, and the Rolling Stones took over rock 'n' roll and the blues. Yet, despite a long list of white Hip Hop/rap artists and groups in the US during the 1980s and 1990s (e.g., Bubba Sparkxxx, Eminem, Kid Rock, Vanilla Ice, Beastie Boys, Limp Bizkit, Korn, 3rd Bass, Young Black Teenagers, and many others), most mainstream rap artists in the US are still African American and few would disagree that Hip Hop is rooted in African American youth culture (Alim 2004a; Smitherman 1997; Touré 1999).[13] Furthermore, white people and institutions traditionally figured prominently as objects of disdain and anger in politically-oriented Hip Hop music from the 1990s (cf. Public Enemy, Busta Rhymes, Cypress Hill, KRS-One, and others).

Yet, instead of taking offense at anti-white lyrics, white fans, according to Wimsatt (1994), "try to distance themselves from the target [and] strive to be *down*" (20). The inherent contradictions mean that Whites (particularly privileged Whites who accrue advantages because of skin color and/

or class status) are often perceived as outsiders and must earn their place in the Hip Hop community in other ways. We can see this in how some white Hip Hop youth attempt to set themselves apart from other Whites in narratives (Chapter 2, this volume). Others achieve authenticity through artistic virtuosity and political activism (e.g., Ivy, a female MC discussed in Chapters 3, 4, and 5, this volume). Still others promote social action like Billy Upski Wimsatt and the members of Zulu Nation/Project Five at New York University. Given the disparate forms of participation, the degree of consciousness that white youth have about their place in Hip Hop varies greatly, and in many cases, appears to reflect a kind of "erasure" by which their own connection to the power structure is rendered invisible (cf. Gal and Irvine 1995).

The meanings of Hip Hop for white youth in the US are therefore quite heterogeneous and get played out at the personal level as well as at the local level. (Witness the highly personalized, subjective lyrics of white rap artists like Eminem). If a global form like Hip Hop can be localized in places like Newcastle, Nairobi, Oslo, and the suburbs of Paris, it can also be individualized to suit the aesthetic and/or personal desires of individual young people anywhere. These multiple meanings are bound up with Hip Hop's extensive commodification and by the globalization and reinterpretation of the African diasporic experience. Yet, in the context of the US, the historical relationship between Blacks and Whites is quite complex and calls for a closer examination of the history of cultural and linguistic borrowing and appropriation.

Cultural Appropriation

It is impossible to talk about white participation in Hip Hop and white use of AAE speech markers without addressing the long history of similar appropriations. Cultural appropriation can be defined as taking from a culture that is not one's own. Although cultural appropriation can be a multidirectional phenomenon, it is viewed primarily as transference from a subordinate culture into a dominant culture (Ziff and Rao 1997: 5). Root (1997) writes of the "white Indians" who announce their affiliation with Native Americans through a conspicuous display of beads and feathers:

> The proclaiming of [this] alliance in a visible, emphatic manner has a performative quality and demands instant recognition . . . [It is] a way of attempting to seize the discursive space from Native People and to the extent that it functions as a demand, this display constitutes an endeavor to extend and underline the authority of the white person (231).

While their displays may reflect a heartfelt and sincere affiliation with the Native Americans, Root claims that "sincerity can be damaging because it can be used as a pretext to gain discursive terrain, while evading the question of who controls, or is trying to control, the discourse" (230).

The relative position of Whites and Blacks in the US is also highly relevant to the white appropriation of AAE-related speech styles. Gal (1988) states:

> Ethnic groups have specifiable structural positions of power or subordination in their regional economy and even groups within socialist states or in apparently peripheral geographic areas are importantly affected by their relation to world capitalist forces. This larger context is crucial in shaping the nature of interactions between and within ethnic groups, the permeability of boundaries, the definitions and evaluations of actions and resources, and the nature of competition across boundaries (247).

Thus, the ways in which Hip Hop culture and AAE are taken up by white Hip Hop youth in the cultural and historical context of the US must be viewed in relation to previous acts of appropriation by Whites and the sociopolitical and historical context of white cultural and political hegemony vis-à-vis African Americans. The historical conditions that prevailed under slavery and legalized racial segregation are not something many Whites connect themselves with, but they loom large in the collective consciousness of many if not most African Americans.

White participation in and appropriation of African American culture and AAE has historical precedents, going back at least as far as the minstrel shows that were the all the rage in big cities like New York during the 1840s. Lott (1993) has written a comprehensive historical account of minstrel shows in Jacksonian America, documenting how white performers—in an act that expressed both fear and desire towards black people—painted their faces black with burnt cork and put on highly essentialized (caricaturized) burlesque performances of black people for largely white audiences. In a panel discussion at New York University in 2000 that centered on the theme of blackface in Spike Lee's film *Bamboozled* (2000), Lott pointed out that blackface or the staged performance of blackness was originally done by Whites and served to reinforce white racist stereotypes about the behavior of black people.[14] Subsequently, the minstrel show was taken over by Blacks, who were then effectively re-presenting images of themselves that fit in with the prevailing stereotypes about black people. Lott argued that in fact much—if not all—contemporary public popular performance by black Americans is filtered through the white gaze. In other words, black public performances such as rap even now, continue to cater in many ways to white conceptions of how black Americans act, think, and talk.

Stanley Crouch, an essayist and critic who sat on the same panel at New York University, made a similar observation when he argued that much of the so-called gangster rap can been seen as a form of minstrelsy in which black rappers perform the types of images and stereotypes that Whites expect to see. He went on to ask why it is that whenever white people think about authentic black males, they imagine some gangster rapper like "Ol' Dirty Bastard."[15] Many white Hip Hop youth do indeed respond to caricaturized images of black males from rap videos, particularly images of gangster types with gold teeth surrounded by luxury cars and scantily clad women. One might also argue that it is a particular kind of black youth culture that gets marketed to and consequently taken up by Whites in the US. The writer bell hooks (1994) refers to this as the "commodification" of black underclass life (152) which is echoed by Potter's observation that Hip Hop has transformed violent black youth culture from a threat into a commodity (Potter 1995: 120).

Music has traditionally played a central role in bringing Blacks and Whites together linguistically and otherwise (McCrum et al. 1986). Rose (1994) writes that white teenagers' interest in rap and Hip Hop culture is quite consistent with the history of black music in America and should be seen in the context of a string of similar appropriations going back to the blues, jazz, rock 'n' roll, soul, and R & B (1994: 5). During the Jazz Age in the late 1920s and early 1930s in New York City, Whites would travel to Harlem to see jazz legends Cab Calloway, Count Basie, Duke Ellington, and Louis Armstrong. According to McCrum et al. (1986), much of Cab Calloway's "jive talk" (expressions such as "groovy," "have a ball," "hip," "jam," and "riff") passed into the mainstream because of the popularity of jazz (224). White audiences and jazz reporters began employing these words and phrases to "show how smart and up to date they were" and little by little the general public followed suit (McCrum et al. 1986: 224).[16]

There were many parallels between the trajectory of jazz and Hip Hop in America. Both forms faced rejection by white and black middle class listeners at the outset and were marketed by independent entrepreneurs and independent labels (Rose 1994). The enormous success of jazz and Hip Hop led to attempts by major labels to dominate production. In the case of jazz, the eventual marginalization of black practitioners was followed by the development of black forms that were less accessible and that required greater knowledge of black language and styles in order to participate (e.g., Be Bop). Gangster rap, like Be Bop, may be regarded as a less accessible form. Potter (1995) notes the ways in which gangster rappers like Tupac began to address his black audience more specifically (as noted earlier). But gangster rap is not an entirely rogue element within rap and has been heavily pushed by major record labels who found that selling hyperbolized images of urban black gangsters appeals to millions of white male teenagers. The emergence of successful, "authentic" white rappers like Eminem in the late 1990s appeared to mark the beginning of greater white infiltration, and the possibility of future domination of rap by Whites, but this has not been the case. As of 2013, the only white rappers who have achieved recognition and commercial success on par with their African American rap contemporaries such as Jay-Z, NAS, P-Diddy, Kanye West, and 50 Cent have been the Beastie Boys, Eminem, and most recently Macklemore and Ryan Lewis.[17]

Literary works such as Norman Mailer's essay, "White Negro" (1959), and Thomas Wolfe's essay "Radical Chic" (1970) have explored the white fascination with black culture in the US. Like the white male adolescent obsession with gang culture in the late 1990s, "radical chic" was the sudden craze among wealthy white socialites in the late 1960s for "primitive, exotic, and romantic radicals" like the Black Panthers, "with their leather pieces, Afros, shades, and shoot-outs . . ." (Wolfe 1970: 42). Wolfe's essay satirizes a party thrown by the then conductor of the New York Philharmonic, Leonard Bernstein, for a group of Black Panthers at which the Panthers were fawned over by New York's elite—an act Wolfe calls *nostalgie de la boue* (literally "nostalgia for the mud"). According to Staples (1995), Tom Wolfe's essay "Radical Chic, is still the best window into the notion that a magical nobility is somehow conferred on the dispossessed" (79).

Norman Mailer's 1959 essay "White Negro" illustrates a similar sort of desire. In it, Mailer describes the emergence in postwar America of the white "hipster"—the cool, non-conformist whose music is jazz, whose drug is marijuana, who lives on the margins of society, and who embodies the opposite pole in a bipolar world from those who are "square." Mailer locates the essence of "hip" in the physical, sexual black man who lives for the moment (1959: 305). What draws the hipster to the black male body, writes Mailer, is the life black men are supposedly forced to live:

> [H]e lived in the enormous present, he subsisted for his Saturday night kicks, relinquishing the pleasures of the mind for the more obligatory pleasures of the body, and in his music he gave voice to the character and quality of his existence, to his rage and the infinite variations of joy, lust, languor, growl, cramp, pinch, scream and despair of his orgasm. For jazz is orgasm, it is the music of orgasm, good orgasm and bad . . . (305).

Mailer describes the "hipster" as a white man who goes about living what it means to be Black so completely that he can be considered black. "So there was a new breed of adventurers, urban adventurers who drifted out at night looking for action with a black man's code to fit their facts. The hipster had absorbed the existentialist synapses of the Negro, and for practical purposes could be considered a white Negro" (Mailer 1959: 306). In his description of the white Negro, Mailer makes reference to his unique style of walking and talking: the hipster "moves like a cat, slow walk, quick reflexes; he dresses with a flick of chic" (335) and "has that muted animal voice which shivered the national attention when first used by Marlon Brando" (334).

The romantic view of the underclass does not emanate solely from privileged Whites. Staples (1995) notes that some black gangster rappers are middle class, which he says is the result of a mentality within African American culture that portrays middle class normalcy as an inferior state of being (80). Staples (1995) notes that some black gangster rappers by education or affluence are middle class, yet project their public persona as black underclass, and in some ways they are not far off track.

Anyone who doubts this might recall Edmund Perry, the black Exeter graduate who was shot to death by an undercover cop in Morningside Heights. At Exeter, Edmund had played the swaggering tough without risk. At home, in the streets of New York, the role reared up and killed him (79).

In short, many white and black middle class Hip Hop youth in the late 1990s and early 2000s appeared to be subject to some of the same fantasies about the black underclass and the "nobility of the dispossessed" as their beat poet and bourgeois intellectual predecessors.

CHAPTER OVERVIEW

In subsequent chapters, many of the themes alluded to in this introduction, i.e., language styling, identity, authenticity, appropriation, and racialization, will be explored through the narratives and performances of a range of young people. Chapter 2 presents the story of "Mike," a White upper middle class teenage boy who was inspiration for much of the work laid out in subsequent chapters. It discusses how "Mike" attempted to project a Hip Hop persona by enacting certain behaviors associated with Hip Hop (membership in a gang, selling drugs, graffiti-writing, fighting, and by using HHNL/AAE). It also looks at this young man's struggles in forming his identity as a teenager, his early identification with African American youth, and the development of his language patterns throughout his teenage years.

Chapter 3 introduces a larger group of young people who affiliate with Hip Hop such as "Ivy," a young woman who moved to Harlem from Ann Arbor to pursue her career as an MC, "G Robot," an NYU student and member of a Hip Hop club, and "Benny" who attended an exclusive Brooklyn Heights private school and hung out with a crew of African American and Latino boys. Drawing on interview data from these and other middle class, white Hip Hoppers in the New York City area, it investigates how they construct themselves as authentic via competing conceptions of the Hip Hop mantra "Keepin' it real."

How successfully do white youth learn and use features of AAVE and Hip Hop language and how do others perceive their speech? Research on linguistic profiling has shown that Americans are quite adept at identifying a speaker's race on the phone, leading to discrimination against African Americans and Latinos in housing and employment (Purnell et al. 1999). Drawing on survey data from 250 undergraduates at three East Coast universities, Chapter 4 examines how outsiders identify the ethnicity of white Hip Hoppers judging on short samples of their speech, showing how many perceive them to be African American or Latino, and suggesting they are actively resisting societal expectations about how they should talk.

Many immigrants and expatriates of European heritage who come to the US are surprised and somewhat offended at having the racial label "white" imposed on them. Chapter 5 focuses on young people who come from a number of eastern European countries (Russia, Ukraine, Armenia, and Bulgaria), as well as one from Israel, who appear to have adopted HHNL as a second language or dialect rather than the local white vernacular or some form of standard American English. These young people's identification with Hip Hop, their language use, and other forms of identity display place them at odds with their compatriots who have chosen to align themselves with the white mainstream and point to the conclusion that Hip Hop culture and black American culture more broadly offer more attractive models for their identity formation than the surrounding white mainstream culture.

Departing from the analysis of sociolinguistic interview data in earlier chapters, Chapter 6 explores televised performances by a white MC who performed in the *Blaze* Battle (2000). The *Blaze* Battle was an annual televised competition between MCs who face one another and take turns generating "freestyle" or spontaneous rhyming insults against their opponents. In 2000, the winner of the *Blaze* Battle was a white male teenager from Minneapolis named "Eyedea" who competed successfully against several African American male MCs. The chapter focuses on how whiteness is foregrounded in the freestyle rhymes of the participants in ways that highlight its marked and problematic status in the Hip Hop worldview.

Chapter 7 continues the exploration of media representations of whiteness, but this time in *Ego Trip's (White) Rapper Show* (2007), a reality TV show in which ten competitors competed to be the "next great white rapper" and win $100,000. In the *(White) Rapper Show*, the contestants are constructed as representatives of different white class and ethnic identities such as "wealthy suburban," "white trash," and "Boston Irish working class" and use features of HHNL/AAE alongside local white vernacular varieties in ways that reflect their origins and the nature of their connection to Hip Hop.

Chapter 8 lays out some of the implications of the above research for our understanding of the role of language in adolescent identity formation. Research on identity points to adolescence as a "psychosocial moratorium," particularly for middle and upper class American children who can experiment with various identities and roles in the process. The analyses described in each chapter suggest that some young people are coming to identify less with traditional social categories such as ethnicity and class and more with diverse "communities of practice" or what Bauman (1991) calls "neo-tribes." Through language and other semiotic markers, white Hip Hop youth signal their ties to a set of practices in ways that go beyond any geographically, ethnically, or class-based identity, connecting them in not always unproblematic ways to the Hip Hop Nation.

The final chapter also discusses some additional implications of research on the language of white Hip Hop youth. The persistence of social dialects like AAE demonstrates that language is a critical dimension of identity and that diverging from "standard English" may be a strategy of resistance among individuals who feel threatened and denigrated by the hegemonic white culture. The book concludes by considering the possibility that the diffusion of HHNL/AAE to middle class white American youth, its appearance in the mainstream media, and the globalization of Hip Hop language and culture may reduce the stigma of AAE and the alienation experienced by its speakers in American society.

NOTES

1. All informants are referred to by pseudonyms.
2. Alim (2002) identified AAVE variants (copula variability and a small number of Southern African American English phonological forms) and investigated their variability in the lyrics of African American rap artists.
3. Most native speakers of American English associate these variables with speakers of African American English (AAE). Indeed, Purnell, Idsardi, & Baugh (1999) found that Americans were able to identify African Americans over the phone with very high degrees of accuracy, even on the basis of a single word. This kind of data is an indication of the salience of AAE features for most Americans.
4. In recent years, the more snugly-fitting jeans style of the early 1990s has returned in New York City, primarily among urban African American male Hip Hop youth, but this time with the jeans pulled further down, well below the buttocks, revealing more of the boxer shorts.
5. Zulu Nation was founded by Bambaataa as a grassroots political organization in 1974. According to the Zulu Nation website, "Afrika Bambaataa is one of the three main originators of break-beat deejaying, and is known as the 'Grandfather' and 'Godfather' of Hip Hop." It describes his successful efforts at co-opting the Black Spades street gang into the music and culture-oriented Zulu Nation for spreading rap and Hip Hop culture throughout the world (www.zulunation.com).
6. DJ battles are contests in which two competitors take turns displaying their ability to mix and "scratch" records on two turntables. MC battles involve two MCs who take turns exchanging ritual insults for one minute each against a backdrop beat provided by a DJ.
7. John Singler (personal communication) observes that in the early 1980s "rap" in Vernacular Liberian English had a connotation similar to the original meaning described by Smitherman (1997).
8. According to a 1998 report filed by Jennifer Ludden for National Public Radio, France was, at the time, the world's second largest market for rap music, and the French rap scene has produced a number of highly successful artists like MC Solaar, F.F.F., and Crew Assassin.
9. Ibrahim (1998) says that his informants come from places as diverse as the Democratic Republic of Congo, Djibouti, Gabon, Senegal, Somalia, South Africa, and Togo (356).
10. The Internet has had a democratizing effect on the music industry by giving musical artists the opportunity to distribute music themselves and the proliferation of internet sharing sites have since made it possible for rappers to disseminate their music much more widely and share it with their fans for free (YouTube) or to keep the profits from sales of their music (iTunes).
11. The New York University (NYU) Zulu Nation club was initially started as a chapter of the Universal Zulu Nation and their meetings and activities

followed the rules of the Universal Zulu Nation. The local NYU chapter student leadership strongly encouraged all student members to apply and eventually become Universal Zulu Nation members, but in order to have club status at NYU, university regulations prohibited the requirement that participants also join the Universal Zulu Nation. By 1998, there was only one remaining Universal Zulu member in the local NYU chapter and she was studying abroad. This caused some problems with the Universal Zulu leadership so the NYU student leadership decided that the group could go on doing what it was doing without necessarily maintaining its ties to the Universal Zulu Nation and the name was changed to "Project Five" to avoid any further confusion or problems (Melissa Manousis, personal communication, 1999).

12. The Free Mumia website describes Mumia Abu-Jamal as "an award-winning Pennsylvania journalist who exposed police violence against minority communities" (www.free-mumia.org). On death row since 1982, Mumia was, according to his supporters, sentenced to death for the shooting of a police officer, a crime which he did not commit. Mumia's fight for a new trial won the support of many prominent organizations and individuals including Amnesty International, Archbishop Desmond Tutu, Nelson Mandela, The European Parliament, Alice Walker, Maya Angelou, Sister Helen Prejean, and Danny Glover. In December 2001, a federal judge threw out Mumia Abu-Jamal's death sentence, ruling that the former journalist and Black Panther is entitled to a new sentencing hearing. In late 2011, Mumia's death sentence was commuted to life in prison without the possibility of parole.

13. The fact that Latinos and Whites were involved in Hip Hop's beginnings is not disputed. However, the most commercially successful element of Hip Hop—rap music—continues to be dominated by African American artists who are effectively the icons of Hip Hop today.

14. Eric Lott spoke on a panel with Stanley Crouch, Margo Jefferson, Clyde Taylor, and Michele Wallace on 2 November, 2000, at New York University.

15. O.D.B. (Ol' Dirty Bastard), founder and member of the popular rap group Wu-Tang Clan, is known for his frequent run-ins with the police as well as his success as a rapper. The Wu-Tang Clan has sold millions of records and has a successful clothing line.

16. I am indebted to my friend Charles Sanson for bringing Harry Gibson to my attention. In 1944, Harry (The Hipster) Gibson, a white singer/piano player, emerged as the jazz sensation of the year. He wrote a short dictionary called "For characters who don't dig jive talk" that included expressions like "cat," "clipster," "fall on down," "freakish high," to "hip somebody," and "same beat groove." Gibson can be seen as a kind of white go-between whose dictionary was clearly written for a white audience. Hewitt (1986) points out the "'Janus-like' role of Whites (like Gibson) whose contacts with African American culture make them a beacon for its promotion amongst White[s]" (1986: 144). In this way words and expressions spread to those who had little contact with African Americans.

17. Macklemore, whose real name is Ben Haggerty, began rapping in the early 2000s. He teamed up with his friend and producer Ryan Lewis in 2005 and their single "Thrift Shop" from their 2012 album, *The Heist*, has been viewed on YouTube over 350 million times, reaching Number 1 on the U.S. Billboard Hot 100 chart in 2013, and selling more than 2.2 million copies. http://en.wikipedia.org/wiki/Macklemore—cite_note-billboard1–3

2   Yorkville Crossing
A Case Study of the Influence of Hip Hop Culture on the Speech of a White Middle Class Adolescent in New York City

INTRODUCTION

Longitudinal Observations

As mentioned in the introduction to this book, the inspiration for this research was a white upper middle class teenager from New York City whose language, dress style, and attitude revealed a deep psychological investment in the "gangsta rapper" image. I had known "Mike" (a pseudonym) since he was 6 years old, as a son of a close friend. I began observing his language practices in the early 1990s when he first seemed to gravitate towards Hip Hop, at age 13. Two years later I began a case study and interviewed Mike individually as well as in group settings with his friends. I was curious as to whether his case bore any similarity to that of "Carla," a 13-year-old white girl who grew up in an African American community (Camden, New Jersey) and was thought to speak AAE. Was Mike able to use phonological as well as morphosyntactic markers of AAE? How did he acquire the linguistic features he was using and was he using them in systematic ways? Was Mike engaging in "language crossing" as described by Rampton (1995) or some other kind of language practice? These were all pressing sociolinguistic questions, but they required a greater degree of ethnographic explanation than an ordinary quantitative analysis would provide, which led me to try to understand more about Hip Hop culture.

The first signs of Mike's identification with Hip Hop were when he began to wear oversized jeans, a backwards-facing baseball cap, and name-brand sneakers, and to listen to rap music. White boys who engaged in these behaviors were often called "wiggas" or "white niggas" at the time, a label that assigned them an inauthentic, wannabe status (Smitherman 1994: 168). Mike also seemed to conform to a local, more specific archetype known as the "prep school gangster" in the popular press (Sales 1996) and portrayed in two contemporary films, *Kids* (1995), and *Black and White* (1999).[1] These films portrayed young, white, urban, middle class, and affluent adolescents who identified with Hip Hop and seemed keen on living out their interpretation of the lifestyle associated with it (dealing drugs to one another, petty theft, forming gangs, etc.). At around the same time, Mike began to change the way he spoke, which initially appeared to be a form of "crossing" (as described by Rampton 1995).[2] At first, Mike's linguistic efforts to employ this language were rather fleeting and tentative, but eventually his casual linguistic style began to reflect notable influence from HHNL and AAE in terms of pronunciation, prosody, and lexis (Hip Hop slang).[3]

Mike's early attempts to modify his speech as an adolescent eventually evolved into a wider range of linguistic forms expressions like "keepin' it real," "yo," and "phat." Like many of the "prep school gangsters," Mike came from an economically privileged family, grew up in a predominantly white neighborhood, attended an exclusive private school, and yet was drawn to a cultural form almost diametrically opposed to his own in terms of class and opportunities.

When Mike was 13 to 14 years old, his affiliation with Hip Hop culture manifested itself in vocal criticism of groups which he viewed to be anti-African American (including Jewish Americans and Korean Americans), and he accused his mother (a native speaker of Spanish) of acting racist when she affectionately referred to one of his African American prep-school friends as "el negrito."[4] He also tried to hide the fact that he lived in an expensive neighborhood in Manhattan by giving out his older brother's Brooklyn phone number to friends and acquaintances.[5]

Mike's self-alignment with Hip Hop seemed to draw on stereotyped conceptions of gangs and African American urban male street culture. Morgan (1994) criticizes many early sociolinguistic studies of AAE for their simplistic depiction of vernacular or core black culture and language as "male, adolescent, insular, and trifling" (328), and indeed a comparable reductionism seems to be at work in the way that many young whites interpret Hip Hop culture. Mike's claims of authenticity took the form of activities he and others associated with urban black and Latino youth: he adopted a "tag" name which he scrawled on the polished granite and limestone walls of banks and exclusive apartment buildings in his neighborhood; he also began experimenting with drugs, joined a gang, and had frequent run-ins with the police. At the end of his first year of high school (at age 14), he claimed to have been beaten by rival gang members, was hospitalized with severe injuries, and subsequently was expelled from the private school that he had been attending since kindergarten.

The following year, when he was 15, Mike began attending another private school (albeit one known as the place where many private schools expellees ended up). He seemed to like the change, got passing grades, and began thinking about college. Although he continued to associate with the same friends and still frequently got into trouble, he learned to vary his speech in the direction of mainstream English forms in the presence of authority figures, yet he continued to use AAE phonology and Hip Hop expressions like "yo" and "know what I'm sayin" with his friends well into his twenties. Mike's life has of course been influenced by much more than his Hip Hop affiliations. Even so, his Hip Hop self-portrayal has been much more consequential for him than notions like "adolescent phase" and "stylistic flirtation" might at first imply.

In many ways, Mike's linguistic and social behavior revealed an essentialized conception of young African American male youth culture. The lengths that he went to in order to live out some sort of "authentic" gang experience are probably not very typical, yet his case can provide useful insight into why many white adolescent males are drawn to Hip Hop as well as their language attitudes. Subsequent interviews with young people that I conducted since the late 1990s reveal distinct ideologies surrounding HHNL and AAE. Some young Whites view their use of HHNL features and involvement in Hip Hop as a form of symbolic political alignment with African Americans and other oppressed or disadvantaged groups (e.g., the Zulu Nation club at NYU). For others, using features of HHNL symbolizes individual alienation and can mark the speaker as an outsider (where Hip Hop is not a mainstream youth style). Increasingly throughout the late 1990s, however, Hip Hop would become a dominant form of youth culture in the US, meaning that many young people were drawn to it by a desire to fit in (cf. Bucholtz 2001) rather than to assert something other than a mainstream identity.

One additional interpretation for the appeal of Hip Hop culture among white adolescent males may be found in essentialized links between black masculinity and "hyper-physicality, hyper-sexuality and physical strength" (Bucholtz 1999: 444). Thus, one interpretation of the white male adolescent fixation with Hip Hop may be that it represents an attempt to overcome a sense of inadequate masculinity and a desire to project a tougher identity (cf. Cornyetz 1994). This was likely part of what drew Mike to Hip Hop culture in general and to gang culture more specifically, but there is likely a great deal of variation between individuals, particularly young white women who might be attracted to Hip Hop for very different reasons.

My long-standing relationship with Mike as a family friend allowed for longitudinal observations over more than five years, but most of the analysis draws on individual interviews, group sessions, and participant observation when Mike was 15 to 16 years old. In 1995–1996, I began recording one-on-one interviews with him. Later on, I was able to tape group sessions with several of his friends, most of whom were also white. On his suggestion, I loaned him a tape recorder so he could record some sessions with his friends, and the resulting data are characterized by self-conscious, playful commentary aimed at the microphone, interspersed with animated interactions between Mike and his friends against a backdrop of Hip Hop and techno music.

SOCIOLINGUISTIC ANALYSIS

A number of studies have commented on the relative ease with which outsiders can acquire phonological (pronunciation) and lexical features (words and expressions) of another language variety as opposed to the morphology and syntax (word and sentence structure; Ash and Myhill 1986; Labov 1972,

1980; Labov and Harris 1983). The present work asks whether the same applies to the acquisition and production of a second dialect or language variety. It also addresses some questions that have relevance to sociolinguistic theory: Are white Hip Hop youth more likely to adopt the so-called "superficial features" of pronunciation and lexis of HHNL/AAE than the structural morphosyntactic features (cf. Butters 1984; Labov 1980)? Is there a relationship between the kinds of features a speaker uses and the investment he or she feels in projecting a Hip Hop identity?

Mike's speech style drew most heavily on phonology, lexicon, and prosody, a pattern observed in a few other cases (Hatala 1976; Labov 1980; Sweetland 2002). Hatala (1976) documents the speech of Carla. A very similar case was the more recent case of Delilah, a 23-year-old white woman who made consistent use of features associated with AAE (Sweetland 2002). Nevertheless, there were important social differences between Mike and these two young women: Carla and Delilah grew up in overwhelmingly African American neighborhoods and school environments (Camden, New Jersey and Cincinnati, Ohio, respectively), whereas Mike lived on Manhattan's well-healed Upper East Side and attended an exclusive private high school. Carla's friends were mainly working-class African Americans, whereas most of Mike's friends were affluent and white. Carla and Delilah's adoption of AAE features reflected an effort to adapt to their respective environments, but Mike's linguistic behavior requires a deeper sociolinguistic investigation into the role of Hip Hop in mediating the use of AAE within a predominantly white peer group.

The idea that white Hip Hop youth can draw on ethnic styles such as AAE is predicated on the assumption that there is an identifiable and somewhat stable set of linguistic features that characterize it. AAE has certain widely recognized patterns with respect to phonology, lexicon, morphology, and syntax (Rickford 1999) which largely overlap with what Alim calls Hip Hop Nation Language (HHNL). Indeed, several scholars have written that HHNL and AAE have essentially the same syntax (Morgan 1993, 2001b; Rickford and Rickford 2000; Smitherman 1997, 2000; Spady, Lee, and Alim 1999). Alim (2001) has identified one important innovation in the speech of African American Hip Hop youth; the tendency to use invariant BE in a larger array of contexts than has been documented for AAE. In Hip Hop lyrics, BE may also be used as an equative copula (e.g., He BE the man) whereas in previous research, it was usually used as a pre-verbal habitual marker of aspect, as is "He BE workin'" (Fasold 1972; Labov 1969; Wolfram 1969).

Phonology

Tables 2.1 and 2.2 below outline the some of the most widely recognized phonological and morphosyntactic features of HHNL/AAE. These features form a kind of stylistic menu white Hip Hop youth use for the construction of a Hip Hop identity.

Table 2.1 HHNL/AAE Phonology (Adapted from Morgan 1993 and Rickford 1999)

	Feature	Example
1	Final consonant deletion or glottalization	[gɛʔ] for 'get'
2	Metathesis (or historical transfer from older variety of English)	[æks] for 'ask'; also [wɑps] for 'wasp'
3	/r/-lessness (Vr##; VrC)	[sɪstə] for 'sister'
4	/r/-lessness or substitution of a glide (VrV; Vr##V)	[sto.wi] for 'story'; [fɑː wei] for 'far away'
5	Nasalization of vowel and loss of final nasal consonant	[mæ] for 'man'
6	Vowel lengthening	[bɔəː] for 'boy'
7	Glottalization of intervocalic /t/ in progressive participles	[sɪʔɛn] for 'sittin'
8	t/d deletion	[mosː] for 'most'
9	Fortition	[fɪt] for 'fifth'
10	Glide reduction of /ay/	A long time [tɑːm] ago…
11	Affrication or stopping of dental fricatives	those [dðoz]; thin [tθɪn]; with [wɪ]
12	"thing" pronounced "thang"	[tθæŋ] for 'thing'

Table 2.2 HHNL/AAE Morphosyntax (Adapted from Rickford 1999: 6–9)

	Feature	Example
1	Invariant *BE* (be2)	He *be* walkin (indicates habitual, repetitive action).
2	Copula *is* absence	He __ walkin' right now.
3	Aspectual *come*	They don't never *come* correct.
4	Stressed *been* (remote past)	She BEEN married.
5	*had* to mark simple past	He *had* went outside.
7	*Ain't* (for didn't)	He *ain't* do it.
8	*Ain't* (for isn't, aren't)	My name *ain't* "yo."
9	Past tense –ed absence	He live_ there five years ago.
10	Completive *done*	He *done* did it. (He already did it.)
11	Double negation	He *don't* know *nothin.*
12	Verbal /s/ absence	She live_ on 3rd Street.

In terms of phonology, many AAE speakers in New York City and many parts of the country tend to omit /r/ when it follows a vowel. This pattern, known as "post-vocalic /r/-lessness" or "non-rhoticity," leading to the pronunciation of "park" as *pahk* and "car" as *cah*. It is not unique to AAE and is found in the wider New York City vernacular among older and working-class white speakers, but not very commonly among young, upper middle class Whites. Labov (1972) lists eastern New England, New York City, and the South (Upper and Lower) as the three major /r/-less or non-rhotic dialect areas. Speakers from Boston, New York, Richmond, Charleston, and Atlanta will show only a "lengthened vowel" in car, guard, or for, and schwa in place of /r/ in fear, feared, care, cared, moor, moored, bore, or bored (13). Among /r/-less or non-rhotic speakers, Labov (1972) showed that African American speakers differ from Whites particularly when a word ending in /r/ is followed by a word beginning with a vowel (as in "four innings"): white /r/-less New Yorkers pronounce a word final /r/ in this position, but for many AAE speakers, /r/ disappears (13).

Today, post-vocalic /r/-lessness (r-Ø) is still common in New York City, particularly among African Americans and working class/older white ethnics (Becker 2009; Labov, Ash, and Boberg 2006). But the tendency to omit /r/ has been disappearing. Nearly four decades ago, Labov wrote that areas like New York City have been "strongly influenced in recent years by the /r/-pronouncing pattern which is predominant in broadcasting," so that "educated speakers, especially young people, will show a mixed pattern in their speech" (Labov 1972: 13). As has been true roughly since World War II, r-Ø in the speech of Whites (and perhaps in the speech of other ethnic groups as well) connotes working class origins and rhotic speech continues to define the US prestige norm (Labov, Ash, and Boberg 2006).

Although little data on r-Ø has been collected in the intervening years, some recent studies note that r-Ø in New York City and other regions is on the decline, albeit slowly (Becker 2009; Fowler 1986; Irwin and Nagy 2007; Nguyen 2006). Fowler (1986) replicated Labov's New York City department store survey and found a small decrease of 5% in r-Ø among younger lower middle class speakers as compared to Labov's 1962 study. Becker (2009) surveyed the Lower East Side in New York City where Labov found that white working-class speakers were virtually 100% r-Ø in the 1960s and found that the average had dropped to 64%. /R/-lessness is decreasing slowly in New England, with the trend more pronounced among African Americans than Whites (Irwin and Nagy 2007). And according to Nguyen (2006), African Americans in Detroit have also decreased their rates of r-Ø from approximately 33% in 1966 to 13% in the past few years.

Despite the social connotations of r-Ø and the general trend towards rhoticity among Whites and African Americans in formerly r-Ø regions, some white Hip Hop-affiliated youth adopt r-Ø as part of their everyday speech style (Cutler 2002a). Although this may be partially a result of contact with white /r/-less New Yorkers, the other putative source is likely

AAE, particularly the varieties found in the speech and/or lyrics of African American rappers (HHNL). Evidence for this comes from a comparison of the ways in which some individuals vary their use of /r/ with different interlocutors (Cutler 2002a). The white rapper Eminem shows variation in his use of r-Ø in a phone interview where he seems to be diverging from the /r/-less Australian English interviewer (8%, N = 108) as compared with a group interview with his African American producer Dr. Dre (50%, N = 28). Fix (2009) notes a similar stylistic shift for Buckwild, a white woman who performed AAE on TV and who varies from 27% r-Ø during her performance of AAE to 0% r-Ø when she switches to her "angry" white style (Fix 2009). Variationist evidence such as this shows how r-Ø functions as a stylistic marker that can signal one's identification with Hip Hop or index a particular stance in interaction.

No one in Mike's immediate family was /r/-less. He wasn't either before the age of 13. However by the time he turned 16, his speech was predominantly /r/-less in pre-consonantal (VrC) position (62%, N = 250). This extended to cases where /r/ was followed by a vowel at a word boundary—a pattern found in the speech of some /r/-less African Americans, but not usually in the speech of /r/-less Whites (32%, N = 54).

Another common phonological pattern found in Mike's speech was the tendency to reduce the glide or second vowel in the /ay/ diphthong. The second element of the diphthong, the vowel /ɪ/, is reduced or deleted and the first element, /ɑ/, is optionally lengthened, resulting in the pronunciation [tɑ:m] for *time* and [rww:m] for *rhyme*. This pattern is found among many speakers in the American South, as well as among African Americans in cities like New York, Philadelphia, and Boston, but not among Whites. Glide reduction of the /ay/ diphthong has been described as a regional marker throughout the American South, the Midlands, and the Outer Banks that has been shared by Anglos and African Americans for at least the past 100 years (Bailey and Thomas 1998). Studies of glide reduction generally look at occurrences of the /ay/ diphthong in open syllables and before voiced consonants (e.g., *buy*, *bide*). Labov, Ash and Boberg (2006) report rates of glide reduction of 100% or close to it in many parts of the South, but a lower percentage in the largest Texas cities of Dallas and Houston, as well as in the Southeast cities of Savannah and Charleston. Speakers in the northernmost regions of the South (Springfield, MO and Richmond, VA) show a minimal amount of glide reduction. Labov, Ash, and Boberg (2006) also report glide reduction before liquids as in words like *miles* and *Irish* and nasals like *time* and *line* among speakers in the South Midland region and in Pennsylvania, but none for the New York City region.

Although glide reduction of /ay/ in *buy*/*bide* is not found in local white vernaculars in New York City, it does occur in the speech of African Americans and Latinos (Coggshall and Becker 2010; Wolfram 1974: 201). Recent studies have begun to question the existence of pan-AAE speech markers (Jones 2003; Nguyen 2006), but some research suggests that in northern cities such as Pittsburgh, glide reduction may still be a resource for African Americans to construct a specifically African American identity (Eberhardt 2010). Purnell (2010) found that middle class African Americans in Milwaukee, reduce the glide in words like *bide* when conversing with one another, but converge to the diphthongal white local norm (indeed overshoot it) when conversing with Whites, implying that this feature is also indexical of African American identity in that region. Its appearance in the speech of white Hip Hop youth in northern cities like New York, along with features like r-Ø, must be analyzed as deriving from HHNL and AAE.

Morphosyntax

In terms of syntax, Mike did not demonstrate any systematic use of benchmark features of AAE such as the Ø-copula or invariant BE. There were a few cases in which he omitted the copula, but it proved difficult to make any claims about his command of this feature, partly because there were no tokens in his recorded speech. He also demonstrated the absence of verbal agreement with non-singular third person subjects where the plural subject is followed by the contracted singular verb "has" as shown in (1) (cf. Wolfram and Fasold 1974: 157):

(1) These **niggas's** got shoes on.

Nor did he produce other benchmark features of the AAE morphosyntactic system such as third singular verbal /s/ absence (e.g., He work_ there), or invariant "be" (e.g., She be trippin') except in a few isolated instances. This suggests that he may have been aware of these features, but for whatever reason, did not incorporate them in his daily repertoire.

Lexical Usage

Lastly, an alignment with Hip Hop showed up in the lexical terms he used in his everyday speech. In the examples below we see some of the expressions that characterized his speech as a 15- to 16-year-old (in bold). The expressions "bomb bitches" (pretty girls), "phat shit" (cool stuff), "yo" (discourse marker), "mad" (very), "the shit" (generic noun), and "chill" (calm down) constitute typical lexical markers of a Hip Hop orientation.

(2) **Yo**, he better know some **bomb** bitches down there!
(3) You ever heard of Frank Frazetta? This is some **phat** shit, **yo**. **Yo**, when the dude dies, this book will probably be worth like a thousand dollars. **Yo**, tell me **that shit** is not **phat**!
(4) This is gonna sound **mad** weird, **yo**. Don't worry, don't worry. I'll put **the shit** off!!! Don't touch it. **Chill**, don't touch it!! Don't touch it!!! I got this over here!

Some of these terms mark Mike as an East Coast Hip Hop fan (i.e., "mad" as a quantifier). Other terms such as "yo" and "phat" have become so widespread in the speech of young Whites that they may not always index speakers' affiliation with Hip Hop. In my observations, white use of Hip Hop slang appears to be primarily imitative and derivative of patterns that emerge in the African American Hip Hop community, a pattern that is consistent with the long history of how Black "slang" has historically entered mainstream American English (McCrum et al. 1986).

DISCUSSION

One of my original research questions when I began interviewing Mike was how white middle class young people pick up features of AAE given that their residential and educational environments are predominately white. It seems quite clear that young people living in New York City have multiple opportunities to observe first hand a variety of linguistic forms in subways, on street corners, in parks, night clubs, etc. Mike spent a great deal of time "chilling" on the street with his friends—something that allowed for some measure of contact with African American and Latino kids. Some of his regular social activities, tagging, playing pool, drinking beer on the street with friends and going out to clubs on the weekends brought him into contact and sometimes conflict with young people from other neighborhoods and ethnic or social groups and may have helped him pick up features of AAE and other New York City vernacular features he would not have otherwise been exposed to.

My initial research also points to a range of other potential sources for linguistic contact. Beyond direct face-to-face encounters, access to AAE also seems to be electronically mediated. As already mentioned, in the 1990s the Internet was emerging as an important source for Hip Hop terms and expressions, and young people could turn to a host of online dictionaries and chat rooms to expand their Hip Hop repertoire. It was also common for rap fans to consult lyric sheets in CD cases, allowing them to learn the latest expressions coming out of New York City and Los Angeles, such that many have become incorporated in the speech of teenagers in many parts of the country.[6] Hip Hop fans also write rap lyrics using Hip Hop orthography and post them on the Internet for others to read (cf. Olivo 2001). For Mike and many others, though, popular music was particularly important. He and his friends were avid consumers of rap music CDs and spent a fair amount of time watching rap-oriented television programming such as VH-1 and MTV.

Mike's case suggests that it may be easier to acquire phonological features and the lexicon of Hip Hop than grammatical features in the absence of everyday face-to-face contact with African Americans, confirming the findings of Labov (1980) and Ash and Myhill (1986). The extent to which this is true for other speakers in the corpus will be discussed in subsequent chapters. Yet another explanation, deriving from an agency perspective, is centered on the idea that speakers make choices about their language use depending on how they want to project their identities in different interactional settings (Cutler 2010). White Hip Hop youth may have a more comprehensive competence with regard to the features of HHNL/AAE than their production would lead us to believe; thus, showing restraint in the range of features one uses may be in part the desire to "keep it real" by using such features in a more symbolic way.

From a cultural standpoint, one might conclude that the fascination for Hip Hop among young Whites represents a cultural rapprochement between African Americans and Whites and perhaps even the creation of a new multiethnic youth culture. But Mike's relationship to African Americans was more complex and more subject to competing pulls. From a position of remoteness from the realities of lower-class urban life, he wanted very much to participate in an essentialized version of urban black male youth culture, but he was uncomprehending about the restrictions, angered about rejection, and worried about being labeled a "wannabe" by his peers. The issues raised by Mike's case, particularly the degree to which other young Whites pattern in similar ways with respect to linguistic variables, attitudes, and behavior will be treated in later chapters.

Clearly, the position of Hip Hop in American popular culture has shifted since Mike entered adolescence in the early 1990s. It appeared that Mike (like many of his peers) was drawn to Hip Hop, especially gangster rap, precisely because it seemed off-limits and represented such a contrast to his own rather protected upbringing. Today, Hip Hop is one of the predominant musical genres and has become more acceptable in the eyes of authority figures and the media, leading the Queens-based African American rapper NAS to proclaim that "Hip Hop is dead," in his 2006 eponymous album. This announcement prompted speculations from cultural critics about the intention and significance of this statement to Hip Hop culture. According to some interpretations, NAS was decrying the commercialization of rap and its waning political influence (Blair 2007). His proclamation also happened to coincide with a steep fall in rap music sales in the US, which fell 44% from 2000 to 2006 according to Billboard Magazine.[7] Despite these trends, rap music continues to enjoy enormous popularity, and rap artists like Eminem and the Black Eyed Peas regularly topped the Billboard 200 Charts in the 2000s. Eminem's album *Relapse* was one of the fastest selling albums of 2009, and he, alongside rappers Ludicris and B.o.B., topped the Billboard 200 Chart during the first half of 2010; in 2013, the white rappers Macklemore and Ryan Lewis emerged to dominate the music charts in the US and around the world with their song "Thrift Shop" from the album *The Heist*. The future of Hip Hop culture and rap music seem bright given these trends, as it continues to be adapted to suit the expressive needs of new generations of young people around the world.

Setting aside the subject of the future of Hip Hop for the moment, I would like to return to one of central themes that runs throughout this book: authenticity. Notably, most of the young people described in this book come from white middle class and upper middle class families and live in predominantly white communities. It is difficult to generalize about the class origins of Hip Hop because quite a few rap artists are college-educated and middle class, but there is a general sense that it originates largely in "the street"—read "black" which implies "black urban ghetto" (Alim 2004a). This poses some psychological challenges for white middle class Hip Hop youth who are socially removed from Hip Hop's creative and ideological space. Their exposure to HHNL/AAE is often indirect and takes place principally through the electronic media—digitally-recorded rap music, rap videos, song downloads, Hip Hop radio stations, and Black Entertainment Television (BET)—rather than through direct face-to-face contact with speakers of AAE.

The white Hip Hop youth in this study adopted these styles as a way to signal their preferences for rap music and or Hip Hop culture, but also often to convey a "don't fuck with me" sort of attitude. Seabrook, a white upper-middle-class journalist and author in his late 30s, embodied something of the aging white male rap consumer demographic in the late 1990s. In his best-selling 2000 book *Nobrow*, Seabrook describes himself walking down the street wearing "expensive black headphones [and] a black nylon convict-style cap," a style which he says he picked up from the homeboys in the rap videos (2000: 3).

> I let the gangsta style play down into my whiteboy identity, thinking to myself, Man you are the illest, you are sitting here on this subway and none of these people are going to FUCK with you, and if they do FUCK with you, you are going to FUCK them up. What's MY muthafuckin' name? (Seabrook 2000: 4).

Although at the time, he was old enough to be the father of many of the young people discussed in this book, Seabrook articulates the appeal of Hip Hop "gangsta" style as a way to assert one's physical strength and the threat of violence. Furthermore, his statements reflect the attitude that Hip Hop style and accessories give the wearer a sense of power and invincibility— something undeniably attractive to many adolescent and post-adolescent males alike (cf. Bucholtz 1999).

Language also functions as a way to project and reinforce this physically tough, "don't fuck with me" stance. In some cases it seems that white youth and others are tapping into what Morgan (1996) calls the "resistance, energy, creativity and brutal honesty" that characterize the new urban language ideology of young African Americans (11). Ideologies of language play a role in how young Whites understand their own language use. Baugh (1992) refers to the "covert prestige" of AAE as stemming from its long-standing public devaluation as "bad English," but also its association with black popular forms of music like such as jazz and other African American verbal art forms (322). As noted earlier, the gender component of Hip Hop is particularly important for many white male youth who view black males as the proprietors of a highly desirable hypermasculinity and who consequently take up aspects of black male behavior (e.g., language, gestures, and dress patterns) to project a bolder, more assertive gender image.

Hip Hop is not and never was exclusively Black, yet the African American urban experience is central to its message and reflective of the fundamental role African Americans have had in its creation (Keyes 1991; Morgan 1993; Rose 1994). Morgan (1993) writes that "the Hip Hop nation is largely constituted through language and communicative practices which are . . . based on urban African American norms and values" (1993: 1–2). She describes the core of the black Hip Hop Nation as "adolescents between 12 and 17 years old who exclusively listen to, memorize and write raps, dress in the current Hip Hop flavor, dance the current style and often tag [spray or write graffiti]" (1993: 5).

Notably, many young people around the world have adapted the metaphor of the black American struggle in the US to their own struggles against racism, marginalization, and authoritarianism. This is true of many young people within the US. Puerto Rican youth in particular have a longstanding tradition of participation in Hip Hop, especially in practices such as "b-boying" (breakdancing) and "graffing" (graffiti art) and are effectively viewed as Hip Hop insiders. Furthermore, in New York City there is a perception that African Americans and Latinos (Puerto Ricans and Dominicans) are culturally, racially, and linguistically close. Indeed, the admixture of Africans in the Puerto Rican, Dominican, and Cuban population often leads to the de facto treatment of some as black within the racially polarized context of the United States (Bailey 2000a, 2000b).

There are also important linguistic ties between Latinos and African Americans in New York City. Several important studies have looked at the acquisition of AAE features among Puerto Ricans in New York City (Fasold et al. 1987; Goldstein 1987; Labov et al. 1968; Wolfram 1974; Zentella 1999). These studies stress the importance of social contact, class, and social position in explaining why many young Puerto Ricans acquire an AAE-influenced form of English. Puerto Ricans have traditionally settled in or near African American communities and share many of the same political, social, and economic concerns as their African American neighbors.[8] The participation of Puerto Ricans and to a lesser extent other Latinos in the New York Hip Hop scene is therefore viewed as natural, given many of the political and social ties between African Americans and Latinos (cf. Morgan 1998). But this is not a generalization that can be extended to most middle class white youth who have trouble claiming authenticity within Hip Hop precisely because of how removed they are from the urban Black (and Latino) working class experience.

The main obstacle for white middle class urban and suburban Hip Hop youth is the centrality of the urban African American experience and the almost mythic significance of the "street" within Hip Hop. Alim (2004a) writes, "In the new millennium, the streets continue to be a driving force in Hip Hop culture" (390). There is a discourse within Hip Hop surrounding authenticity encapsulated in the expression "keepin' it real" which means being true to your roots, and not "frontin'" or pretending to be something you are not (Rickford and Rickford 2000: 23). White participation has sparked a debate within Hip Hop, centering on the lack of "realness" of those who do not come from urban black or Latino neighborhoods, stemming from the idea that "the body must be the center of all authentic Hip Hop" and that "[those] who do not participate in its street space or in a black cultural context are seen as not having experienced Hip Hop at all" (Rebensdorf 1996: 38). This leads many young white Hip Hop fans (and white rappers like Vanilla Ice) to justify and validate their participation in Hip Hop by claiming (whether true or not) that they grew up in the "ghetto" or near to one, or that they attended schools with a high proportion of black students.[9] Unlike Vanilla Ice, the white rapper Eminem actually grew up near a poor black neighborhood in Detroit and suffered the same sort of deprivation as his black neighbors which lends him cultural authenticity (Rubin 2000). Thus, Vanilla Ice and Eminem serve as competing models of whiteness within Hip Hop, embodying the inauthentic wannabe (Vanilla Ice) case and the cultural insider (Eminem).

Traditionally, the continuum of authenticity in US Hip Hop placed urban black youth at its core and Whites of privilege on the periphery, so the closer one is in some sense to the urban black underclass experience, the more "real" one can claim to be (although this appears to be changing). By exploring language practices and attitudes, we can begin to understand how young white Hip Hop youth negotiate cultural and linguistic appropriation in a subcultural milieu where whiteness (including "talking white") and class privilege constitute a handicap (Fordham and Ogbu 1986). Subsequent chapters in this book will analyze the competing and often contradictory ideological pulls underlying white use of HHNL and affiliation with Hip Hop, and examine how each plays a role in the individual experiences of white youth. Chapter 3 takes up some of these questions in analyzing a larger group of white Hip Hop youth and the ways in which they attempt to overcome de-authenticating aspects of their identities, namely their whiteness and their class status.

NOTES

1. In the US, "prep schools" are private, often rather exclusive schools that prepare young people for attending college or university.
2. Crossing refers to a range of sociolinguistic practices including the dominant outgroup use of prestigious minority codes, pejorative secondary foreigner

talk, and marking (Rampton 1996). It describes momentary, ritualized instances of outgroup language use rather than the everyday language style(s) that speakers employ as an expression of the self.

3. I use African American English (AAE) as a cover term for the collection of standard and non-standard, or "vernacular," varieties or dialects used by people of African American descent in the US while acknowledging that not all African Americans speak AAE, nor are all of its speakers African American. White Hip Hop youth use a speech style that draws on the language used by rap artists and young, urban African Americans which Alim (2004a) has termed "Hip Hop Nation Language."

4. The expression "el negrito" does not have the same racial charge in Spanish as its translation might have for English speakers. Diminutive expressions like "el rubito" (the blond guy) or "la morenita" (the dark-haired girl) are common, somewhat endearing terms used to refer third persons in conversation.

5. Brooklyn is one of the boroughs where Hip Hop emerged and flourished in the 1970s and 1980s, has enormous cachet in the Hip Hop market place.

6. The emergence of Whites who "talk black" is hinted at in the 1999 rap movie *Whiteboys* (directed by Danny Hoch). The film satirizes three teenagers from rural Iowa freestyle-rapping and beat-boxing in a barn.

7. Record (CD) sales began to fall in the early 2000s across all musical genres as the prevalence of downloading music on the Internet increased. In an era of declining record sales overall, rap still outpaced the industry average decline of 25% (Blair 2007).

8. Goldstein (1987) provides an important example of how Latino male youth make choices about which group(s) they wish to identify with, which is often reflected in their use of AAE variants.

9. In the 1990s, white rappers like MC Serch, Kid Rock, and Eminem were very careful to distance themselves from Vanilla Ice and to assert an alternative sort of authenticity based on white poverty and the dysfunctional family. MC Serch sings "I'm on a Serch to crush a Milkbone/I'm Everlasting/I'll melt Vanilla Ice like silicone (Strauss 1999: 29)." Kid Rock boasted in 1999 "I ain't straight outta Compton, I'm straight out the trailer" (Strauss 1999: 29), and Eminem raps about his mother's addiction to crack and the struggles of growing up in a trailer park in Detroit.

3 "Keepin' It Real"
White Hip Hoppers' Discourse on Language, Race, and Authenticity

INTRODUCTION

Following up on the theme of authenticity touched on in Chapter 2, this chapter investigates how white youth attempt to qualify and justify their participation in Hip Hop discursively. It also explores the ways in which Hip Hop mediates the adoption of an African American English-influenced speech style by such young people and how this phenomenon complicates traditional patterns of identity formation. Although Hip Hop has a multicultural ideology, there is a discourse that privileges the urban black street experience as the locus of authentic Hip Hop (Alim 2004a; Rose 1994). This creates an intriguing double-bind for white middle class Hip Hop youth whose race and class origins distance them from this socially located space.

Authenticity in Hip Hop

The expression "keepin' it real" is practically a mantra in Hip Hop exhorting individuals to be true to their roots, and not to "front" or pretend to be something they are not (Rickford and Rickford 2000: 23). Hip Hop is ostensibly a multiracial and multicultural movement, yet its origins and creative force, as well as most of its well-known rap artists, come chiefly from urban African American communities (Blake 1993). Boyd (2002) writes that young African Americans in the post-Civil Rights era have the possibility and the choice to join mainstream society but many are choosing quite defiantly not to. As such, Hip Hop constitutes what Rose (1994) calls an oppositional youth identity that stands diametrically opposed to the white middle class establishment.

There is a powerful discourse within Hip Hop that privileges the black body and the black urban street experience. According to Boyd (2002), "Hip Hop and basketball are spaces where blackness has been normalized, and whiteness treated as the Other" (23). This creates an interesting double-bind for many white Hip Hop youth whose race and class origins are thrown into stark relief by the normative blackness that characterizes Hip Hop. One is reminded of Du Boisian "double-consciousness," or the inability to see oneself except through the eyes of others. Du Bois invokes it to describe the plight of black people within the hegemonic white culture of the United States. "It is a peculiar sensation, this double-consciousness, this sense of always looking at one's self through the eyes of others, of measuring one's soul by the tape of a world that looks on in amused contempt and pity" (Du Bois 1903: 3). In this case it is white youth who are compelled to see themselves through the eyes of black Hip Hop youth and try to measure up to that group's standards of authenticity, achievement, and knowledge.

Overstepping the boundaries of appropriate behavior leaves white Hip Hop youth open to the charge that they are "wannabes." Their efforts to walk the line are particularly evident in public Hip Hop performances, especially MC battles in which two opponents take turns testing their verbal skill by "dissing" or berating each other for one minute, usually in front of a group of onlookers who determine the winner. African American battle competitors routinely "out" white competitors in a number of ways, e.g., calling them "Vanilla Ice" (the white rapper who lied about growing up in the ghetto when he really grew up in a white middle class suburb) or by telling them to "go back" to some space like MTV or rock 'n' roll where whiteness is the norm. Outside the world of Hip Hop, white Hip Hop youth experience pressure from other Whites, particularly authority figures or peers, to "act white." This dual pressure results in an underlying sense of insecurity among white Hip Hop youth, particularly if they lack strong interpersonal connections to African American Hip Hop youth. This can manifest itself in the sort of overt, performative behavior typified by the proverbial white "preppie gangsters" (Sales 1996),[1] but also evident in the way many white young people talk about their own participation in Hip Hop and in the ways they negotiate the license to claim a Hip Hop identity (cf. Wimsatt 1994).

Hip Hop began in the 1970s in New York City but only broke into the all-white music video world of MTV in 1989 with the launch of "Yo! MTV Raps" (Rose 1994). In 1999, it was dubbed "the most important [musical] genre in America" by the *New York Times* (Strauss 1999: 28), and has arguably been one of the dominant youth cultures in the United States since the early 1990s. According to Morgan (1996), the mass appeal of Hip Hop among Whites has led to the "emergence of a new urban youth identity constituted in part through African American linguistic symbols" (14; cf. Jacobs-Huey 1997; Bucholtz 1997). Some of Hip Hop's popularity among white youth today is undoubtedly due to the widespread commodification of Hip Hop culture, especially music and fashion, as they emerge from the urban African American community.

The collective of individuals who identify with Hip Hop culture often refer to themselves as members of the "Hip Hop Nation" or simply the "nation." Touré (1999: 10) writes, "the nation has no precise date of origin, no physical land, no single chief," but it exists "in any place where Hip Hop music is being played or Hip Hop attitude is being exuded." Back (1996) describes the Hip Hop Nation as a multiracial group of young people with a unique worldview. He writes that Hip Hop was designated as a "culture for the kids" that made "black symbols and emblems equally accessible" (Back 1996: 215). According to Back, the Hip Hop Nation has a black culture but its citizens are multiracial (215), making it open to all. The criteria for membership would appear to have more to do with one's commitment to a particular ideals world view, rather than to one's racial, ethnic, or economic background. In some sense the Hip Hop Nation is like an imagined community as described by Anderson (1983) in that it is constituted by imagined rather than face-to-face relationships. This is particularly true of white Hip Hop youth whose ties to the young urban African Americans who create Hip Hop culture are often tenuous or non-existent.

Bauman's formulation of neo-tribes or consumption-based collectives is also useful here (Bauman 1991). Neo-tribes are the somewhat unstable, fleeting, collectives that make up our contemporary society, reflecting the need of individuals to find meaning by bonding with others. Such self-defined communities often rely on the exclusion of "the other" which may be marked by overt signals such as dress and language or by basic value orientation. The continuity of the group is dependent upon maintaining these boundaries. Indeed Hip Hop youth often define themselves as in opposition to mainstream society in terms of language, dress, values, and orientation (Bucholtz 1997). Alim (2004a) writes that this sensibility reflects a rejection of "'standard' notions of correctness and appropriateness" by members of the Hip Hop Nation whose values and aesthetics, ways of thinking, and lifestyle choices differ from the majority culture (396). White Hip Hop youth participate in this symbolic display of group affiliation although their authenticity and their license to participate may be contested by both Blacks and Whites. Hip Hop culture and the language associated with it are clearly not racially exclusive. Rap music, Hip Hop language, Hip Hop fashions, and the kinesics of Hip Hop style are highly commodified and widely accessible. As Sweetland (1998) usefully reminds us, ethnic boundaries, although powerful, are not insurmountable, observing that racializing languages—or youth culture for that matter—can obscure the more subtle and intriguing process by which linguistic (and cultural) patterns unexpectedly diffuse across cultural boundaries.

My initial interest in studying white Hip Hop youth was to explore their motivation to adopt linguistic patterns they had not grown up with—specifically those associated with African American English (AAE)—and to answer questions about who speaks AAE and what it means to do so. This led to an exploration of the ways in which Hip Hop mediates the adoption of AAE-styled speech by non-African American youth, and what (if anything) such speech styling signals about identity—particularly ethnic identity given the associations listeners have between certain ways of talking and certain ethnic groups. An additional issue I wanted to explore was the question of authenticity given that so many of the young people I spoke to reported incidents in which their right to participate in Hip Hop was challenged—either by African American youth or by other Whites.

Methodology

The data for this chapter is drawn from two years of sociolinguistic fieldwork collected in New York City involving 35 white middle and upper middle class teenagers and young adults who affiliate with Hip Hop and who style their speech with features of HHNL and AAE. I conducted roughly one third of the sociolinguistic interviews myself, but as a white female academic, I found it was often difficult to get speakers to employ the kind of speech they would use among their peers. Consequently I decided to hire two under-graduate and five high-school-age research assistants to conduct interviews among their friends and acquaintances. The data discussed in the chapter come from sociolinguistic interviews with seven high-school-age young people who were living in New York City, three of which were conducted by me, and four by my research assistants. The research questions pertaining to this particular analysis were motivated by the seeming inauthenticity of white youth who appeared to me to be appropriating a speech style that didn't belong to them and who identified with a culture (Hip Hop) that seemed to be off-limits to them. I wondered how white Hip Hop youth saw themselves and what kind of linguistic and semiotic work they did in order to authenticate themselves within Hip Hop. The analysis focuses on the respondents' responses to questions about what "keepin' it real" meant to them and how they reconciled their whiteness and their affiliation with Hip Hop.

PREVIOUS RESEARCH ON THE LANGUAGE OF HIP HOP

Alim (2004a) calls Hip Hop Nation Language (HHNL) a language unto itself and one that defines the Hip Hop Nation (HHN). Although there is not a consensus about what to call it nor is there a clear understanding about the exact nature of its relationship to AAE, there are a few small quantitative studies that have examined variables such as copula absence. Alim (2002) examines variation in the speech of two rap artists, showing that rates of copula absence in musical performance far outweigh the rates found during taped interviews. Alim also argues that Hip Hop artists pay a great deal of attention to their speech and that they consciously manipulate it as a way to maintain their street credibility. The white middle class young people in this study also use speech in quite deliberate and conscious ways to perform a Hip Hop identity, varying their use of features depending on their interlocutors and when they participate in rap performances of various types (ciphers, MC battles, freestyling).

At the level of discourse, direct questions about the meaning of "keepin' it real" elicited two main themes in the data: 1) the idea that people should present themselves for what they are and not "front," and 2) the idea that "real-ness" has to do with being connected to "the street" or the urban ghetto. This chapter explores how speakers discursively construct themselves as authentic within Hip Hop. When looking at specific examples in which young people discuss issues of identity and authenticity, two patterns emerge. In my experience, the youth who are involved in Hip Hop practices like MC-ing and DJ-ing often feel more secure about their right to be in Hip Hop and are quite candid about race and class than those whose participation is largely consumption-based (i.e., clothing, CDs). Furthermore, these more active participants do not feel the need to signal their Hip Hop identity in linguistically overt ways. The more peripheral Hip Hop youth tend to orient more to the idea that authenticity is rooted in a connection to the street or the urban ghetto. They feel obliged to establish their credibility by placing themselves in a semiotic sense closer to the urban ghetto and by obscuring the racial and class boundaries that separate them from the urban African American community.

There are a number of related studies looking at speakers who make use of ethnically marked outgroup language varieties: these include an analysis of a 13-year-old white girl from New Jersey who was thought to speak AAE (Hatala 1976), an examination of heteroglossia and "crossing" within multiracial adolescent peer groups in Britain, (Rampton 1995), an ethnographic study of the discursive construction of white identities through AAE among high school students in the Bay Area (Bucholtz 1997), and the authentic, ingroup use of AAE by a white woman in Cincinnati (Sweetland 2002). These studies have drawn quite different conclusions regarding the nature and significance of outgroup language use. Labov's interpretation of Hatala (1976) suggested that Whites could perhaps imitate the phonology of AAE, but not the morphosyntax (Labov 1980). In contrast, Sweetland's work suggests that Whites can acquire AAE and be accepted as authentic speakers within African American networks despite claims to the contrary.[2] Rampton (1995) claims that the ethnically diverse adolescents in his study in the UK have created a new, "de-racinated" ethnicity constructed via commodified ethnic symbols such as language and contesting social and governmental practices of racial categorization. Bucholtz found no such attempt to establish cross-ethnic bonds of solidarity in the white teenagers' use of AAE. Rather, it was a way to construct "cool" white identities. My own work suggests that white Hip Hop youth have complicated and often contradictory relationships to HHNL/AAE and Hip Hop and struggle to authenticate themselves in the culturally black space that constitutes Hip Hop culture (Cutler 2003a, 2010).

This chapter first explores how some of the young people who participated in the study define the expression "keepin' it real." Next, it explores differing interpretations of "realness," particularly how white Hip Hop youth construct themselves as authentic and how they deal with the question of identity and Whiteness within Hip Hop. Lastly, it takes up the issue of language ideologies expressed in how these young people use language and what they say about their language practices. Their comments reveal an awareness of the prevailing language attitudes surrounding AAE and the social consequences of using a variety that bears a quite negatively overt stigma within the mainstream white American culture.

DATA

One of the central questions addressed by this research is how young people construct their identities in a post-modern world where cultural markers are widely commodified and can be adopted and reworked to create new ethnicities (cf. Hall 1988; Rampton 1995). Some general patterns emerged in the larger data set of 35 speakers pointing to a connection between an individual's participation in Hip Hop activities such as MC-ing or DJ-ing and use of HHNL/AAE. The vast majority of the young people in the study participated in Hip Hop largely as consumers of rap music and Hip Hop fashions. The latter group paradoxically tended to make much bolder use of HHNL/AAE—at least in the interview data I collected—whereas the former group was more quite conservative in their linguistic display.

These patterns are shown for the subset of speakers discussed in this paper in Tables 3.1 and 3.2 below. Table 3.1 divides the speakers into two groups: those who are involved in Hip Hop as MCs or DJs, and those who

Table 3.1   White Hip Hop Youth Included in the Analysis

Hip Hop Performers

Benny (male, age 18)—participates in staged Hip Hop performances; hangs out with African American and Latino "crew."

Ethnicity: Jewish American

Ivy (female, age 18)—emerging MC; performs in progressive Hip Hop venues in New York City and is a member of a women's Hip Hop collective.

Ethnicity: Israeli American

Trix (male, age 18)—Hip Hop DJ; white and Greek American peer group.

Ethnicity: Greek American

Hip Hop consumers

Bobo (male, age 17)—listens to rap music and wears Hip Hop clothing; plays on mostly African American football team.

Ethnicity: Russian-Jewish American

Clay (male, age 19)—undergraduate student at private university. Hangs out with Latino and Asian peer group.

Ethnicity: Jewish and Hispanic American

Ghetto Thug (male, age 16)—listens to rap music and wears Hip Hop clothing. Hangs out with Puerto-Rican peer group.

Ethnicity: Armenian American

PJ (male, age 17)—consumes rap music and wears Hip Hop clothing. Hangs out with white and Asian peer group.

Ethnicity: Russian-Jewish American

---

are fans and consumers of rap music. Some speakers selected their own pseudonyms (Trix, Bobo, Ghetto Thug, and PJ); the remainder were chosen by me. It is noteworthy that so many of the young people who participated in the study were from immigrant or white ethnic backgrounds. This was in part due to the fact that most of my informants attended public schools that drew from a solidly middle class population in the boroughs of Brooklyn and Queens. Demographically, there are neighborhoods within them that have notable ethnic enclaves (e.g., Borough Park, which has a large eastern European Jewish population, Bensonhurst, which is dominated by Italian Americans, and Astoria, which is known as a Greek American neighborhood). The small number of white youth from more privileged backgrounds in my study tended to live in Manhattan, and were more likely to attend private schools, which proved to be much more difficult for me to gain access. They also tended to live in predominantly white neighborhoods where no single white ethnic group was dominant.

Among the performer group, Ivy is arguably the most involved in Hip Hop culture; at the time of her interview, she had just graduated from high school in Ann Arbor, Michigan and moved to Harlem where she had joined a women's Hip Hop collective. Benny, who attended a private school in Brooklyn, appeared on stage with his African American "crew" in various rap performances, and Trix, who attended a large public high school in Brooklyn, was a Hip Hop DJ who worked at local events in his Greek American neighborhood.

The second group is made up of young people who express their Hip Hop affiliations mainly in terms of clothing and consumption of rap music. PJ and Ghetto Thug were notable for the degree to which they professed some kind of connection to the "ghetto" although they lived in solidly middle and upper middle class white neighborhoods respectively. Bobo mainly identified with Hip Hop fashions and rap music. Peripheral Hip Hop youth, particularly PJ, stood out linguistically in terms of their recurrent use of the *ain't* construction, as well as habitual *be* and multiple negation. The core speakers rarely, if ever, used these features.

We can get a sense of each speaker's linguistic performance in Table 3.2. Index scores were arrived at by adding up the raw percentages of a speaker's use of five linguistic variables found in HHNL/AAE: postvocalic and intervocalic /r/-vocalization, /ay/ monophthongization, t/d deletion, verbal /s/ absence, and copula absence.[3] Although speakers varied to some extent in the extent to which they used any given linguistic variable, there was a general correlation in the use of most of features. The higher a speaker's index score, the more he or she employed all of these features combined.

The data here show that two of the more marginal participants (PJ and Ghetto Thug) were actually bolder in their use of particular features than Ivy the MC. Data from a radio interview with Eminem is included here to show that he patterns somewhat in the middle with respect to the white

Table 3.2 Speakers' Index Scores for Use of 5 AAE Variables

Speaker	Score
PJ	3.52
Ghetto Thug	3.27
Ivy	2.24
Trix	2.13
Eminem	2.12
Benny	1.72
Bobo	1.10

Hip Hop youth in this study. Unlike the informants discussed here, Eminem actually grew up around African Americans, yet he is quite conservative in his use of AAE features. The reasons for these patterns may be difficult to decipher, but it may be that Whites like Eminem have to be especially careful not to appear to be "wannabes" because they are in regular contact with African Americans. On the other hand, there are Whites who are well integrated in African American communities and accepted as part of the African American speech community (cf. Sweetland 2002; Cutler 2010). It is difficult to determine why some speakers make more overt use of AAE than others. Contact with African Americans is certainly a major factor in acquiring more native-like linguistic structures, but individual speakers may have a range of social and psychological reasons for styling their speech in different ways depending on the setting, the interlocutors, and other interactional constraints. One such constraint appears to be the ideology of "realness" or "keepin' it real" in Hip Hop culture.

Discursive Expressions of Authenticity

Being real or authentic in Hip Hop is a complicated construct that depends on many factors, but one component involves socioeconomic, ethnic, and cultural proximity to the urban African American community where Hip Hop is created and disseminated, i.e., "the street" (Blake 1993). Alim (2004a) makes reference to this when he describes the street as "the center of Hip Hop cultural activity" and not just a physical space, but a "site of creativity, culture, cognition, and consciousness" (390–91). Establishing one's connection to the street is *de rigeur* for rappers themselves, but it is such a defining element of Hip Hop that many middle class white youth try to play up their connections to the actual ghetto or some imaginary ghetto by forming crews and engaging in certain "gang"-style activities (cf. the "preppie gangsters" documented in Sales 1996).[4] Direct questions about the meaning of "keepin' it real" in my corpus elicited two main themes: 1) the idea that realness has to do with being connected to and achieving respect on the streets and, 2) the idea that people should present themselves for who and what they are.

White Hip Hop youth often cite the two enormously famous white rappers Vanilla Ice and Eminem as embodying opposing poles of an imaginary spectrum of authenticity. Vanilla Ice is often cited as the personification of "frontin'" because he made false claims about growing up in the ghetto when he really grew up in a white middle class suburb (Rose 1994). He is now widely perceived to be a creation of music industry moguls who were trying to tap into the white suburban rap audience (although, in all fairness, he was widely popular in his own time). Eminem, on the other hand, does come from a poor neighborhood in Detroit and was discovered and promoted by the African American Hip Hop icon, Dr. Dre. He is seen as the embodiment of white authenticity within Hip Hop and is the standard against which many white Hip Hoppers measure themselves.

Thus Eminem has become an icon of "realness" for white Hip Hop youth, essentially giving them a right to participate and claim authenticity in Hip Hop, and although Eminem's upbringing was very different from that of most of my informants, they see his success as proof that "white people can rap too." This indexicality is visible in (1), where PJ argues that ghettos are not the sole domain of Blacks and implies that Whites living in ghettos can be "real" too.

(1) "PJ" (age 16, 2000); interviewed by classmate Lien.

1	Lien:	Can you be white and be "real" in Hip Hop?
2	PJ:	Definitely. I mean, you—you—you know, you got white ghettos.
3		**Ain't no** [-INVERSION/-CONCORD] just black ghettos. . . .
4		The white people Ø goin' through the same **shit** as black peo-
5		ple Ø goin' up through every day.
6	Lien:	But you didn't go through that same experience . . .
7	PJ:	No, not me, but people like Eminem might have. You know, I
8		don't know his exact biography or what his life's about, but, you
9		know, not all white people are perfect, just like every other kind
10		of person.

When Lien (an Asian American female research assistant) challenges him about his first-hand knowledge of ghetto life, PJ invokes Eminem as a representative for Whites whose urban Detroit roots can stand in for Hip Hop youth like himself. Although PJ acknowledges here and again later on in the interview that his neighborhood in Brooklyn isn't very "ghetto," he does claim that "it will do" referring to Brooklyn's special status as the home to many African American rappers. These attempts at self-legitimization—via Eminem and via Brooklyn—to Hip Hop's authentic space are two strategies that PJ and other white Hip Hoppers employ.

Bobo, a 17-year-old who also lives and attends school in Brooklyn, expresses feelings about Eminem in (2), when he says that the white rapper's respectability rubs off on other Whites like himself and licenses their participation in Hip Hop.

(2) Bobo (age 17, 2000); interviewed by classmate Kitoko.

1	Bobo:	He's—I mean, I have really liked him [Eminem]. I like his
2		new song. I like his—I like—he's a cool guy, I don't know. I
3		mean, I'm not going to like debunk him for being white—
4		I mean, you know, that—that gives me a little bit of an
5		advantage, you know, in my lifestyle in some ways, you
6		know, people say, "You know, Eminem's white, you know.
7		Maybe other white people that are cool like that"—and,
8		you know, he—he's obviously white, but, I mean, if you
9		talk to the guy, you wouldn't know he's really white.

More than most of my informants, Bobo affiliates with more mainstream commercial rap as opposed to gangster rap. Similarly, he projected a clean-cut studious image in contrast with the ghetto image some young white male Hip Hoppers aspire to. In lines 8–9, Bobo implies that perhaps some of Eminem's authenticity stems from the idea that he could pass for black based on his language.[5] However, the brief discussion of Eminem's conservative use of AAE features above suggests that he may not really pass as a native-speaker (except perhaps according to Whites) or may not really want to.

Contrasting Definitions of Authenticity in Hip Hop

Turning now to sections of talk in which white middle class Hip Hoppers define "keepin' it real" in their own words, we can identify references to the two definitions alluded to earlier. In (3), Ghetto Thug makes a connection between a particular kind of lifestyle and "realness."

(3) Ghetto Thug (age 16, 2000); interviewed by classmate Andrew.

1	G Thug:	**Nah**, you know what it is? It's like—where—with Hip Hop
2		music, the rappers or whatever, **keep it real**. Like—like–like
3		you don't' really have that–with like—with other types of
4		music. It **ain't** like real.
5	Andrew:	I understand what you're sayin'.
6	G Thug:	[You know what it is?
7	Andrew:	I understand what you're sayin'.
8	G Thug:	[You know what it is? It's like—it's like—like– like I could
9		associate with like—I could associate it with my life. So,
10		**you know what I'm sayin'?**

11	Andrew:	[Really? Living in Forest Hills which isn't exactly the—
12	G Thug:	[Well no, I'm sayin'—
13	Andrew:	[ghetto neighborhood of—
14	G Thug:	((early rising contour)) No, I'm sayin,' but—
15	Andrew:	[ghetto capital of the world.
16	G Thug:	Of course, of course now, but I'm sayin' like—like just
17		because my parents live here don't [-AGR] mean that I **chill**
18		here . . .
19	Andrew:	Yeah, so right, your friends live in mostly ghe—ghetto neigh-
20		borhoods, high crime areas?
21	G Thug:	Whatever . . .

When Ghetto Thug says that rappers "keep it real" as opposed to artists from other musical genres, he is alluding to the fact that many rappers are active participants in a vibrant and very real street culture. Andrew (a white friend and classmate) challenges Ghetto Thug's personal knowledge of this culture. As the product of private schooling and a resident of a well-to-do part of Queens (Forest Hills), Ghetto Thug justifies his "realness" by claiming that he doesn't hang out near home. Later on, when Andrew asks if he means to say that he hangs out in "high crime" ghetto areas, Ghetto Thug replies with a very non-committal and /r/-less "whatever."

The ideology of ghetto-proximity emerges in Ghetto Thug's response to questions about who, if anyone, should not participate in Hip Hop, as we see in (4).

(4) Ghetto Thug (age 16, 2000); interviewed by classmate Andrew.

1	Andrew:	Do you think Hip Hop's for everybody?
2	G Thug:	No.
3	Andrew:	Who isn't it for?
4	G Thug:	Like what type of people?
5	Andrew:	Yeah.
6	G Thug:	. . . for—for—for people that like—for like rich people.
7	Andrew:	All right.
8	G Thug:	It **ain't** for rich people. Not for like—not for like, you
9		know, like high class white boys **and shit**. It **ain't** for that.
10	Andrew:	We have several friends like that (( )) and they listen to it.
11	G Thug:	[They **ain't**—they **ain't** high class WHITE boys! I'm talkin'
12		'bout the fuckin' Beverly HILLS **niggas**. Like fuckin' rich
13		**niggas** with like fuckin'—((falsetto pitch)) *I* 'onno **nigga**!
14		Like fuckin' **niggas** that own like—condos **and shit**. *I*
15		'onno. **Niggas** with **loot**.

Here, Ghetto Thug constructs wealthy white people from places like Beverly Hills as archetypal outsiders to Hip Hop, and by emphasizing how much wealthier they are than he is, constructs himself a more legitimate participant than they are. It is by contrasting himself in this way to these other Whites that he attempts to establish his own legitimacy and to counter the discourse about who can or cannot participate in Hip Hop. These attempts to differentiate himself from other Whites on the basis of class, income, and/or geographical residence is a way of placing himself in a semiotic sense via place deixis closer to the urban black "street" culture. The closer one is to the "street" the more authentic one is.

In the next example, Benny, who attends a private school in Brooklyn, alludes to the two contrasting discourses within Hip Hop of what constitutes "realness" or authenticity.

(5) Benny (age 18, 1999); interviewed by author.

1	CC:	What does—what does "keeping it real" mean to you?
2	Benny:	I think it's just being—being true to yourself, like don't
3		act—don't act like, you know, someone that's not you; and
4		some people—some people like they keep it real with a gun
5		or something, like they get a lot more heart when they're
6		holding a gun, and they change; and when they put the gun
7		down, you know, it—they—they don't act the same. I've—
8		I've seen that a lot, and it's like a lot of people try to keep
9		it real by being **mad** hard and—these are like questions that
10		are just like—I mean, I like the questions 'cause they're
11		not easy. It would kind of be boring if you kept asking like
12		really simple stuff to answer like—
13	CC:	It's hard, right?
14	Benny:	Yeah.
15	CC:	Nail it down. What does it mean to you, though?
16	Benny:	Well, me? I think—to me, I—I could just say I **keep it real**
17		because I don't—I don't want to—I don't try to deny any-
18		thing that I am– I don't try to be black, but I'm not trying
19		to be white, 'cause you don't try to be anything. I'm just
20		trying to—I'm just trying to *be*, you know?

The first discourse appears in lines 2–3 where he talks about being "true to yourself" and acting like yourself. The second definition appears in lines 4–8 when he says that some people "keep it real" or gain respect on the streets by wielding a gun or by being "mad hard" ("very tough"; See Smitherman 1994: 131)—similar to Ghetto Thug's interpretation where realness has a connotation of streetwise toughness and a knowledge of how to hold one's own.[6] The first theme emerges again in lines 16–20 when Benny defines realness in terms of his own experience. He says that he keeps it real by not trying to deny who he is and by not trying to be black. These examples show how authenticity is defined both in terms of space, i.e., the literal or symbolic proximity to the urban African American core Hip Hop community, and honesty or truthfulness about where one comes from. White kids are torn between the maxim that requires some kind of connection to the street and the need to acknowledge racial and class identities that separate them from that space. Eminem's status as a highly respected and successful white rapper mitigates some of the anxiety they feel in this regard, but speakers also discursively construct themselves as "real" by distancing themselves from people who "try to be black" or who are "too rich" to be legitimate participants.

The Construction of the Self and the Other

Turning to specific examples of young people discussing issues of identity, it is evident from the numerous discussions I had that many white Hip Hoppers are quite conscious of their race as participants in Hip Hop. There is also an underlying sense that part of "keepin' it real" is acknowledging one's whiteness. Ivy, a talented Hip Hop MC who performs regularly at venues like SOBs (Sounds of Brazil) and the Nuyorican Poet's Café in New York City, is one example. Ivy grew up in Ann Arbor, the child of academic parents. She became interested in Hip Hop when she was about 10 years old and established connections with the Detroit Hip Hop scene as a teenager. Shortly after graduating from high school she moved to New York City (specifically to Harlem) to further her career as a rap artist. Ivy constructs herself linguistically as part of the AAE speech community, but when she performs as an MC she is constantly reminded of her whiteness and must continually acknowledge it within the industry and culture of Hip Hop. Here, she discusses how she was called out for being white when performing at an MC battle.[7]

(6) Ivy (age 18, 1999); interviewed by author.

```
 1  CC:  Have you ever had a hard time or has anyone ever given you
 2       a hard time for being white?
 3  Ivy: That's why I lost the battle! ((suck teeth))[8]—the Blaze Battle,
 4       'cause they brought up the fact I was white ((rising contour on
 5       white)). And you know, ((falsetto pitch)) makin' ra—racist ref-
 6       erences, "Oh, you're a racist. Oh, you're a racist. I'mo lynch
 7       YOU. Oh, you Ø racist." You know, just sayin' shit, callin'
 8       me a white bitch and whatnot and um . . .
 9  CC:  It would be hard not to take that personally.
10  Ivy: Right, but you can't. ((falsetto pitch)) That's my race card,
11       that's MY CARD! How'm I gonna let someone pull my card?!
12       That's—they don't know shit about my card! You know what
13       I mean? That's how you can't take it personal, because they
14       actually don't know what they're talkin' about and so . . .
15       ((suck teeth)) I 'onno. In that—in that instance, I played the
```

16   role. I was like, "Oh, I re—you want me to be racist, so I'll be
17   racist. Look, I'm a racist, look, here's my KKK—sheet—here's
18   my—you know—here's my—here's my rope—and um fuck
19   you too," you know, and then that's not the way to go, but
20   you know, I was cynical about it the whole way, but you know,
21   it's like, I've got—yeah, I've gotten probably equal amounts
22   of **shit** for being—white and a woman and—and you know,
23   probably ten times the **shit** for those combined um—((whis-
24   pery voice quoting imaginary speaker)) "*Wow, I've never seen
25   a white girl who can rap.*" It's crazy.

Ivy lost the battle because she wasn't able to recover from her opponent's
charge of racism in her rebuttal. She quotes her opponent in lines 6–7 but
does not quote him in ways that differ considerably from her own speech.
Although the contracted form "I'mo" for "I'm going to" may be indexing
an AAE speaker, it's also a form that she uses quite often herself and one
that many white New Yorkers use as well. She also generally preserves
intervocalic /r/ in her own speech and does so in quoting her opponent in line
6 ("you're a"). Similarly, she reduces the /st/ clusters in "racist" in all three
instances of the word—something she tends to do herself at quite a high rate
in her normal speech (63%, N = 127). This can be analyzed as an example
of what Bakhtin (1984) refers to as "uni-directional double voicing," as Ivy
is not at odds with this voice.[9] She is simply reflecting an aspect of the Hip
Hop world which she has experienced but still has come to terms with.

Ivy also employs a paralinguistic feature known as "suck teeth." Sucking teeth or "suck teeth" according to Rickford and Rickford (1973) is an
Africanism which has survived in the New World among West Indians,
Guyanese, and African Americans. It refers to the gesture of "drawing air
through the teeth and into the mouth to produce a loud sucking sound" and
is generally an expression of anger, impatience, exasperation, or annoyance
(165–166). With regard to its function (based on my own impressions),
teeth sucking has expanded to new domains of use among young African
Americans beyond those described in Rickford and Rickford (1973). It represents a kind of contextualization cue, to borrow a term from Gumperz
(1982) that signals a speaker's definition of the situation. It can have different meanings ranging from neutral to negative and is used with a high
degree of frequency in casual conversation to signal a speaker's affective
stance.

The implication of Ivy's use of "suck teeth" seems to be that she sees
herself as part of the same speech community as the black speakers she
voices. This contrasts with most of Bucholtz' informants who differentiated
themselves in subtle linguistic ways from black speakers (Bucholtz 1998,
2011). Ivy also draws on the ideology of oppression that pervades some
rap music. As a young white woman participating in an African American
male-dominated art form, she too has been the victim of gender and racial

bias and discrimination. She closes the narrative by voicing an imaginary, presumably African American speaker. She creates a mental image of someone whispering his or her astonishment on seeing a white female rapper, but not in a way that suggests a dichotomy between herself and the person she voices. She does not alter her phonology in any way or intimate through extra-linguistic cues that she is shocked or dismayed by this type of attitude. Indeed, it is within the realm of what she has come to expect as a white female rapper.

Although Ivy has been made to feel aware of her race within Hip Hop, she expresses a heartfelt solidarity for others within that community and clearly feels herself to be a part of it. In (7), she employs collectivizing pronouns to link herself deictically to African American Hip Hoppers.

(7) Ivy (age 18, 1999); interviewed by author.

1 CC: Did you follow that controversy about Tommy Hilfiger?
2 Ivy: What controversy?
3 CC: That I mean supposedly he said he didn't even like black people
4   or something like that . . .
5 Ivy: It doesn't surprise me. I mean, I remember there was a thing
6   with Timberland back in the day—um—where they Ø sayin,'
7   you know, "We're not tryin' to market to—to that audience,"
8   you know. **We're** like, "Yo, **we** buy like fifty percent of your
9   gear!" like—like maybe even more, you know. "**We're** the rea-
10   son why you're—why you're makin' your money. It's not hikers
11   buyin' Timberland," you know and you know, they didn't give
12   a fuck but—but you—I'm not surprised. That's why I don't
13   sweat it. I don't—I really don't go and buy the labels 'cause
14   they're labels, 'cause I know it's, you know, just exploiting this
15   culture, and it's not giving back to it. You know. So if **I'mo** buy
16   a label it's gonna be someone who I know who's doin' good.

Clothing designers like Tommy Hilfiger, Calvin Klein, Ralph Lauren, and Timberland have traditionally targeted the affluent yuppie/country club class. Over the past decade, however, they have become hugely successful among urban black and Latino teenagers (and of course among the white teens who adopt urban Hip Hop style). In the mid-1990s, there was a rumor that the clothing designer Tommy Hilfiger said he did not really like black people, spurring a debate within the Hip Hop community about whether people should wear his clothing or that of any other typical white-owned brands that were popular at the time. In expressing her indignation about the behavior of companies like Timberland vis-à-vis African Americans, Ivy uses the pronoun "we" in lines 8–9 to link herself deictically to the black Hip Hop community referred to in lines 3–4. The pronominal indexicality here can be seen as attempt to downplay racial difference within Hip Hop in line with the progressive political and social ideology of unity within the Hip Hop Nation.

Although she is linguistically more conservative in her use of AAE morphosyntactic features than PJ and Ghetto Thug, Ivy has mastered the phonological and intonational system of AAE and can pass as a speaker (Cutler 2010). She also sets herself apart from other Whites by marking them linguistically in her discourse (cf. Bucholtz 1997). In (8), Ivy positions herself vis-a-vis other white speakers by "marking" their speech as different from her own.

(8) Ivy (age 18, 1999); interviewed by author.

```
1   CC:   Are there other expressions that you just wouldn't use now?
2         Things that are really dead kind of?
3   Ivy:  Um . . . I don't pay attention that much to slang. There's
4         stuff I brought back. Let me think. I didn't say "homegirl"
5         or "homeboy" for a long time. I brought those back 'cause
6         they fit. Rather say that than ((stylized white voice)) "This
7         is my girlfriend and my boyfriend—and my friend" to my
8         homegirl. I don't say "funky fresh in the flesh" anymore. I
9         think that's some—that's some eighties shit.
```

Ivy has also been reminded of her whiteness by the music industry. She has been offered (and has turned down) several record contracts by companies that saw her whiteness as a way to market her music. Some company representatives saw her as the "female Eminem" while others saw her as a kind of rap/folk singer. Here she says that she stopped using terms like "homeboy" and "homegirl," because they had ceased to be fashionable, but she soon started using them again for a couple of reasons: first, because these terms fill a lexical gap in English, i.e., the lack of a neutral, ingroup expression for "male friend" or "female friend." Secondly, the alternatives "boyfriend" and "girlfriend" would be pragmatically inappropriate for interactions with other Hip Hoppers because they have a distinctly "white" ring to them (at least for Ivy), as evidenced by the way she stylizes a white speaker in lines 6–7. This indexical marking of a white speaker is accomplished by the use of a squeaky, high-pitched voice, the enunciation of the final /d/ in "girlfriend," "boyfriend," and "friend," and the absence of AAE phonology, all of which contrast with her own personal style. The implication is that these terms of address are hyper-feminized, white, silly, and thus inappropriate for her to use.

Ivy is perhaps more conscious about her whiteness than many of the other young people I interviewed because as an aspiring rapper, she interacts with a lot of African American Hip Hop kids who challenge her legitimacy. As a white female, she has had to fight an uphill battle to earn her place as a performer within an art form that is dominated by African American males. She thus has a large personal stake in promoting the multicultural, progressive ideology of the Hip Hop Nation. She clearly sees herself as part of the Hip Hop community and has earned herself a place based on her talent as an MC. Many of the other informants expressed similar assertions about an identity rooted primarily in Hip Hop and secondarily in race.

Ambivalence about Whiteness

Benny says he did not make the decision to be white and says that he had no choice in the matter. In (9), he reports that his friends tease him about being "black on the inside" (line 14). The fact that many of these friends are black (in contrast to most of the other informants whose friendship groups are primarily white) lends him a greater degree of credibility.

(9) Benny (age 18, 1999); interviewed by author.

1	Benny:	I don't think I made a decision to be white. I'm just—I was
2		born and this is my—you know, it's not even a situation.
3		It's just who I am. I don't know if—I don't even know if my
4		friends look past it or not, but it doesn't matter to me.
5	CC:	Do the—do your friends ever say anything to you?
6	Benny:	Oh—
7	CC:	Do they ever give you a hard time?
8	Benny:	—Of course. All the time.
9	CC:	What do they say?
10	Benny:	Like, "Yeah, I think he's black." They're like—they are
11		always—they're always saying something like that, like –
12	CC:	As a joke, though, or seriously?
13	Benny:	I don't know. Sometimes, they seem so serious; and they're
14		like, *"This kid is black on the inside,"* and I know how to
15		(( )) **and shit**; and it's like, "All right." Oh, my God, ask me if
16		they fuck around with me? ! ((slow, rhythmic speech, AAE
17		intonation)) All the time—of course; but, you know, we're
18		all friends.

In line 17, Benny answers his own question in a markedly slower, AAE-influenced style that indexes his integration in the group despite the fact that he gets teased about being white. This is evident in his vocalization of /l/ in *all*, the affrication of the voiced fricative in *the*, and the reduced glide in the /ay/ diphthong in *time*. The intonation patterns are also reminiscent of patterns found among some AAE speakers, i.e., elongated syllables, low pitch, and creaky voice. For Benny, part of "keepin' it real" is not trying to deny his whiteness, and this earns him a badge of honor among his friends—that of being called "black on the inside."

The issue of race also arises in another discourse among Hip Hop youth concerning the origins of Hip Hop culture. Some white Hip Hop youth are keen to point out that white people were involved in the creation of Hip

Hop from the very beginning, perhaps as a way to legitimize themselves.[10] Others are aware of this participation, but acknowledge that its roots are African American. In the next example, Benny acknowledges the African American origins of Hip Hop and asserts Hip Hop as his primary identity.

(10) Benny (age 18, 1999); interviewed by author.

1	CC:	Do you think—do you think Hip Hop is really multicul-
2		tural?
3		Is it open to everybody?
4	Benny:	Oh, it's—it's open to everybody; but I don't think you
5		can—you can lie and say it's not a—a black—a black
6		music. You know, its—its origins are African American. Its
7		mass-audience is African American. Its mass-performers are
8		African American—and if you try to—if you try to front
9		like—like, "Oh, no, white people have just as much say in
10		it," you're just lying to yourself because, you know, you
11		gotta give credit where credit is due.
12	CC:	Do you think there are white people, though, who want to
13		kind of pretend like that's not the case or it—
14	Benny.	Oh, yeah, of course. There's always people like that. Not
15		everybody sees it—I mean, some people probably have a
16		problem with what I'm saying. They're like, "No, that's
17		not true." Right, but I'm like, "Hey, I give credit where
18		credit is due," and, you know, I *humble* myself as a—you
19		know, as someone in the Hip Hop world, 'cause it's—this is
20		not—this is not my—my—I consider my culture Hip Hop
21		culture. I don't consider my culture like white. I'm a—
22		you know, I'm a white kid in the Hip Hop culture. I don't
23		consider—but I just consider, you know, I'm in the Hip Hop
24		culture—but I—I give credit where credit is due, you know.
25		They originated it. It's theirs, but it's mine, too, now.

Unlike some informants who want to minimize or erase the central role of African American culture in the creation of Hip Hop, Benny says that "you gotta give credit where credit is due." The third person pronouns "they" and "theirs" in line 25 unambiguously index African Americans who he says originated Hip Hop. He objects to those who "front" or overstate the participation of Whites in the origins of Hip Hop (lines 8–11). He then makes a very interesting distinction regarding his identity in lines 20–24, saying that he considers his culture to be Hip Hop culture, not white cul- ture, and he identifies himself as a "white kid in the Hip Hop culture." Once again, Benny acknowledges race while claiming that it is secondary to his Hip Hop identity. This is a crucial example of the way many white Hip Hoppers have come to see themselves within Hip Hop.

Clay, an undergraduate student talks about himself somewhat more overtly as black and affiliates with issues that he feels affect black people. Although he says he has reservations about saying it himself, he reports that many of his friends refer to him as black.

(11) Clay (age 20, 1998); interviewed by author.

1	Clay:	I don't consider myself an African American or even like—
2		and I—I—I have reservations about calling myself black,
3		but—but—but they'll—but—but some of my friends here
4		will refer to them and me as being black, even—and—and
5		it's—like my—my—I rhyme with a Dominican kid. He's
6		the one—like one of my best friends, and—and we're
7		((the)) "Latin Sensations," and he—he says—he says—he
8		says, "Clay, you're my **nigga**."

As was the case for Benny, Clay's friends occasionally refer to him as black. The neutral/positive ingroup use of "nigga" in white peer groups where Hip Hop plays a central role is ubiquitous (Cutler 2002a; Kennedy 2002). When Clay quotes his friend, he is not trying to say that there is something remarkable about him, a white boy, being called "nigga." The implication is that his Dominican friend accepts him entirely and sees him as part of the group.

Yet Clay aligns himself with African Americans in other ways that are much more personal. In (12), Clay says that he feels like his "mind patterns" and his intelligence are more like that of African Americans than white people. Earlier in the interview, he spoke about how he experienced discrimination in high school because he had learning disabilities which gave him insight into what it must feel like to experience racial discrimination.

(12) Clay (age 20, 1998); interviewed by author.

1	Clay:	. . . my mind patterns is like—my whole—my whole intel-
2		ligence scale, the way it—it—it sums up is almost more like
3		in the range of an African American than the typical white
4		person, very interestingly enough and so it's—it's—it's very,
5		very strange that—that I have been—I've had this skin.

Another interpretation of these comments could be that Clay seems to identify with African Americans due to his perception that like him they too suffer from low scholastic achievement. In spite of the rather troubling conflation he makes between his own learning disabled condition and the intelligence scale of African Americans, Clay sincerely feels he can understand racial discrimination because he too is a victim of a kind of oppression. He sums up by saying that he feels it's strange that he ended up with the skin color he has, implying that under the circumstances he really ought to have been born black. It is obviously difficult to judge exactly what Clay's views of African Americans actually are from this brief exchange. The tenor of the interview made me think that his comments mostly stem from a naïve and simplistic conception of African Americans rather than from any sort of deep-seated racism.

Clay's self-portrayals contrast with that of PJ, a high school freshman whose claims of identity go further than third-party ascriptions of blackness. Interestingly, PJ is much less involved in Hip Hop than young people like Ivy and Benny, yet comes closest to constructing himself discursively as black.

(13) PJ (age 16, 2000); interviewed by Lien.

1	Lien:	What words and expressions are out?
2	PJ:	"Phat." You don't say "phat" no more. *That shit* been out a long
3		time ago.
4	Lien:	What about "dope?"
5	PJ:	"Dope?" Only white people use that word.
6	Lien:	Do you use that?
7	PJ:	No, but I consider myself **blackinese**.
8	Lien:	Blackinese?
9	PJ:	**Blackinese**.
10	Lien:	What does that mean?
11	PJ:	That I'm a white person that's got a little bit of black in me.
12		That's basically what it means—

PJ identifies himself as Russian and Jewish at the beginning of the interview, but later on in instances like this, he distances himself when he says that Whites are the only ones to use "dead" expressions like "dope." He then claims to be different from other white people, identifying himself as "blackinese," a neologism which he glosses as "a white person with a little bit of black."

These examples show that white Hip Hop youth feel that they occupy a liminal space in terms of identity and must constantly negotiate their participation with respect to African American Hip Hop youth as well as other Whites. These examples suggest that white Hip Hop youth grapple with issues of race in different ways. Some, like Ivy and Benny, invoke the ideology of inclusiveness within Hip Hop to downplay racial difference. Yet they are careful to acknowledge race in line with their interpretation of "keepin' it real." Others try to obscure or downplay their own whiteness by citing others' ascriptions of their blackness, or in PJ's case, by creating a novel racial category. For many young people, to be in Hip Hop is to step outside one's identity and become something else, perhaps similar to what Hall (1988) has referred to as the emergence of "new ethnicities" (cf. Rampton 1995). But the normative role of blackness in Hip Hop still forces white Hip Hop youth to confront their race and class in ways they are usually not obliged to do. They must acknowledge their whiteness in order to be accepted as "real" and any individual who tries to claim he or she is black risks being accused of "frontin'."

Language Practices and Ideologies Surrounding AAE

We can also talk about "keepin' it real" in terms of language. In general, white Hip Hoppers seem quite sensitive to questions of authenticity, given the importance placed on "realness" within Hip Hop culture. Yet their adoption of African American cultural signifiers, particularly language, seems contrary to the idea that one should not "front" or pretend to be something one is not. I have suggested in previous work that linguistically most white Hip Hoppers do not match the speech of African American rappers in a quantitative sense and furthermore that there are many features of AAE that they do not use (Cutler 2002a). In the previous chapter, I refer to these patterns as "styling," which involves a straightforward and stable relationship between language use and identity. Speakers style their identities through the use of speech variables linked to identity categories for constructing social meanings, social categories, and identity (Eckert 2008). Coupland (2007) describes *social styles* as the language and clothing resources people use to make personal and interpersonal meaning and *styling* as the activation of this stylistic meaning (2–3).

Here, the stylistic use of HHNL/AAE features is a form of indexicality. Irvine and Gal (2000) write that "linguistic forms, including whole languages, can index social groups [and] can become a pointer to (index of) the social identities and the typical activities of speakers" (37). Outgroup referee design (Bell 1984) helps us account for the fact that even the nominal use of features from another language variety can signal to audience members which group of speakers is being referenced. Outgroup refereee design is when speakers lay claim to a speech and identity which are not their own but which hold prestige for them on some dimension. They diverge from the speech of their ingroup and thus form their own "natural" speech towards an outgroup with which they wish to identify (188). Employing HHNL/AAE is therefore a way to connect speakers to the high status of African Americans and AAE that exists within Hip Hop. Yet in terms of authenticity, there is also a sense that trying to sound "too black" might actually make one less "real" because it would be trying to be something one is not; that is, respecting ethnolinguistic boundaries is an essential part of "keepin' it real" because it is an acknowledgement that one is not trying to be black.

Turning now to actual speech performance, we can observe how white Hip Hop youth "keep it real" or fail to "keep it real" in terms of their language use. White Hip Hop artists, particularly MCs like Ivy, must display their ability to perform a number of verbal genres from freestyling to rapping and battling—genres that have a long tradition in the black community—while being ever mindful of their audience and acknowledging their whiteness. But many of the more marginal white Hip Hop youth may not be as sensitive to linguistic boundaries. PJ is one such case. In (14), PJ is asked to follow up on his friend's accusation that he tries to *sound black*.

(14) PJ (age 16, 2000); interviewed by Lien.

1	Lien:	What do you think that means when someone tells you that you
2		sound black?
3	PJ:	I mean, I—*ain't* nobody [-CONCORD; -INVERSION] ever
4		told me I sound black. This is the first time I hear such—
5		such bullshit. Anybody here want to say anything?
6	Jing:	Yeah. You sound like you want to be black.
7	PJ:	Whatever, man. You sound like a wannabe Chinese person.
8	Jing:	What's your point, kid?
9	Lien:	But he is Chinese.
10	PJ.	All right. Well, you might have a point this time, all right—
11		but, anyway, I'm just—I'm just handlin' my own. I'm just
12		doing what I got to do, you know. If I have (( ))—it's a
13		(( )) a free country. It's like I'm in—I'm in—I'm in Russia
14		or **shit**.
15	Jing:	I don't know, but we just got to listen to you all day, you
16		know.
17	PJ:	For real, and, yeah, you—and you got to put up with **my shit**.
18		You got to love it or leave it, ((for)) **real**.

This example illustrates PJ's linguistic competence in terms of his use of multiple negation, and negative inversion (line 3)—all well-documented morphosyntactic features of vernacular AAE.[11] But at times, his speech seems so much like a performance that the young Asian American high school student who is interviewing him (Lien) breaks out in laughter.

PJ openly identifies his own speech as "Ebonics" which he glosses as the language of "Hip Hop," but his highly stylized speech prompts his peers to challenge his authenticity.[12] Although PJ vehemently denies that others identify his speech as black, he concedes that people have called him a "wannabe." His comments also illustrate the erasure of blackness. He shows an awareness that AAE exists and perceives this to be what he speaks, but he denies that anyone would think he is trying to "talk black." He interprets his language as coming from Hip Hop but does not accept that there is a connection between the way he talks and "sounding black."[13] His denial about sounding black elicits a challenge from his Chinese American friend "Jing" who says that PJ sounds like he *wants* to be black. PJ doesn't really know how to reply to this statement and accuses Jing of sounding like a "wannabe Chinese person." This reply backfires because Jing, as a Chinese American, cannot presumably act like he wants to be Chinese so PJ must concede the point. Jing's complaint about having put up with PJ's speech "all day long" implies that he regards it as an affected and thus inauthentic way of talking.

Speakers who were linguistically more conservative than PJ in their use of HHNL/AAE were also challenged by their peers about the way they speak. In the next example, Trix, in a discussion with his friend Eugene, describes how his present girlfriend didn't want to go out with him because she thought he "sounded black."

(15) Trix (age 18, 2000); interviewed by Eugene.

1	Trix:	Well, I've been going out with my girlfriend now for like
2		eight months; and like it was hard to get her because the
3		reason she didn't want to go out with me is because she said
4		I sounded black, like she—
5	Eugene:	And that was actually a big—a really big thing for you?
6	Trix:	Yeah. You know, like I would always like say, "**Son**, this,
7		**son**, that," you know—"**Get the fuck out of here**," this and
8		that, you know; but it's not that she like—she's like, "*It*
9		*doesn't go on you, you know. It's just not—like it doesn't*
10		*fit your character*," 'cause like I'm a really nice person, you
11		know; and I'm—I'm not like the type of person to be like
12		hardcore and stuff like that. So, whatever, she just like—
13		yeah, I've been told I act—I act black; but that—at that
14		time was like that's how all my friends were acting, you
15		know, so it was like my friends were acting like that, I was
16		acting like that, you know?

Trix's girlfriend apparently thought he was "too nice" of a person to talk "black" and her criticism made him aware of the need to shift his speech according to the context. In terms of language ideologies, Trix's girlfriend's comments reveal an iconic link between AAE and certain qualities and attributes that do not coincide with being a "nice" person.

The reactions they get from adults and peers make white Hip Hop youth sensitive to the social meanings attached to HHNL/AAE. Although their communicative competence within the African American speech community is generally limited, white Hip Hop youth are quite sensitive to mainstream societal norms about when it is or is not appropriate to use Hip Hop- or AAE-styled speech. Speakers almost uniformly acknowledge the need to switch in the presence of adults or in the workplace.

Here, PJ says that he talks differently around his parents out of respect or maybe even fear.

(16) PJ (age 16, 2000); interviewed by classmate Lien.

1	Lien:	Do you always talk like this? I mean, do you change your speech
2		patterns?
3	PJ:	I mean, when I talk to my parents, yeah, I try to just kind
4		of respect, **you know what I'm sayin'**. I mean, if—they brought

5   me into the world, they kick me out, **you know what I'm sayin'.**
6   So I got to—I got to handle my business around my parents; and
7   when I'm outside, it's a completely different horizon; and I (( ))
8   my horizon around, you know, when I'm outside or inside, I
9   gotta change the vibe.

Trix echoes this sensitivity toward the reception of HHNL/AAE in the continuation of a metalinguistic and metapragmatic discussion about how his girlfriend made him change his speech when they started going out together.

(17) Trix (age 18, 2000); interviewed by classmate Eugene.

1 Eugene: So (( )) to your girlfriend.
2 Trix: Oh.
3 Eugene: Do you think—do you think if you do talk to (( )) is there any
4   repercussions over that?
5 Trix: Repercussions like? Why use SAT words, man? No. Like
6   the first thing that she stopped making me say was the word
7   **buttas**; and I used to love that word. Everything was—like
8   it's—it's like **whoa** right now. Everything was **buttas**, but
9   like—I don't know, she just like—she didn't make me stop
10   saying it, but she made me realize that like soon you're
11   going to have to stop saying it, you know, if you want to
12   be like—go out in the *real world* and like get like a job and
13   stuff . . .
14 Eugene: Are you really trying to break that habit because of her or is
15   there anything that's—?
16 Trix: Like it's not that I realize that she's right, but like she had—
17   she did have a point, you know; and like how things are
18   going to be later on, you know; and considering that next
19   year I'm going to be a senior, you know, you—it's like I
20   really have a job right now. I'm a waiter, you know; and
21   I can't go up to the customer and be like, "*Yo, what up,*
22   *nigga*?" you know, "*What* [-AUX] *you wanna eat*?" you
23   know, you gotta be serious at certain points, you know.
24   When you're with your friends, you're with your friends;
25   and you don't want it to just slip out, like by accident,
26   when you're not, when you're with an adult or something.

Trix concedes that his girlfriend had a point because this language might inadvertently "slip out" and offend someone. He gives an example of what one might accidentally say to a restaurant customer in lines 21–22. "Yo, what up, nigga?" you know, "What [-AUX] you wanna eat?" Although he seems to be offering this example in all seriousness, its patent absurdity as something a waiter regardless of his or her ethnicity would ever say to a restaurant patron makes for a subtle but interesting counterpoint to his girlfriend's argument.

These statements are particularly revealing with regard to language ideologies. In these excerpts, AAE becomes an icon for a particular class of people. It is constructed as a language or style of the street—the opposite of "SAT" language" (line 5)—and as a language that will prevent one from getting a job and having a secure future in the "real world." This attitude stems in part from the widely held belief among Whites that one's language, dialect, or ethnolect is a legitimate reason to deny someone employment, particularly African Americans (cf. Morgan 2002; Lippi-Green 2010) and that if only they would change the way they speak, they would have better job opportunities.[14]

Although they flirt with a speech variety that has enormous prestige within Hip Hop culture, white Hip Hop youth seem to become more and more aware of the potential personal consequences of continuing to use it as they grow older. Bourdieu (1991) predicts that young people with linguistic capital (i.e., access to the prestige language) will eventually embrace this identity and the "material and symbolic profits" it can secure them (245). Most of the white Hip Hop youth in this study possess a high degree of sociolinguistic awareness, and their comments suggest that they are increasingly aware of the social consequences of their linguistic choices.

CONCLUSION

This chapter has explored the ways in which white Hip Hop youth talk about identity, authenticity, and language and has shown that there are many ways one can be a Hip Hopper. The emergence of white rap artists like Eminem has made it easier to be white in Hip Hop—something that was more difficult in the past. But white Hip Hop youth still struggle to authenticate themselves because Hip Hop was and still is perceived to be an African American cultural form in the context of the US. Unlike in some other countries where Hip Hop is effectively a celebration of blackness often in the absence of black people (cf. Bennett 1999), in New York City, white Hip Hop youth encounter African American Hip Hop youth on a daily basis in the streets and subways, and also sometimes in school. There is a resulting dialectic between Hip Hop's rootedness in underprivileged urban African American neighborhoods as well as its inherent anti-establishment ideology and the participation of white youth who are perceived to represent that establishment. The analysis illustrates how the authentic-inauthentic dichotomy that operates within Hip Hop as a whole is projected at another level in the ways that white Hip Hop youth assert their "realness." Some white Hip Hop youth like PJ and Ghetto Thug do this by asserting their connections to the street, citing third-party ascriptions of blackness, drawing heavily on HHNL/AAE markers, and/or by borrowing authenticity from white rappers like Eminem. Others do it by becoming Hip Hop artists or political activists and aligning themselves with causes that affect the African American community (e.g., Ivy and Benny).

It is important to recognize the highly personal, subjective appeal of Hip Hop as well, particularly within the highly individualistic culture of the US. Hip Hop can be a way to rebel against parental authority, express a distinct form of masculinity or ethnicity, or a way to express resistance to the socio-economic/political system. Many young people view rap and related forms such as spoken word as the most effective way to express their personal feelings and frustrations about who they are and where they come from. Despite the progressive reasons many young Whites have for being involved in Hip Hop, their adoption of black cultural symbols, particularly language, is not always perceived as neutral or unmarked, even in the multicultural milieu of Hip Hop. Racial differences produce power differences that white Hip Hop youth may overlook or erase even when they buy into the anti-racist, progressive ideology of Hip Hop. Yet in spite of the risk of misunderstanding and resentment, white participation in Hip Hop ultimately has the potential to raise awareness of the perspective of African Americans and the normative status of whiteness in US culture.

NOTES

1. Deborah Root (1997) writes of the "white Indians" who announce their affiliation to Native Americans through a conspicuous display of beads and feathers: "the proclaiming of [this] alliance in a visible, emphatic manner has a performative quality and demands instant recognition . . . [It is] a way of attempting to seize the discursive space from Native People and to the extent that it functions as a demand, this display constitutes an endeavor to extend and underline the authority of the white person" (231).
2. Sweetland (2002) contradicts Labov's assessment of "Carla," a 13-year-old white girl who grew up in a predominantly black neighborhood in New Jersey and was thought to speak AAE. Labov (1980) found that Carla's performance of AAE was mainly in terms of phonology, intonation, and lexical usage and that she had not acquired the tense and aspect system of the language.
3. I recognize that not all of these features are unique to AAE and HHNL. Yet there is justification for choosing them because of the fact that they do not generally characterize the speech of young, middle-class Whites in New York and the Midwest. /R/ vocalization or /r/-lessness is of course common in New York City, but not among young middle-class speakers. Glide reduction of the /ay/ diphthong is found in white vernaculars, but not in the North.
4. One of my informants in New York City recounted that there were at least five all-white crews on Manhattan's affluent Upper East Side in the late 1990s: NUTS (Never Underestimate the Style), 10–7, CWB (Crazy White Boys), HFL (Hoods for Life), and Breeds.
5. However, others have commented to me that there is something very "white" and "geeky" about Eminem's voice and that in their view this is why it is accepted by people like Dr. Dre and African American audiences.
6. Smitherman (1994: 131) writes that "hard" describes someone who is tough or has been hardened by life and experience.

7. MC battles are one of the most visible and potentially humiliating ways for an MC to demonstrate his or her rhyming and freestyling skills. Two MCs face one another and each is given a fixed amount of time (usually 30 seconds to a minute) to perform a spontaneous, or "freestyle," rhyming litany of insults at his or her opponent. In most cases, MCs draw on a mix of spontaneous and pre-written rhymes, using hooks like "on the mic" and fillers like "yo" and "check it" to keep their rhymes flowing. A battle ends in defeat if the MC can't think of another rhyme during the allotted time period or if the rhymes are obviously written ahead of time rather than generated spontaneously. The audience chooses the winner by applauding louder for one opponent than the other at the end of the battle. Crucially, each competitor tries not to take all of this criticism personally lest he or she lose face and the backing of audience. The MC battle Ivy participated in was sponsored by *Blaze* magazine. It is important to note that battles sponsored by magazines and cable television channels are highly commercialized and differ significantly from the informal battles that takes place on street corners, parks, parties, or other places where black Hip Hop youth gather.

8. See Cutler (2002a) for an expanded discussion of suck teeth among white Hip Hoppers.

9. As Rampton (1999) notes citing Bakhtin (1984: 89), double-voicing is the narrator's use of someone else's discourse (or language) to insert "a new semantic intention into a discourse which already has . . . an intention of its own." There are two kinds of double-voicing: uni-directional—involving the use of someone else's discourse in the direction of one's own particular intentions—and vari-directional—when the speaker employs someone else's discourse but introduces an opposing semantic intention.

10. Whites who were involved in Hip Hop in the 1980s include Rick Rubin, who produced many early rap groups including Run D.M.C., LL Cool J, and the Beastie Boys; the Beastie Boys (a white rap group from Brooklyn); 3rd Bass (mixed race rap group from New York City); and Zephyr (early white graffiti artist).

11. PJ's overall rate of verbal /s/ absence was 10% (N = 50). He averaged 42% copula absence (N = 36).

12. Cutler (2002b) analyzed a survey of 108 undergraduates at New York University about what ethnicity they judged PJ and several other of my informants to be. PJ was judged to be African American by 44% of the respondents. An almost equal number (45%) judged him to be Latino, and just 11% thought he was European American. These results suggest that PJ is at the very least trying *not* to sound white.

13. Several non-linguists have made similar comments to me. There is a perception that what linguists call AAE is just "street talk" or "slang." That is to say, people do not perceive it to be a language that is associated specifically with African Americans. See Trechter and Bucholtz (2001: 8–9) for a succinct critique of the way sociolinguists often link particular kinds of speakers with particular linguistic practices.

14. Morgan (2002) makes reference to several writers who try to justify racist hiring practices based on language tests. She describes the logic of these writers as follows: "since Whites believe that AAE usage reflects ignorance, criminality and immorality, African Americans should not use it" and that by doing so, they would "remove one more barrier to employment discrimination" (70).

4 Hip Hop, White Immigrant Youth, and African American English
Accommodation as an Identity Choice

INTRODUCTION

Sociolinguistics has a long history of trying to establish linguistic group norms and identify socially stratified speech patterns. More recently, the focus has shifted to the idea that speakers, although always somewhat constrained by the sociocultural field, exert some degree of agency on the way they express themselves. This chapter explores language choice among white ethnic immigrants who live in New York City and affiliate with Hip Hop culture. It examines what appear to be conscious choices by these young people to style their speech in the direction of what they perceive as African American English (AAE) and Hip Hop Nation Language (HHNL) and, in one case, New York Latino English (NYLE).[1] As such, it aligns with a Gilesian conception of linguistic accommodation that involves social identification and preferences for self-identification (Giles, Coupland, and Coupland 1991). The fact that people choose to mark themselves linguistically and/or by other means as members of groups other than their own points to the role of individual agency in resisting the social pressures to conform to group norms. These various identity orientations were evident in the speech patterns exhibited by each individual in terms of morphosyntax and phonology, as well as in the ways they were identified on the basis of their speech in a blind perceptions survey of students at three East Coast American universities.

THEORIZING AGENCY AND ACCOMMODATION

Agency, according to Ahearn (2001), refers to the "socioculturally mediated capacity to act" (112), meaning that people are controlled to some degree by social expectations and norms of the society in which they live. A question that arises in theorizing agency is the degree to which it involves free will exercised by completely autonomous people. The balance between social constraints and individual agency is exemplified by the ways in which Hip Hop youth define themselves as both local and global members of the global

Hip Hop community. Alim (2009: 123) points to the agentive force of Hip Hop youth in how they "create styles and languages that (re)mix dominant styles and languages in relation to those already in their repertoires," calling for a greater focus on linguistic agency in linguistic anthropological studies of globalization.

The concept of agency can also be linked to the competing theories of accommodation. According to one view (Giles et al. 1991), accommodation involves adapting one's speech to the speech of an interlocutor (convergence), or away from it (divergence), the focus being on conscious or unconscious identification with another group. The role of black America (and associated speech styles such as AAE and HHNL) as a key frame of reference in Hip Hop culture (Alim 2009) suggests that the emergence of local Hip Hop language style is indeed a case of conscious identification with another group as well as a desire to project local distinctiveness. A related way to analyze this type of conscious identification is the Acts of Identity model (LePage and Tabouret-Keller 1985), which argues that convergence-type behavior is possible if and when speakers can identify, access, and analyze the speech patterns of the target group and have a motivation and the ability to modify their own speech in the direction of the target group.

Previous work has examined the idea that immigrant minority youth make some stylistic choices (albeit limited ones) in how they speak, using language in ways that contest their own social categorization and suggest new forms of social alignment while drawing on the shared local meanings of particular language varieties (Auer and Dirim 2003; Fagyal 2005; Fought 2003; Ibrahim 2003; Queen 2006; Quist 2000; Nortier and Dorleijn 2008; Rampton 1995, 2006). In other cases, the choice to accommodate their speech towards that of another group is constrained by how speakers (e.g., immigrants) are perceived by the host society. Youth who are racialized by their appearance and presumed membership in certain socially defined groups (such as East African immigrants in Canada) may contest this process by taking ownership of the category into which they are placed (Ibrahim 2003).

Researchers use a number of terms to describe the various orientations that speakers adopt when they use, appropriate, or voice linguistic features from other group. As described in Chapter 1, the terms *styling, stylization,* and *language accommodation* are theoretically distinct but also somewhat related. Departing from the Labovian conception of *style* as attention paid to speech on a continuum of informal to formal, *styling* involves the use of variables linked to identity categories for constructing social meanings, social categories, and identity discursively (Eckert 2008). Styling is when individuals adopt ways of speaking that are linked to particular social groups to project their identity in different situations and with different interlocutors; it's akin to the ways in which individuals style their appearance in terms of hairstyle, clothing, makeup, gait, etc., in ways that are deeply personal, but also according to the constraints of the situation. *Stylization* is removed from the projection of the self and entails the performative deployment of stylistic variables in sometimes playful and fleeting ways that deviate from the expected forms for a given speaking context (Coupland 2001; Rampton 2006). *Language accommodation*, on the other hand, refers to the tendency to converge towards or diverge away from the speech of one's interlocutor (Giles et al. 1991). Although accommodation generally refers to temporary linguistic behavior in interactional settings, it has implications for under-standing how speakers adopt or affect new linguistic patterns within and across speech communities and over time, and may in turn trigger language change. As such, it overlaps with the concept of *styling*, which also involves the use of variables that index social groups. In line with Bigham (2010); Blake and Shousterman (2010); Purnell and Yaeger-Dror (2010); Strand et al. (2010); and Watt et al. (2010), I use the term *accommodation* to refer to the general tendency of speakers to converge towards the speech of another group (African Americans or New York City Latinos) while recognizing that their speech may vary in different interactions, depending on whether they are attempting to converge or diverge from their immediate interlocutor.

The emergence of *ethnolects* or ethnic-based language varieties (Nortier 2008) among immigrant youth has been documented in Hamburg, Ger-many, where youth from a variety of different ethnic backgrounds use Turk-ish words and expressions as a way to express varying degrees of affiliation with Turkish culture, youth culture, and a subcultural or minority orienta-tion (Auer and Dirim 2003). Related work in other European cities has shown how languages other than the dominant or national code function as resources to signal a variety of orientations (Quist 2000; Nortier and Dorleijn 2008). In other cases, youth in Europe express (or index) more than one identity through the use of symbolic resources from more than one language (Fagyal 2005; Queen 2006). Similarly, in the southwestern US the predominance of Mexican/Chicano heritage among Spanish-English bilinguals leads immigrants of other origins to adopt linguistic features associated with Mexican Spanish (Fought 2003). Other recent sociolinguis-tic work in the US addresses the question of accommodation with respect to AAE, showing that African Americans are able to vary in their use of phonetic features with different interlocutors (Weldon 2004; Scanlon and Wassink 2010). Yet in other cases, extensive, direct contact with a group (e.g., African Americans) does not seem to be a requirement for speakers (e.g., Hispanics in North Carolina) to learn and use AAVE features (Dun-stan 2010).

In sum, some of the recent research that touches on the question of agency and accommodation shows that people do make choices about how they use the language(s) and varieties in their linguistic repertoires. In some cases, these choices reflect a degree of language contact resulting from exposure to another group. In others, choice may reflect the racializing discourses that place individuals outside the mainstream, leading them to identify with one or more other ethnic minorities and adopt associated youth speech styles as a symbolic resource. The present study deals with youth who come from countries whose inhabitants are often considered white, although a wide range of physical differences exists within them. Perhaps more so than for people of color living in Europe and North America, these young people can assimilate to the normative white mainstream culture in the US in terms of their appearance. Linguistically, their friends and families expect them to assimilate towards some form of mainstream Local Vernacular English (LVE) or National Vernacular English (NVE), yet they resist this process to varying degrees, choosing instead to project ethnolinguistically ambiguous identities that result from a conscious desire to signal an affiliation with Hip Hop.

For each of the individuals discussed in this chapter, Hip Hop culture is a common point of reference. The ties between Hip Hop culture and urban African American youth culture are well established (Alim 2002) and the speech patterns associated with Hip Hop culture clearly derive from AAE (Alim 2002, 2009; Smitherman 1997, 2000). Thus, youth from various ethnic backgrounds in the US adopt local or supra-local AAE features in order to express their affiliation with Hip Hop culture. Using AAE- and NYLE-styled speech does not necessarily always reflect a strong attitudinal orientation towards young urban African Americans or Latinos, but rather towards Hip Hop culture, whose language of expression and cultural roots are African American. Accommodation of this kind is of an indirect nature and reflects the use of language by speakers in order to construct themselves and others as *kinds* of people (Eckert and McConnell-Ginet 1995: 470). The input varies from speaker to speaker, but for some, it involves mainly listening to rap music, and transcribing and memorizing rap lyrics. Other individuals have African American and/or Latino friends, attend public school with African American and Latino students, and play on sports teams with them.

DATA AND METHODS

The data for this chapter come from some of the same informants who appeared in Chapter 3 (Bobo, Ghetto Thug, Ivy, and PJ), however, in this case, the focus is on their status as foreign-born or second-generation immigrants with foreign-born parents. I wanted to examine these four young people in greater detail because they display differing degrees of accommodation towards AAE and NYLE. Were they making conscious choices in how they styled their speech? Was their immigrant status or their appearance a factor in the linguistic choices they made? Finally, how did others perceive their speech and could they pass as members of another ethnic group (i.e., African American or Latino) on the basis of their speech? I focused on three phonological and one syntactic feature for the analysis.

The variables of /r/-lessness, /ɑy/ glide reduction, t/d deletion, and copula deletion are all found in AAE and NYLE. Although /r/-lessness and glide reduction are found in the speech of Whites in various regions, they are not typical of the speech of young, middle class white youth in New York City and therefore suggest some degree of convergence towards AAE and/or NYLE. Copula (*is*) deletion is not found in the speech of Whites (although *are* deletion is found among Whites in the South), so it quite clearly points to AAE and/or NYLE as linguistic targets. For two of the variables (r-Ø and t/d deletion), the data from these four speakers is compared with radio interview data (recorded and analyzed by the author) from the African American rappers/producers NAS (from New York City) and Dr. Dre (from Los Angeles), as well the white rapper Eminem (from Detroit). The four speakers are identified in Table 4.1.

Bobo was born in Moscow and identified himself as Jewish Russian. He and his family lived in Italy briefly, and then moved to the US when he was four. Bobo has dark, straight, closely cropped hair and pale skin and would most likely be classified as white on the basis of his appearance. He lived in a Russian neighborhood (Brighton Beach), attended a large, academically oriented public high school in Brooklyn, and played on the mainly African American football team. He participated in Hip Hop mainly as a consumer of rap music.

Ghetto Thug, although born in the US, identified himself as Armenian. He described himself as having an olive complexion, dark-colored eyes, and thick, curly hair, and says that people think he is either Hispanic or Middle Eastern when they first meet him. He lived in a wealthy neighborhood in

Table 4.1   List of Informants

Pseudonym	Age	Appearance	Country of Origin/ Ethnicity	Gender	Gender/ Ethnicity of Interviewer	Age on Arrival in US
Bobo	17	dark straight hair, fair skin	Russia (Jewish)	Male	African American female (age 17)	4
Ghetto Thug	16	thick, curly hair, olive skin	Bulgaria (of Armenian descent)	Male	White male (age 16)	2nd generation
Ivy	18	blond, fair skin	Israel (Jewish)	Female	White female (age 35)	7
PJ	16	dark hair, fair skin	Russia (Jewish)	Male	Asian American female (age 17)	5

Queens (Forest Hills) and attended the same public high school as Bobo, but "hung" with a primarily Latino (Puerto Rican) male crew and demonstrated systematic use of certain NYLE features such as apical /l/ in onsets (Slomanson and Newman 2004) and syllable timing (Anisman 1975), along with AAE features such as copula deletion. He listened to rap music and saw himself as living the Hip Hop lifestyle in terms of his dress style and peer affiliations.

Ivy was born in Israel where she spent the first seven years of her life before moving to Ann Arbor in 1988, where her parents were employed at the University of Michigan. Ivy spoke only Hebrew when she arrived and claimed that she learned English by rapping to Hip Hop lyrics. Ivy has blond hair and light eyes and looks Northern European. She moved to Harlem (near 125th street and Broadway) the day after she graduated from high school (approximately one year prior to the interview) and was the only white girl in an all-female rap crew. At the time, she performed frequently as an MC in venues around New York City and saw herself as an aspiring rap artist.

PJ lived and attended high school in a Jewish enclave of Brooklyn (Borough Park). As noted in Chapter 3, he describes himself in the interview as a conservative Jew and later as *Blackinese* which he defined as "white with a little bit of Black." His peer group was somewhat mixed but contained no African Americans. PJ heavily identified with Hip Hop culture and claimed that he spoke "Ebonics," yet his friends contested his status as an authentic speaker, accusing him of "trying to talk Black."

The racial/ethnic makeup of the area where each informant grew up is listed in Table 4.2, as is their self-proclaimed predominant reference group. It is clear from the data that all of the informants were raised in predominantly white communities. In the case of Bobo, Ghetto Thug, and PJ, it is also evident that they were living in white ethnic enclaves given that Whites in New York City constitute approximately 45% of the population on average (US Census 2000). Based on the demographics of Brighton Beach, Borough Park, Forest Hills, and Ann Arbor, it is unlikely that the speakers would have been in close contact with speakers of AAE or NYLE in their immediate neighborhoods without making special efforts to seek out such contact. Ivy stands out as having moved from a white enclave (Ann Arbor) to an African American one (Harlem) after graduating from high school.

Ghetto Thug and Bobo were each interviewed by one of their own high school friends, a strategy to collect more naturalistic data than the author—a white, female academic—might have been able to obtain herself. Clearly, the identity of the interviewer may have had some effect on the language used by each speaker, although it is difficult to determine the direction of the effect because multiple interviews with different interlocutors were not conducted. None of the interviewers is involved in Hip Hop nor do they display any tendency to use AAE or NYLE-styled speech in the recordings, so it is difficult to determine what if any effect this had on the speech of the interviewees.

Table 4.2   Racial/Ethnic Makeup of Informants' Primary Residence

Pseudonym	Locality	White	African American	Hispanic
Bobo	Brighton Beach, Brooklyn	73.1%	5.9%	8.5%
Ghetto Thug	Forest Hills, Queens	71.3%	2.5%	10.8%
Ivy	Ann Arbor	74.7%	8.8%	3.3%
	Harlem, NYC	18.5%	59.7%	19.4%
PJ	Borough Park, Brooklyn	68.4%	3.9%	7.3%

US Census 2000 for Forest Hills and Ann Arbor; Borough Park Data Report, Harlem and Brighton Beach Data Report (*New York Times Real Estate*)

Each interview was approximately one hour in length and was recorded on portable Sony TCM-5000EV tape recorders with clip-on Lavalier microphones. The coding was done by the author, based on the first 30 minutes of the interview, and was impressionistic. The following four sections examine each of the variables: copula deletion, t/d deletion, the reduction of the glide in the /ɑy/ diphthong, and post-vocalic /r/-lessness.

FINDINGS

Copula Deletion

Research on morphosyntactic patterns such as copula deletion among African Americans, and more specifically those involved in Hip Hop culture, shows that there are correlations with socioeconomic status, geographic origins, and gender (Alim 2002). The female African American rapper Eve was shown to have lower rates of *is* deletion than the male African American rapper Juvenile in their respective interviews (8% vs. 61%). Alim attributes these differences to social factors including gender, region of residence, social class, and educational opportunities (Alim 2002: 297–98).[2]

Alim (2002) points to the role of vernacular AAE style and stylistic variation in symbolizing street credibility. Similarly, omitting the copula for white youth is a symbolic way to lend themselves an aura of street credibility while not necessarily representing any actual ties to the street. The young people in this study have not been socialized in African American communities and did not grow up speaking AAE, so their use of features of AAE like copula deletion, albeit not at the rates we find among African American male rappers such as Juvenile, must still be analyzed as a choice that deviates significantly from NVE and the surrounding white vernacular.

We see a wide range of inter-speaker variation in Table 4.3 which is indicative of more general patterns for each speaker as well as an indicator of a general orientation towards street culture.[3] Bobo, a studious, college-bound young man who associates with African Americans on the high school football team, never omits the copula, whereas Ivy and Ghetto Thug do, but only to a small degree. Three of these speakers actually surpass the African American female rapper Eve in terms of their rates of copula deletion in an interview setting, but none comes close to the African American male rapper Juvenile, who averaged 61% deletion in his interview data. This points to the symbolic role that features like copula deletion may also play in indexing street personae for many white Hip Hoppers.

t/d Deletion

The following section examines t/d deletion in the speech of the four informants and compares it with two additional speakers: Eminem, a well-known and successful white rapper from Detroit, and NAS, an equally famous African American rapper and producer from Queens.[4]

In his analysis of t/d deletion, Guy (1991) shows that it is possible to determine the extent to which speakers are deviating from their individual expected rate of t/d deletion based on the exponential relationship between the rate at which they retain monomorphemes (M) and bimorphemes (B) in regular verbs (R) versus irregular verbs (I). The exponential model predicts these relationships among rates of final coronal stop retention in monomorphemic (underived) words (M), irregular past tense verbs (I), and regular past tense verbs (R) as follows:

$$M = R^3$$
$$I = R^2$$

Thus, speakers whose rates of t/d retention deviate from this pattern can be said to be style shifting in either a more vernacular or a more standard

Table 4.3   A Syntactic Feature: Individual Rates of Copula Absence (Is) in Interviews

Speaker	Rate of Absence	N
Bobo	0%	30
Eve*	8%	—
Ghetto Thug	10%	25
Ivy	15%	37
PJ	42%	36
Juvenile*	61%	—

*Data from Alim (2002)

direction. Those whose rates of monomorphemic retention (M) exceed the cube of their rate of regular verb past tense markers and whose rates of retention of irregular verb past tense markers exceed the square of the rate of retention of regular verb past tense markers ($M > R^3$; $I > R^2$) are theoretically shifting their speech in a more vernacular direction. When the opposite conditions hold ($M < R^3$; $I < R^2$), a speaker is shifting in a more standard direction (Guy 1991).

The results for each speaker appear in Table 4.4.[5] The figures in the final column indicate the degree to which a speaker is deviating from his or her unmarked style. The figure is arrived at by subtracting the cube of the rate of t/d retention in regular verbs from rate of retention of t/d in monomorphemes.

These results are illustrated graphically in Figure 4.1. The bold vertical zero line represents neutrality or no shift (Ghetto Thug, Eminem). Speakers to the left of the line are shifting towards AAE (Bobo, PJ, and Ivy). Data points to the right of the line (NAS) indicate a shift towards NVE. Note that shifts in either direction are all relative to a speaker's underlying, unmarked rates of t/d use, indicated by his or her placement on the vertical Y-axis.

Unlike PJ, Bobo, and Ivy, Ghetto Thug and Eminem appear to be using their natural or unmarked style in this data, as indicated by their location on or near the zero line. Note that although Ghetto Thug's data show little perceptible style shifting, he greatly exceeds the deletion rates of all other speakers, including NAS. As already noted, he stated in his interview that he "hangs" with a crew of Puerto Rican boys in a part of town isolated from the well-to-do part of Queens where he and his parents live. Wolfram (1974) found that consonant cluster reduction among Puerto Ricans was potentially traceable either to Spanish or to AAE and was more frequent among some Puerto Rican speakers than among African Americans (cited in Slomanson

Table 4.4 A Morphophonological Variable: t/d Deletion, Retention, and Style Shifting

Speaker	No. deleted t/d tokens	Total no. of t/d tokens	Freq. of t/d deletion	Rate of M retention	No. of retained (R) tokens	R^3	Measure of style shifting (Rate of M retention - R^3)
NAS	47	66	71%	0.11	24	0.16	−0.05
Eminem	27	55	49%	0.24	35	0.25	−0.01
Ghetto Thug	50	62	81%	0.09	16	0.08	0.01
Ivy	66	109	61%	0.37	9	0.27	0.10
PJ	60	92	65%	0.29	11	0.09	0.20
Bobo	14	32	44%	0.52	6	0.30	0.22

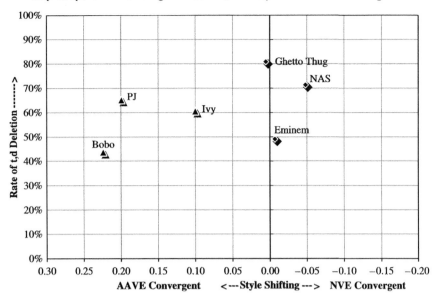

Figure 4.1   t/d Deletion as a Measure of Identity Performance

and Newman 2004: 201). Slomanson and Newman (2004) point out that rates were higher for speakers with high rates of contact with African Americans than for those who had fewer contacts, suggesting that the Spanish and AAE influences converged to yield a higher rate of deletion than either would have produced by itself. This sort of generalization may be relevant to the high overall rates of t/d deletion shown for Ghetto Thug because he is presumably emulating the patterns used by his Puerto Rican friends.

The data presented here suggest that Ghetto Thug has successfully internalized characteristics of the vernacular of his chosen reference group. Eminem was raised very near to the African American community in Detroit so it is possible that his rates of t/d deletion reflect a pattern he acquired as his "native" variety or that he subsequently internalized as he was exposed to AAE as a child. NAS, on the other hand, appears to be engaging in some kind of linguistic convergence towards a more standard model in line with a Labovian view of style as attention paid to speech. Bobo, PJ, and Ivy are deleting t/d at a rate higher than their unmarked style and are thus shifting their speech towards AAE, but the largest shifts are found for Bobo and PJ (whose friends thought of him as a "wannabe" or someone who tries to act and sound black). PJ's style shifting data appear to confirm this interpretation. Bobo, on the other hand, is quite conservative overall in terms of his use of other AAE patterns—at least judging by the data in his interview. Although he shows a significant style shift towards more t/d deletion, he still has one of the lowest rates of deletion in the corpus, paralleling his conservative use of the other features under investigation here.

Ivy's rather modest shift was somewhat surprising given the extent of her involvement in Hip Hop as an aspiring MC, and the fact that many listeners in a blind survey believed her to be African American (as discussed below). But she does report having learned English at the age of seven by practicing rap lyrics which may have caused her, like Ghetto Thug, to internalize many AAE patterns. Additionally, she is the only one being interviewed by a white academic, which may cause her to converge toward the NVE.

Glide Reduction of the /ɑy/ Diphthong

Labov, Ash, and Boberg (2006) report rates of glide reduction of 100% or close to it in many parts of the South, but a lower percentage in the largest Texas cities of Dallas and Houston, as well as in the Southeast cities of Savannah and Charleston. Although glide reduction of /ɑy/ in *buy/bide* is not found in New York among Whites, it does occur in the speech of African Americans and Latinos (Wolfram 1974:201; Coggshall and Becker 2010). Although recent studies have begun to question pan-AAVE speech markers (Jones 2003; Nguyen 2006), Eberhardt (2010) suggests that in northern cities such as Pittsburgh, glide reduction may still be a resource for African Americans to construct a specifically African American identity. Purnell (2010) found that middle class African Americans in Milwaukee, Wisconsin reduce the glide in *bide* when conversing with one another, but converge to the diphthongal white local norm (indeed overshoot it) when conversing with Whites, implying that this feature is indexical of African American identity in that region, but that AAVE speakers are aware of and are able to accommodate their speech to local white norms.

Wolfram (1974: 202) shows that African Americans reduced the glide at a rate of 77%, followed closely by Puerto Ricans who had extensive contact with African Americans at 70%, while Puerto Ricans who had little contact with the African American community had a much lower rate at 40%. Slomanson and Newman (2004) also found that Latino members of the Hip Hop peer culture, with its strong cultural and demographic ties to the African American community, tend to reduce the glide more than members of other Latino groups, despite the fact that they had relatively few African Americans in their immediate peer group.[6]

Given the ubiquity of glide reduction in the speech of the white Hip Hoppers, it appears to be an entry-level marker of Hip Hop affiliation (Cutler 2002b). The presence of glide reduction in the speech of white youth in New York City suggests Hip Hop culture and AAE as reference points (Slomanson and Newman 2004), although it might also reference more generalized patterns associated with popular music genres, as Trudgill (1983) has suggested. Glide reduction is extremely common in the performed musical lyrics of countless American pop singers; however, there is one crucial difference: white Hip Hop-affiliated youth use this feature in their everyday speech (as opposed to strictly in performance), which may point to a greater personal investment in the social meanings of AAE-styled speech than is the case for vocalists. Table 4.5 shows the rates of /ay/ glide reduction among the four speakers in the sample.

It is rare to find frequencies for glide reduction in the contemporary literature. Current analyses of glide reduction in New York City and Detroit look at F1/F2 formant values (Coggshall and Becker 2010; Nguyen 2006), allowing only for comparisons with Wolfram's data from the 1970s and Fix's data for white women who perform AAVE on television (Fix 2009). The patterns in the present data on white, Hip Hop-affiliated youth seem to match up with the ethnographic data presented earlier for each speaker. Bobo once again has the lowest rate at 39%, coming very close to Puerto Ricans in New York City in the 1970s who had minimal contact with the African American community at 40% (Wolfram 1974: 202).[7] Ivy's rate of 70% approaches, and Ghetto Thug and PJ both exceed, the rate of African Americans in New York City in the 1970s cited in Wolfram (1974). Ivy's rate also approaches that of the two white women profiled in Fix (2009) who performed AAVE on television and averaged 74% (Fix 2009). We might expect Ghetto Thug to approximate the rate of Puerto Ricans who have extensive contacts with African Americans, yet his rate well exceeds theirs, as well as African Americans, coming close to categorical glide reduction. PJ's rate also exceeds the rate found among African Americans in New York City in the 1970s, suggesting that he and Ghetto Thug are engaged in hyper-accommodation (Yaeger-Dror 1992a, 1992b) to the linguistic target.

Post-vocalic, Pre-consonantal /r/-lessness (r-Ø)

The fourth variable under consideration is particularly interesting precisely because it appears to be disappearing and is notably less common in the speech of younger people than it was even a few decades ago. In AAE, as in many dialects of American English, there is a general tendency to omit post-vocalic, pre-consonantal /r/. Labov (1972) lists eastern New England, New York City, and the South (Upper and Lower) as the three major /r/-less dialect areas. Today, /r/-lessness (r-Ø) is still common in New York City,

Table 4.5 Phonological Variation: Glide Reduction of /ay/

Speaker	Rate of glide reduction	N
Bobo	39%	142
Ghetto Thug	94%	162
Ivy	70%	220
PJ	86%	170
Eminem	94%	172
Dr. Dre	99%	102

particularly among African Americans and older and/or working class white ethnics (Becker 2009; Labov, Ash, and Boberg 2006).

Yet, the tendency to omit /r/ has been disappearing in the all of the regions listed above. Nearly four decades ago, Labov (1972:13) wrote that areas like New York City have been "strongly influenced in recent years by the /r/-pronouncing pattern which is predominant in broadcasting," so that "educated speakers, especially young people, will show a mixed pattern in their speech." As has been true roughly since World War II, r-Ø in the speech of Whites (and perhaps in the speech of other ethnic groups as well) connotes working class origins, and rhotic speech continues to define the US prestige norm (Labov, Ash, and Boberg 2006).

Although little data on /r/ has been collected since the 1960s, some studies in the intervening years note that r-Ø is on the decline in New York City and elsewhere (Becker 2009; Fowler 1986; Irwin and Nagy 2007; Nguyen 2006). Fowler (1986) replicated Labov's New York City department store survey and documented a small decrease of 5% in r-Ø among younger lower middle class speakers as compared to Labov's 1962 study. Becker (2009) surveyed older white speakers on the Lower East Side in New York City (where Labov showed that white working class speakers were virtually 100% r-Ø in the 1960s) and found that the average had dropped to 64% r-Ø. Irwin and Nagy (2007) established that r-Ø is also decreasing slowly in New England, with the trend more pronounced among AAE speakers than white speakers, and Nguyen (2006) found that African Americans in Detroit have also decreased their rates of r-Ø from approximately 33% in 1966 to 13% in recent years.

In light of these trends, the appearance of r-Ø in the speech of many young white middle class Hip Hoppers at rates that exceed older white working class speakers must be viewed as a reverse tendency. There is variation between speakers who grew up in New York City where r-Ø is part of the surrounding local white vernacular (Bobo, Ghetto Thug, and PJ), versus those from the inland north (Eminem and Ivy) where it is not. Although this difference may be attributable to the presence or absence of r-Ø in the local vernacular, the target is likely to be AAE/HHNL. Evidence for this comes from a comparison of the ways in which some individuals vary their use of /r/ with different interlocutors. The white rapper Eminem shows variation in his use of r-Ø in a phone interview where he seems to be diverging from the /r/-less Australian English speaker (8%, N = 108) as compared with a group interview with his African American producer Dr. Dre (50%, N = 28; Cutler 2002a). And Buckwild, the white woman who performs AAVE on television discussed in Fix (2009), ranges from 27% r-Ø during her performance of AAVE to 0% when she switches to her "angry" white style.

Table 4.6 shows the distribution of pre-consonantal, pre-pausal r-Ø (VrC) for the four speakers in the sample plus radio interview data from Dr. Dre and the white rapper Eminem.[8]

Table 4.6   Phonological Variation: r-Ø

Speaker	VrC	N
Bobo	0%	33
Ivy	27%	123
Eminem	50%	28
Ghetto Thug	72%	161
Dr. Dre	77%	142
PJ	82%	201

Table 4.6 also illustrates the very wide interspeaker variation in /r/ usage: Bobo's speech is entirely rhotic, which seems to match the rather conservative way he patterns with respect to the other variables. Ivy and Eminem occupy a middle ground, ranging from 26%–50%and surpassing rates of r-Ø found among African Americans in Detroit (Nguyen 2006). Finally, Ghetto Thug, Dr. Dre, and PJ have the highest rates of r-Ø (VrC) ranging from 72%–82%, all of which exceed the rates of older white working class New Yorkers. The local indexical meanings of r-Ø may vary from one speech community to another, but its continued presence in the speech of many young urban African Americans (as well as in rap lyrics) makes it a resource for young Whites who want to project their orientation towards Hip Hop culture.

Ethnic Identity Survey

What follows is a discussion of how three of the four informants in the present study were identified in terms of ethnicity in a survey of undergraduates conducted at three East Coast campuses in 2002–2003: 142 students from New York University (NYU), 117 from Stony Brook University on Long Island (SBU), and 29 from the University of North Carolina, Chapel Hill (UNCCH; Cutler 2002b). The original survey included a total of nine speakers who were chosen because they all demonstrated some use of AAE features. Due to the limitations of time in administering the survey, Bobo was not included.

The respondents' schools and self-reported ethnicities appear in Table 4.7. The third column lists the percentage of the overall incoming first-year class from a particular state (CityTownInfo.com), giving some general indication of the make-up of the respondents in any given class. Going by these numbers, we would expect about 40% of the NYU students and almost 90% of the SBU students to be at least familiar with different varieties of New York City English, whereas most of the UNCCH students would be at least familiar with different varieties of southern American English, including local varieties of AAE. The students at NYU are broken into two classes, which each heard a different selection of speakers: NYU 1 heard PJ and Ivy's samples; NYU 2 heard Ghetto Thug's sample.

After hearing 12–15 second samples from each speaker, the respondents were asked to identify each speaker's ethnicity from five categories: African American, European American, Asian American, Latino/Hispanic, and a blank space (Other) to write in another ethnicity. The main objective of the survey was to measure the extent to which any of the speakers might be identified as African American or something other than European American, given that the speech style they employ overlaps with AAE, and in some cases, NYLE.

Table 4.8 shows how Ivy, PJ, and Ghetto Thug were identified in terms of ethnicity by the undergraduate respondents at each school. Although the results vary somewhat between schools, it is noteworthy that a majority of the respondents identify Ivy as African American at all three schools.[9] It is also interesting to note that the group that was most convinced that she is African American was from North Carolina and also happened to be 83% white (24/29 students). The more ethnically and geographically diverse students at NYU and SBU were less likely to identify her as African American. It is also striking to compare the relatively low percentage of respondents who identify each speaker as white. On average, PJ and Ghetto

Table 4.7   Respondents by School and Ethnicity

School	N	%Local*	%White	%African American	%Latino	%Asian	%Other
NYU1	107	42%	43%	7%	15%	16%	19%
NYU2	35	42%	23%	29%	9%	11%	28%
SBU	117	89%	42%	2%	8%	36%	12%
UNCCH	29	80%	83%	10%	0%	7%	0%

*%Local pertains to entire freshman class; local defined as NY, NJ, CT for NYU and SBU; NC for UNCCH.

Table 4.8   Perception of Speaker Ethnicity by School

School		Ivy			PJ			Ghetto Thug	
	N	AA	EA	HA	N	AA	EA	HA	N	AA	EA	HA
NYU	107	57%	24%	15%	107	40%	24%	15%	35	26%	17%	57%
SBU	117	67%	18%	13%	117	53%	7%	36%	117	20%	11%	65%
UNCCH	29	76%	14%	10%	29	36%	36%	25%	29	21%	10%	62%
Average	253	64%	20%	14%	253	45%	13%	38%	181	21%	12%	63%

(AA = African American; EA = European American; HA = Hispanic American)

Thug are identified as white by just 13% and 12% and Ivy by 20% of the respondents.

The results for PJ are the most variable overall. The percentage of students who identify him as African American is somewhat similar in all three schools, but there is much more variation between European American and Hispanic. On average, he is perceived to be African American by a lower percentage of the students than Ivy and a higher percentage than Ghetto Thug.

Ghetto Thug's results are the most closely matched between schools. A majority of the respondents at all three schools believed him to be Hispanic, followed by African American and European American, with little variation between schools. The students at SBU are the most convinced, followed closely by students at UNCCH. Notably, it is the students at SBU with the highest proportion of students who might be predicted to be most familiar with NYLE who are most convinced that he is Hispanic.

Listeners' judgments are valuable for what they are—quick assessments of a speaker's ethnic identity, much like those made every day by people talking on the phone to an unfamiliar person. Given the accuracy with which listeners are typically able to identify the ethnicity of a speaker over the phone (Purnell et al. 1999), these results show the degree to which speech styling can confound the judgment of listeners.[10] However, analyzing what particular features listeners were attuned to when they identified each speaker is difficult to determine, because many factors may be involved, including voice quality, intonation, morphosyntax, word choice, and/or content. In more general terms, listeners may have been cuing into features or lexical items that index Hip Hop, which in turn led them to conclude in many cases that the speaker was African American.

What is remarkable about these results is the fact that the speakers lacked role models in their immediate social networks prior to adolescence and then attempted to accommodate their speech towards AAE or NYLE either via direct or indirect contact. As a result, they are now able to convince a large proportion of the listeners that they are something other than white.

DISCUSSION AND CONCLUSION

Figure 4.2 shows in more graphic form a consistent pattern across variables for each speaker, with speakers like Bobo showing the least overall convergence towards AAE and the others showing greater convergence. Clearly, this does not capture the full spectrum of individual accommodation, but it does show how speakers tend to converge towards AAE and/or NYLE across a number of variables. Greater convergence also results in speakers being identified as African American or Latino, although not in predictable ways. PJ and Ghetto Thug's rates are higher than Ivy's across most variables, yet she is judged to be African American by more listeners than either.

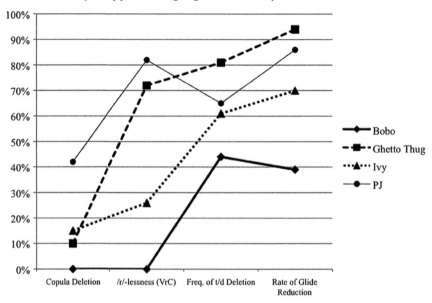

Figure 4.2   Phonological and Morphosyntactic Variation

I turn now to a discussion of these findings in terms of speaker agency and accommodation. Slomanson and Newman (2004) suggest that Latino youth in New York City experience the substrate pull of Spanish and the social pressure to assimilate to African American- and European American-oriented peer groups. Arguably, youth who move to New York City from other places (e.g., Russia, Ann Arbor) may experience some of the same pressures, although they may not necessarily have the same degree of contact with African Americans as many Latinos in New York City. Their choice or "act of identity" to accommodate towards AAE or NYLE is thus somewhat unexpected, save for the influence of Hip Hop culture and/or their peer groups. Historical analyses of groups like Irish, Italian, and Jewish Americans have traced the process by which these groups "become white" (Brodkin 1999; Ignatiev 1995). But in the present case, these particular immigrant youth seem to resist whiteness in their linguistic and cultural orientations (Cutler 2008a), pointing to the role of Hip Hop culture and the appeal of Hip Hop-oriented African American youth culture in disrupting the expectation they will automatically take up the mantle of whiteness and NVE in their projections of personal identity.

While it may be impossible to determine the extent to which identity is "intentional, habitual, consciously projected, the result of interactional negotiation, a construct of others' perceptions" or yet other factors (Bucholtz and Hall 2005), these data show that in some cases, it may be quite intentional. Bobo, Ivy, Ghetto Thug, and PJ might not be aware of the microlinguistic features they use in the process, but their speech styling involves at the very least an active and conscious desire to sound like someone else—speakers of AAE or NYLE—in order to project qualities that they associate with speakers of those varieties and/or their affiliation with Hip Hop.

These findings show that individuals can go quite far in their styling of the other as a way to define themselves (Bell 1999), and in some cases, actively resist societal expectations about how they should talk. Furthermore, these young people did not have the kind of contact that would lead to unconscious accommodation towards AAE and had to make concerted and conscious efforts to speak the way they do. Models that make predictions about speech behavior on the basis of unconscious input and contact such as exemplar dynamics and Trudgillian accommodation cannot predict these results, because they do not take into consideration the effects of social and psychological orientation towards a particular group.

A more nuanced analysis of the perception results and the specific features that respondents may have responded to is needed before making definitive claims about whether these speakers are reaching their respective linguistic targets. In conclusion, these examples support a view of accommodation that emphasizes the role of attitudinal orientation towards a target group (Auer and Hinskens 2005; Giles et al. 1991), but also that speakers are orienting towards a subculture (Hip Hop) that is associated with particular varieties (NYLE/AAE), rather than a particular group of people (African Americans or Latinos). Furthermore, this sort of accommodation emerges from a complex, long-term identity project, pointing to the role of agency as an explanation for accommodation, and showing that individuals can accommodate to the speech of another group in the absence of systematic contact.

NOTES

1. I use the term *AAE* (African American English) to refer to the range of variable patterns associated with the speech of African Americans in the US, while acknowledging that there are significant regional and social differences among speakers. Other researchers cited in this chapter employ the term AAVE (African American Vernacular English), a choice which I chose to respect when discussing their findings. Slomanson and Newman (2004) identify a number of features that characterize NYLE, or New York Latino English, including apical or *light* /l/ onsets and monophthongal /ay/, /ey/, /ow/, and /uw/. Syllable timing has also been identified as a feature of New York Puerto Rican English (Anisman 1975).
2. Note the fact that Eve is from Philadelphia, a city where speakers do not typically use copula deletion, whereas in Louisiana, where Juvenile comes from, it may be common even for non-African American speakers (Dubois and Horvath 2003).
3. Copula (*is*) deletion was calculated using Labov's formula, by adding the total number of deleted forms of "be" (D) and dividing them by the sum of the deleted forms plus contracted forms (D+C). The formula reads D/(D+C) (Labov 1969).

4. The data for these six speakers comes from Guy and Cutler (2011). Tokens of t/d deletion were only counted if the following word began with a sound other than a coronal stop.

5. Eminem and NAS' data were culled from interviews broadcast on the radio; Eminem was interviewed over the phone for ABC (Australian Broadcasting Company) radio in 2000, and NAS was interviewed on the 1xtra radio show for the BBC in 2003.

6. There are also cases of non-American English speakers using glide reduced /ay/. Trudgill (1983) analyzed the sung lyrics of two British rock 'n' roll groups, the Beatles and the Rolling Stones, finding that they used Southern American pronunciation patterns such as glide reduced /ay/ (as well as /æ/ instead of /aː/ in *last*, and the flap for intervocalic /t/). His work suggested that, early on, their lyrical pronunciations were highly influenced by Southern US patterns, but that they later came to sound more British as the need to imitate American music diminished. Similarly, singers like Bob Dylan use glide reduced /ay/ in words of the BUY or BIDE classes (perhaps in order to reference older American folk singers like Woody Guthrie) although not apparently in everyday speech (Malcah Yaeger-Dror, personal communication).

7. I only looked at glide reduced /ay/ in open syllables or syllables with voiced coda consonants. Tokens were recorded as glide reduced if there was any audible tendency to reduce the second element (/i/) in the diphthong.

8. In this corpus, pre-consonantal /r/-lessness refers to the absence of /r/ following a vowel and preceding a consonant (e.g., CARD, CARED). Tokens of /r/ that occurred at a sentence boundary (Vr##) were treated as pre-pausal and were grouped with the pre-consonantal tokens (e.g., He's in the CAR.##). Eminem and Dr. Dre's data on r-Ø come from a joint radio interview on BBC radio that aired in 2000.

9. The differences between schools were not statistically significant.

10. Contra Purnell et al. (1999) and Foulkes and Barron (2000) found that a tightly-knit network of ten young British men had difficulty reliably identifying their own peer-group members (as well as themselves) on the basis of eight- to ten-second speech samples.

5 Brooklyn Style
Hip Hop Markers and Racial Affiliation among European Immigrants in New York City

INTRODUCTION

In the US, race is perceived as an utterly natural way to identify people and there is widespread recognition of racial categories at the societal, institutional, and governmental levels. Immigrants to the US are assumed to affiliate principally with one of several racial or ethnic categories such as Black, Hispanic, White, or Asian—labels that leave little room for the disparate class, racial, linguistic, or gender experiences they bring. For example, some immigrants from the Caribbean and Latin America are labeled "black" even though they do not define themselves that way nor are they identified as such in their homelands (Bailey 2000a, 2000b). Omi and Winant (1994) argue that the black-white racial polarity is a system of representation that still plays a very real role in shaping social structures and individual experiences in the US. In recent years, other categories such as Asian, Latino, and Middle Eastern have emerged as recognizable identities that are distinct from both black and white categories. Understanding one's place in the system of racial categorization is less of a dilemma for speakers born in the US where such categories are often perceived as natural, but for those born elsewhere such categories are not necessarily meaningful. Most immigrants from Europe, including countries such as Russia, the Ukraine, and the Balkans, are usually classified as white in the US. Yet whiteness may not be a category that is part of their self-definition, and their understanding of the meanings attached to whiteness might differ from those of people who have grown up in the US.

This chapter continues the analysis of data from five teenage first- and second-generation immigrants to the United States who originate from a number of eastern European countries including Bosnia, Russia, Ukraine, Armenia, and Bulgaria. These young people were interviewed by me or one of my research assistants. In contrast to Chapter 4, the focus here is more broadly on identity and the ways in which these young people grapple with the ethnic labels applied to them and how they signal their rejection of whiteness discursively and pragmatically. My research questions centered on how young immigrants come to terms with the black-white binary system of racial identification in the US, and the extent to which they use HHNL/AAE and Hip Hop culture as semiotic resources to resist whiteness.

There is nothing particularly distinctive about immigrants from Eastern Europe as opposed to other European immigrants in terms of how they experience race in the US. What connects the young people in this study is their identification with Hip Hop, an identity they express through stylized language and lifestyle practices such as the consumption of rap music and Hip Hop fashions and participation in cultural practices such as writing rhymes, DJ-ing, and MC-ing (cf. Newman 2004).

In American Hip Hop culture, adopting a Hip Hop-styled speech (HHNL) that is rooted in African American English (AAE) is also part of the way that Hip Hoppers (regardless of ethnic background) project their identities (Alim 2004a; Smitherman 1997). When it comes to white youth, this sort of linguistic appropriation may be read by some as a "desire to be black" or as a rejection of a white identity (Bucholtz 1999; Cutler 2002a). Given the social and economic advantages that whiteness confers in the US context, projecting an ambiguous racial identity can be a chancy endeavor for young immigrants who risk alienating their friends and families or sabotaging their educational and economic prospects. It is also an affront to standard language ideologies about the need for immigrants to speak Standard English for their own benefit (cf. Jaspers 2008).

Yet for some, Hip Hop culture and black culture more broadly offer more attractive models for identity formation than the surrounding white mainstream culture. This is not only true for first and second generation immigrants to the US, but also for native-born youth who are drawn to Hip Hop's defiant symbolism. Ibrahim (1998) has documented a similar trend among East African immigrant youth in Canada. The result has been the emergence of a kind of Hip Hop- and AAE/Hip Hop-flavored speech style among urban and suburban youth across North America that Alim (2004a) has dubbed "Hip Hop Nation Language" (HHNL). It has certain common features and crosses ethnic, cultural, and socioeconomic lines, but its speakers are not necessarily trying to project a single type of ethnic or Hip Hop identity. Hip Hop offers a range of social, cultural, and linguistic features that anyone can experiment with, and immigrant youth in particular seem drawn to the possibilities for self-definition that these symbolic resources can offer. This is evident in verbal interactions at both the linguistic and discursive level as they negotiate a place in their adopted homeland.

This chapter also examines the orientation of young immigrants to race and how their language practices tie into notions of "linguistic crossing" (Rampton 1995) and the possible emergence of a new ethnolect (Cornips 2000; Nortier 2001). Immigrants in the US who come from European countries may feel pressure to self-identify as white, and while most eventually give into these pressures, some attempt to resist whiteness. Many come from countries where color-based racial distinctions are not institutionalized the way they are in the US (e.g., Bosnia), making it more difficult for them to identify themselves with a racial category. Hip Hop culture can be a way of deferring this forced identification by providing young people with a way to "embrace the rituals of American popular culture" (Maira 1999: 44) while confounding or putting off the question of racial identification. Using a speech variety other than the standard allows these young immigrants to define and express themselves on their own terms rather than being positioned by the discourses of either dominant or minority ethnic cultures (Cornips 2000; Ibrahim 1998, 2003; Nortier 2001; Rampton 1995). Taken together the data examined here point to the mediating role of Hip Hop culture in the process of acculturation and its role in resisting racializing discourses.

PREVIOUS WORK ON IDENTITY FORMATION AND RACIALIZATION IN THE NORTH AMERICAN CONTEXT

The drive for immigrant groups to become defined as white or to distance themselves from blackness is historically rooted and seemingly natural given the political, social, and economic dominance of Whites in the US (Brodkin 1999; Ignatiev 1995; Roediger 2006). Indeed, some immigrants are shocked to discover that they are considered black when they arrive in North America, a category that confers on them a subordinate, disadvantaged identity. Some immigrants resist blackness while others embrace or at least accept it (Bailey 2000a, 2000b; Ibrahim 1998). Yet, placing too much emphasis on the black-white binary obscures the growing multidimensionality of the ethnic mix in places like New York City where Latinos, Asians, South Asians, and many others have distinct, widely recognized identities and where children with diverse ethnic backgrounds are more common than in many parts of the country. Thus, a more nuanced way of looking at the racial binary might therefore be to see whiteness as a category that sits ambiguously in a relationship with either "Minority" or with "Non-white."

A number of studies have looked at how young people experience and resist processes of racialization (Bailey 2000a, Bailey 2000b; Bucholtz 1999; Cutler 1999; Ibrahim 1998; Maira 2000; Rampton 1995). Dominican immigrant youth, the majority of whom have some sub-Saharan African ancestry, do not identify themselves as black or white, but rather in terms of ethnolinguistic identity, as Dominican/Spanish/Hispanic (Bailey 2000a, 2000b). For them, skin color does not equal racial identity, much as it does not in the Dominican Republic. In contrast, East African youth in Ontario embrace blackness and take ownership of blackness through AAE-styled speech and affiliation with Hip Hop (Ibrahim 1998).

For many young people born in the US, Hip Hop culture and HHNL/AAE-styled speech are a vehicle for transcending certain aspects of identity. Affluent white youth in New York City identify with Hip Hop culture in order to project a more streetwise, masculine identity than their private school and affluent family backgrounds would normally afford them (Cutler 1999; 2002a). In northern California, AAE is used by some white youth to construct a certain type of masculinity which they associate with blackness

(Bucholtz 1999). White male adolescents position black masculinity as physically powerful and locally dominant in contrast to white masculinity. This view is shaped by racist ideologies and white anxieties that link black masculinity to "hyper-physicality, hyper-sexuality and physical strength" (Bucholtz 1999: 444). Thus white male adolescent fascination with Hip Hop may represent a rejection of conventional white forms of male identity, in the desire to project a more virile physical masculinity.

Youth in other parts of the world use language in ways that contest racial categorization. Rampton (1995) employs the term "language crossing" to describe the playful and fleeting use of Creole, South Asian English and Punjabi within multiethnic adolescent peer groups. Crossing, particularly into Creole, symbolized toughness, coolness, but also opposition to authority and alienation from middle-class white culture. Significantly crossing also seemed to project a deracialized identity and represented a resistance to racism. The use of outgroup languages to express a racial otherness has also been documented in Germany. In Hamburg, youth from many different ethnic backgrounds use Turkish words and expressions as a way to express varying degrees of affiliation with Turkish culture, youth culture, and a subcultural or minority orientation (Auer and Dirim 2003). A few such young people used Turkish (alongside other markers such as rapper style clothing) to signal their ties to street culture and affiliation with Turks. Thus, in large urban centers, a minority language such as Turkish can function as a way to disassociate oneself from mainstream German or other mainstream cultural orientation. The Turkish language and culture seem to offer an alternative pole to which immigrant as well as native-born youth can orient themselves. A similar pattern is found among South Asian "Desi" youth in New York City (Maira 2000). Hip Hop culture allows them to "defer the question of 'black or white' through the ambiguity of adopting black style in an otherwise ethnically exclusive space" (Maira 2000: 339).

In sum, recent work on language and identity has shown that many young people in different parts of the world now actively resist hegemonic racial categories, often preferring to identify with groups other than the white mainstream. This counters a longstanding trend for immigrant groups to try to identify with white culture and to distance themselves from blackness in the US. Immigrant youth who affiliate with Hip Hop and use black-stylized speech may do so in order to resist the constraints of being defined as a member of a particular racial or social category, although the meanings they attach to Hip Hop and how they choose to orient themselves vis-à-vis youth culture, mainstream culture, and racial categories may vary from individual to individual.

ACTS OF IDENTITY: THE EMERGENCE OF AN ETHNOLECT?

The existence of a distinctive speech style among Hip Hop-affiliated youth has been theorized by a number of researchers (Alim 2002, 2004a, 2004b;

Bucholtz 1999; Cutler 2002a; Morgan 1993, 1996, 2001; Smitherman 1997). The research thus far seems to concur on a number of key points: (1) that the language style associated with Hip Hop is rooted in AAE communicative practices (Morgan 2001; Smitherman 1997), (2) that it is just "one of many language varieties used by African Americans," and (3) that it is "widely spoken across the country and is used, borrowed and transformed by African Americans as well as non-African Americans in and outside the US" (Alim 2004a: 393–394; cf. Bennett 1999; Bucholtz 1999; Cutler 1999; Morgan 2001; Smitherman 1997).

The use of symbolic resources from HHNL/AAE constitutes an "act of identity" (Le Page and Tabouret Keller 1985), signaling a range of possible orientations towards ethnicity, Hip Hop, mainstream American culture, and youth culture. The bundling of symbolic means of expression that have sociocultural meaning for informed members of a community constitute what Auer and Dirim (2003) call "socio-cultural styles." Linguistic resources that index Hip Hop affiliation come largely out of urban African American youth culture. This fact connects young European immigrants to a range of language practices that Rampton has called "crossing." Rampton (1995) describes crossing as "a range of ways in which people use language and dialect in discursive practice to appropriate, explore, reproduce or challenge influential images and stereotypes of groups that they don't themselves . . . belong to" (421). The same is true for other language varieties that these young people draw on. One young man in this sample (Ghetto Thug) also draws on New York City Latino English (NYLE) features in conjunction with HHNL/AAE features to express his membership in a Latino male peer group and his affiliation with Hip Hop (cf. Slomanson and Newman 2004). As has been noted in previous chapters, styling one's speech on an ethnolect does not necessarily imply a desire to affiliate with a particular ethnic group (although in Ghetto Thug's case, it did); in most cases, it indexes qualities and attitudes associated with speakers of that variety, e.g., toughness, street smarts, masculinity which are associated with AAE speakers and perhaps also NYLE speakers.

The act of adopting HHNL/AAE-styled speech by non-African Americans is political; it contests preconceived notions of who should speak what language and which racial groups people, especially immigrants and the children of immigrants, ought to identify with; it also challenges language ideologies insisting on the need for immigrants to use the standard language for their own benefit (Jaspers 2008). Deviation from these norms leaves young people open to social censure from members of their own community or their peers. Their ethnic loyalty is questioned and they are accused of wanting to be black. On one level, linguistic features may be associated with a particular ethnic group, but they are available to anyone and can be used for different purposes and in different ways. Importantly, affiliating with Hip Hop and projecting this on the linguistic level can often signal a rejection of racial categories and a resistance towards racializing practices.

The young people in this study resist whiteness as a category both linguistically and discursively even though many of them concede that others will probably always see them as white. The data does not point to a straightforward interpretation of the ways in which young European immigrants define themselves; rather it suggests that resisting racial categories opens the door for many different identities and alignments.

INFORMANT BACKGROUNDS

The speakers in the sample (Dimebag, Ghetto Thug, Isko, Kin, and PJ) are all of European origin and live in New York City. All but one of the five informants (Isko) attended the same high school in Brooklyn and were connected through networks of friends who identified with Hip Hop. Although they are not all part of the same peer group, they do constitute a community of practice, a group of people who engage in some common endeavor (such as Hip Hop culture) and who come to share ways of doing things (talking, dress style, beliefs, values, etc.; Eckert and McConnell-Ginet 1992).

Young people who affiliate with Hip Hop signal this in how they dress (e.g., oversized shirts and pants for boys), the values they share such as "keepin' it real" (representing yourself for what you are), and language (drawing on AAE features to stylize their speech; Alim 2004a; Cutler 2003a; Rickford and Rickford 2000; Rose 1994). As noted in Chapter 3, many individuals who actively participate in Hip Hop as rappers, DJs, and social activists also come to internalize a cultural hierarchy that privileges blackness (Boyd 2002; Cutler 2005). Although there is certainly variation in how Hip Hop youth express their membership in this community of practice, most are consumers of or participants in activities such as writing (graffiti art or "graffing"), b-boying (break dancing), DJ-ing, and MC-ing.[1] It is important to point out, however, that probably only a minority of Hip Hop-affiliated youth actually participate in any these practices on a regular basis; most display their participation through a set of lifestyle practices that revolve around the consumption of rap music and Hip Hop fashions. This was certainly true of the young people discussed here.

Table 5.1 shows the age and national origins of each of the speakers. The data for this research were collected between 1999 and 2001 in New York City. Dimebag, Ghetto Thug, Kin, and PJ were recruited via networks of friends who participated in Hip Hop culture at a Brooklyn high school; Isko was attending college in Manhattan and was recruited through a college Hip Hop club. All of the speakers range in age from 16–18 and were living in the boroughs of Queens or Brooklyn in New York City at the time the interviews were conducted. The lack of gender diversity in the sample reflects an overall skewing towards male participation within Hip Hop culture and its associations with masculinity (cf. Bucholtz 1999).

Table 5.1   Informants

Pseudonym	Age	Country of origin	Gender	Age on arrival in US
Dimebag	18	Ukraine	Male	8
Ghetto Thug	16	Armenia	Male	2nd generation
Isko	18	Bosnia	Male	16
Kin	18	Bulgaria	Male	8
PJ	16	Russia	Male	5

Stylistic Markers of a Hip Hop Orientation

Table 5.2 outlines the range of HHNL/AAE linguistic markers that typify the speech of young people in the sample as well as those many others affiliate with Hip Hop more generally (Alim 2004a; Morgan 1996; Smitherman 1997). Variation according to topic and interlocutor for some of the features including post-vocalic r-Ø, /ay/ glide reduction, t/d deletion, verbal /s/ absence, and copula absence has been empirically demonstrated (Alim 2002; Alim 2004b; Cutler 2002a; Guy and Cutler 2011). There is also wide inter-speaker variation in how speakers in the present study employ these features; some display a more systematic use of phonological, morphosyntactic, and paralinguistic elements while others display only emblematic use of these features.

Stylistic practice involves reworking linguistic variables that are available to everyone for the construction of social meaning on a local level (Eckert and McConnell-Ginet 1992). Speakers make connections between attitudes, stances, and activities of people and their ways of speaking, appropriating elements of style to project the meanings that they associate with those individuals (Irvine 2001; Irvine and Gal 2000). Irvine and Gal write that "linguistic forms, including whole languages, can index social groups [and] can become a pointer to the social identities and the typical activities of speakers" (2000: 37). Thus HHNL/AAE-stylized speech indexes qualities people associate with African American youth culture, which may include a range of meanings depending on the speaker and what he or she is trying to convey. Thus the features above serve not as a way to claim blackness or any other ethnic designation, but rather as a way to project traits or characteristics associated with blackness and/or black Hip Hoppers such as coolness, not being uptight, and possessing a more physical type of masculinity. The use of HHNL/AAE-styled speech may also signal distance from whiteness or a general sense of ethnic otherness.

Getting Racialized: Other Ascriptions of Whiteness

One important reason for studying these young immigrants is to try to understand the meaning behind their cultural and linguistic affiliation with

Table 5.2   Hip Hop Speech Markers among Immigrant Youth

	Coda and syllabic /l/ vocalization post-vocalic r-Ø, e.g., car > *kah* monophthongization of /ɑy/ diphthong, e.g., rhyme > *rahm* glottalization of alveolar stops in codas, e.g., hitting > [hɪʔɪn]
Phonological Features	didn't > [dɪʔɪn] t/d deletion in coda consonant clusters, e.g., bes' offer

Paralinguistic
Features
	Wide intonational range
	   Falsetto voice
	   Low pitch
	   Suck teeth (alveolar lateral click)

Morphosyntactic
Features
	Habitual "be," e.g., She be workin'
	   Equative copula "be3," e.g., He *be* the man
	   Copula absence, e.g., She Ø comin' home
	   3rd person verbal –s absence, e.g., He live_ here
	   Negative inversion, e.g., Didn't nobody laugh
	   Multiple negation, e.g., He *don't* know *nobody*
	   Use of "ain't" in place of negated copula
	   Lack of subject-verb agreement, e.g., They *is* goin' too

Discourse and
Lexical Features
	Yo (vocative or tag)
	   You know what I'm sayin'?
	   I 'onno (truncation of "I don't know")
	   Nigga (in group form of address)
	   mad (very)
	   chill (calm down)
	   my boy (my friend)
	   nah (no)

Hip Hop and the extent to which this has an impact on how they construct their identities (cf. Newman 2001). The young people in the sample cannot be identified as from any single group: some socialize with a wide range of young people from many ethnic backgrounds, including African American youth, rather than strictly with members of their own immigrant community (Isko, Kin, PJ), while others affiliate primarily with white youth (Dimebag) or Latino youth (Ghetto Thug). In some cases they even reject close identification with other immigrants from their own countries of origin (PJ, Kin). They see Hip Hop as something that sets them apart from their compatriots in New York City, connecting them to what they see as the coolest, most appealing form of American youth culture, giving them a space where they can experiment with aspects of identity.

In the first excerpt, we see an example of how Kin, who immigrated to the US from Bulgaria at age 8, finds himself pressured by "J," his Bulgarian female friend to identify with whiteness. It shows how he uses language symbolically and discursively to distance himself from attitudes he associates with a white identity. In previous turns, Kin spoke about how many of his own family members regard black people as "beneath them" and how they can't understand why he wants to "act black." But Kin explains that it's not only his family members who have these kinds of attitudes; he then recounts how "J" has been telling him that he's "not like black people" and that one day he'll realize "who he really is." Kin voices his friend's manner of speech by shifting into a higher-pitched, feminine-sounding voice thereby distancing himself from her and the attitudes she expresses. In voicing "J," he eliminates his usual use of AAE features such as copula absence (Ø), and post-vocalic /r/-lessness (r-Ø), and adopts certain super-standard, white talk identified by features such as the rhotic realization of post-vocalic /r/ (r-1) (Clark 2002).

(1) "Kin" (Bulgaria/Armenia, age 18); interviewed by Andrew Marshall.

```
 1  Kin:       You know who recently starting to act really racist?
 2  Andrew:    ((Who?))
 3  Kin:       I [ɑ:] don't know if you know this, "J."
 4  Andrew:    Yes, alright (( ))
 5  Kin:       She is PISSIN' me off! All the shit she's sayin'. I [ɑ:] feel like
 6             smackin' 'em. I'm [ɑ:m] like, "Ø you stupid? Do you hear
 7             what you're (r-Ø) sayin'?
 8  Friend 1:  //in the background// What'd she say?
 9  Kin:       She Ø **mad** racist! Like, "fuck." (falsetto) She Ø talkin'
10             'bout (suck teeth), ((voices "J"; higher pitch, softer tone)),
11             "*Kin, you're* (r-1) *not like that. You're* (r-1) *bringing your-*
12             *self* (r-1) *down to their* (r-1) *level. You're* (r-1) *gonna realize*
13             *that one day – you're* (r-1) *– you're* (r-1) *gonna realize that*
14             *one day that you're* (r-1) *not the same – you're* (r-1) *not the*
15             *same as them. You're* (r-1) *not them.*"
16  Andrew:    So . . .
17  Kin:       //still voicing "J"// "*You're* (r-1) *different and you're* (r-1)
18             *gonna realize it. You're* (r-1) *gonna come back to what you*
19             *really* ARE (rr).
20  Andrew:    Is she talking about black people or the Hip Hop culture?
21  Kin:       She Ø talkin' 'bout—she Ø talkin' 'bout BLACK [blæʔ]
22             people!
```

This example illustrates the kinds of features that many Hip Hoppers use to signal their Hip Hop affiliation: /ay/ glide reduction, /r/-lessness, Ø copula, and the use of *mad* as an intensifier, Discursively, it illustrates how young people get racialized by those around them and the pressure they are under to conform to societally prescribed notions of personhood and racial affiliation. Linguistically, it shows how speech styles can symbolize different orientations towards ethnic groups. Kin constructs his own way of speaking in opposition to white styles which he associates with racism and intolerance towards black people.

Many immigrants to the US can recall their first experience of being labeled or having to identify their ethnic group on an official form. Isko is a Bosnian refugee who came to the US on a high school soccer scholarship during the war in Yugoslavia. At the time he was interviewed Isko was attending university in New York City. The interviewer, a friend of his from a campus Hip Hop club, asks him about racial categories in his homeland. Unsurprisingly, Isko seems a bit shocked when asked if Bosnians think of themselves as white as we see in the following exchange below. The most salient HHNL/AAE features in the excerpt are phonological: Isko's reduction of the /ay/ glide, post-vocalic /r/-lessness (r-Ø), and wide-ranging intonation.

(2) "Isko" (Bosnia, age 18); interviewed by Sarah Siebold.

1	Sarah:	Is everyone considered white in Bosnia? Does everyone think
2		of themselves as white?
3	Isko:	**Hell no. Hell no.** White? Like how would you consider (r-Ø)
4		yourself (r-Ø)—like what is their—oh, it's like you can't
5		consider (r-Ø) yourself (r-Ø) white, 'cause there (r-Ø) was =
6	Sarah:	(( )) nothing else to compare it (( ))
7	Isko:	= nothing else, you know, compare it to—and Bosnia's more
8		like—you know, especially since the war is religious division.
9	Sarah:	Really, religious distinction.
10	Isko:	Yeah, divisions or (r-Ø) whatever (r-Ø).
11	Sarah:	Do you consider yourself a White?
12	Isko:	Right now, yeah.
13	Sarah:	Right now?
14	Isko:	Like—yeah, but like when I [ɑː] came here, it was like, "You're
15		(r-Ø) white." I [ɑː] was like, "I [ɑː] am?" You know, like I [ɑː]
16		was like, "All right. Yeah. I'm [ɑːm] white, you know, skinned,
17		whatever," (r-Ø) you know. I [ɑː] probably didn't even know
18		I [ɑː] was like—you know, like—I [ɑː] mean, I [ɑː] knew, but
19		in—it was like my [mɑː]—I [ɑː] knew it. I [ɑː] was educated I
20		[ɑː] was white, but it was just like so unusual to people to say
21		like, you know, when they say, "What—what race are (r-Ø)
22		you?" I [ɑː]—at the—you know how they =
23	Sarah:	Yeah.
24	Isko:	= sometimes [səmˈtɑːmz] you have those—
25	Sarah:	(( )) check boxes or something.
26	Isko:	Yeah. They say like what—I [ɑː] used to put like "Bosnian"
27		under—in Bosnia, like what race are (r-Ø) you—like—and I
28		[ɑː] used to put—like just check "Bosnian."
29	Sarah:	Right.
30	Isko:	'Cause like, you know, that's—that's really not common to
31		me, like to say, "Oh, you're (r-Ø) white." You know, that's—
32		nobody really sees themselves as white in Bosnia.

Isko's comments reveal a range of responses to being racialized at the discursive level. At first, he's surprised. Then he accepts that this is how many people see him, but he resists this process in his own way. He refers to the common experience of filling out official documents that ask one to identify one's race or ethnic background, and reports that he rejects these received categories and just writes "Bosnian." Isko is somewhat unique in this group because he did not spend his formative years in the US; consequently his awareness of the process of racialization was probably higher than for others in the sample. Linguistically, his use of HHNL/AAE markers mirrors his resistance to received categories such as "white," allowing him to complicate and confound the way he is perceived by others.

Many of the other speakers expressed less resistance to being labeled white and have come to regard this process as inevitable and one over which they exert little control. Julia asks her friend "Dimebag," a Ukrainian immigrant, how he would define himself. Dimebag who affiliates with a mostly white peer group, first identifies himself as white. He qualifies this by claiming that it doesn't really matter how you see yourself because "it's all one world," but then it comes out that perhaps one reason he defines himself as white is because that's how he's classified "in society."

(3) "Dimebag" (Ukraine, age 18); interviewed by Julia Bonsignore.

1	Julia:	All right then, how do you define your ethnicity and why?
2	Dimebag:	I [ɑ:] consider myself [mɑ:sɛlf] a white person. It doesn't
3		where I come from like I said, 'cause I'm a white person. I
4		consider myself a white person because that's (( )) just the
5		way I see it. I don't see . . . it doesn't matter where you're
6		born. Like—it just—like it's all one world. It's just that
7		we're all different colors and stuff like that. And that's what
8		I'm classified in society—I THINK. So when I co—when I
9		walk down the street, people don't see me as where I come
10		from, they just see me as white.
11	Julia:	I understand you're an immigrant. Does that in any way
12		affect you?
13	Dimebag:	No! I still. I fit in well—among Americans quote unquote.
14		I mean, this country's built on immigrants, **know what I'm**
15		**sayin'**? [no:msey:n] It's just like—just like that. I just still
16		see myself [mɑ:sɛlf] as a white person. It doesn't where I
17		come from like I said, 'cause I'm just still—a white person.

Dimebag expresses acquiescence about being labeled white and this seems to be reflected at the linguistic level with only a few tokens of /ɑy/ glide reduction (lines 2 and 16) and just one salient Hip Hop expression in lines 14 and 15, "know what I'm sayin'?" a pattern that is quite consistent throughout the interview. Expressing neutrality or distance from whiteness is only a part of the identity work that young immigrants accomplish through speech. In some cases, they embrace racial identities other than black or white.

Identifying with the Other

Ghetto Thug, a second generation Armenian American, affiliates with a mainly Latino peer group and has adopted a speech style that blends Spanishized-English features such as light "l" (cf. Slomanson and Newman 2004) along with Hip Hop expressions such as "boys" (friends), "nah" (no), "chill" (cool), "I onno" (I don't know), and "niggas" (guys). Ghetto Thug, who lives in a mostly white, affluent part of Queens and attended mostly white private schools prior to high school, has clearly sought out and cultivated friendships with Latinos. His Hip Hop affiliation is mediated and shaped by this cultural lens.

(4) "Ghetto Thug" (Armenia, age 16); interviewed by Andrew Marshall.

1	Ghetto Thug:	Nah, I'm [ɑːm] sayin' like—like (light /l/), you mean **my**
2		[mɑː] **boys**?
3	Andrew:	Yeah you know =
4	Ghetto Thug:	I'm [ɑːm] cool with people.
5	Andrew:	= closest friends?
6	Ghetto Thug:	But, like (light /l/), **nah**, in terms of boys—**nah**, you
7		know—**mos'** of 'em **is** [-AGR] Hispanic.
8	Andrew:	umm hmm.
9	Ghetto Thug:	'cause like . . . (light /l/)
10	Andrew:	Why do you think that is? Like did they, they went
11		to your same school or whatever it is or you just like
12		associating with that group?
13	Ghetto Thug:	**Nah**, I'm [ɑːm] sayin' it's more than that. It's like it's
14		like, **I onno**. Hispanic **niggas is** [-AGR] **chill** (light /l/).
15		You know ((suck teeth)). I [ɑː] feel—I [ɑː] find, I [ɑː]
16		find that like—**I onno**. Like (light /l/) I [ɑː] got more in
17		common with them than with most other people that—
18		**I onno**.

The proximity of black and Latino culture in terms of institutional racism and exclusion in New York City allows for the relatively easy blurring of racial divisions. It also confers a status on Latinos within Hip Hop that is not available to most Whites. This is especially apparent in New York City Hip Hop culture, allowing Ghetto Thug to associate with a group that has high status within the local Hip Hop scene.

A number of these young immigrants professed to have a strong identification with black people, although few made any claim to a black identity or were socialized in black communities. The closest most come is asserting that they like hanging out with black kids or that somehow they feel more at ease around them that around Whites. Asserting proximity to blackness is an important way in which many Hip Hoppers try to establish their authenticity within Hip Hop culture and their license to participate in what is viewed to be a black cultural space (Cutler 2003a).

In (5), Isko and his friend Sarah are discussing how they both feel more comfortable in black households than in white ones. Isko's experience with one family left him with the impression that a lot of white people are "uptight" or uneasy around strangers. Isko relates a story about a white family who invited him to dinner and served pork which he as a Muslim had to refuse. The whole thing was terribly embarrassing for the family and for him. The awkwardness was only exacerbated when Isko's friend "flipped out" on his mother. Isko's story constructs this middle class white family as tense and uncomfortable with themselves and others. Isko contrasts this experience with visits to his black friend "E's" house where he says he feels like he's a part of the family. Isko's orientation towards the more relaxed, uncomplicated family life he observes at his black friend's house points to his sociocultural orientation towards blackness.

(5) "Isko" (Bosnia, age 18); interviewed by Sarah Siebold.

1	Isko:	I [ɑː] went to this other—my [mɑː] other friend's house—he's
2		white—and the—while in high [hɑː] school, and his mother
3		(r-Ø) was trying [trɑːn] to—she can't—she couldn't cook. So
4		she was trying [trɑːn] to like impress me or whatever (r-Ø)
5		with this cooking 'cause I'm [ɑːm] a Bosnian kid, you know.
6		All of a sudden, I'm [ɑːm] someone special. They never seen a
7		Bosnian, like just now I [ɑː] told you I [ɑː] never saw a black
8		person before (r-Ø); and she made like a—like a roast pork
9		(r-Ø), and I don't eat pork (r-Ø). I'm [ɑːm] Muslim.
10	Sarah:	Right. I don't eat pork either (( ))
11	Isko:	So—so I [ɑː] came up. I [ɑː]—I was like, "Oh." I [ɑː] was like,
12		"Well, I'm [ɑːm] sorry, I [ɑː] really"—you know, I [ɑː] felt bad
13		tellin' them no –
14	Sarah:	Yeah.
15	Isko:	—but I [ɑː] had to tell them. You know, "I [ɑː] just can't eat
16		it."
17	Sarah:	Right.
18	Isko:	I [ɑː] was like, "Like I [ɑː] don't eat pork (r-Ø). I [ɑː]"—and
19		like they just like looked at me. "We—we apologize. We Ø so
20		sorry. You know, we don't—we didn't know you were—like
21		you Muslim or whatever," (r-Ø) and **my** [mɑː] **boy** flipped out
22		on his mom. He's like, "I told you not to like do anything. Ask
23		me. You should have asked me first!" you know. I [ɑː] was
24		like, "**Yo**, it's—it's not bad. There's (r-Ø) like potatoes. There's

25   (r-Ø) a little chicken on it, too. You know, don't worry about
26   it! You know, I'm [ɑːm] not like—I [ɑː] haven't ate meat in two
27   years. This is all right, you know. It's all right." So like =
28 Sarah: So—
29 Isko: = those kind [kɑːn] of things like made me—made me—even
30   though like, you know, I [ɑː]—I [ɑː] felt uncomfortable eating
31   other (r-Ø) people's houses, period. You know, like I [ɑː] can-
32   not really just **chill** like in other (r-Ø) people's houses. I [ɑː]
33   don't like to sleep over (r-Ø) people's places =
34 Sarah: Yeah.
35 Isko: = 'cause, you know, it's not my [mɑː] bed or whatever (r-Ø)—
36   but E's ((Isko's black friend)) house was—oh, it was just **chill**
37   like it was my [mɑː] house. You know, his mom, like, you
38   know, they'd never (r-Ø) looked under your (( )) like any (( ))
39   **you know what I** [ɑː] **mean**, you know?
40 Sarah: Yeah.
41 Isko: So, you know, she was cool. Everybody was nice to me. You
42   know, I [ɑː] was cracking jokes with them, whatever (r-Ø).
43   So that—so with that family I'm [ɑːm] **mad** comfortable, you
44   know. I [ɑː] was no different from whatever (r-Ø).

Isko's orientation towards blackness and use of AAE-styled speech parallels
the ways in which German youth use Turkish and orient towards Turkish
culture. Auer and Dirim (2003) found that young peoples' use of Turkish in
Germany could symbolize a very positive orientation towards the Turks and
Turkish culture, which in some cases bordered on idealization. Similarly,
Isko seems predisposed towards highly positive images of black American
culture that border on desire (shown in (6)). When asked about how he
got interested in Hip Hop, Isko admits that he was fascinated by images of
black people from films like *Shaft* before he ever saw a black person.[2] His
interest in Hip Hop stemmed from a view of black people as exotic and tan-
talizing, which also played a role in his desire to come to the US.

(6) "Isko" (Bosnia, age 18); interviewed by Sarah Siebold.

1 Sarah: So—okay. So how did you—I [ɑː] mean, how did you get into
2   Hip Hop or like how did you (( ))
3 Isko: I [ɑː] think to me—to me—to me, this is—to me, in every
4   movie, like when I [ɑː] used to watch movies, this is like the
5   black people **was** [-AGR] always cool to me.
6 Sarah: Was always what?
7 Isko: Cool. They were always –
8 Sarah: Yeah.
9 Isko: – cool like. Whenever (r-Ø) I [ɑː] see like the—the movies with
10   black—black people inside, they were like—I [ɑː] was like,

11		"Damn, they look cool," **you know what I'm saying**? When
12		the first time I [ɑ:] saw *Shaft* in Bosnia, there was (( )) and
13		"((up the easy))"—and, umm (( )) it was—and, you know, the
14		whole—like I [ɑ:] always—like I [ɑ:] always wanted to come
15		to the United States.
16	Sarah:	Yeah.
17	Isko:	It was one of my [mɑ:] dreams; and like every time, I'd like—
18		you know, I'm [ɑ:m] never (r-Ø)—I [ɑ:] haven't seen a—like a
19		person—a black person. I've [ɑ:v] seen a black person once in
20		my [mɑ:] first 15 years of my [mɑ:] life.
21	Sarah:	Wow!
22	Isko:	Once! And that's because there (r-Ø) was this um . . . African
23		student—in my [mɑ:] town—that—he—he went to medical
24		school . . .

Isko's comments reveal how his conception of African Americans was actually formed before he ever met an African American. Yet the essentialization of African American culture is not unique to immigrants whose only exposure to black Americans prior to their arrival in the US was on television or in the movies. In (7), we see how PJ (a Russian immigrant who came to the US at age 5)—like many native born white male teenagers—is drawn to highly commercialized media images of young African American men from rap music videos that emphasize the accumulation and display of wealth, expensive cars, and beautiful women.

(7) "PJ" (Russia, age 16); interviewed by Lien Ly.

1	Lin:	Okay. Do you like rap music?
2	PJ:	**Hells yeah.** I [ɑ:] like everything about it, the style [stɑ:l], the
3		rappers, the women they get, the cars they have, the money they
4		**be** spending. **Shit.** That was me? I'd [ɑ:d] die [dɑ:] a happy **nigga**.

DISCUSSION AND CONCLUSION

These last two examples illustrate how complicated identification with another group can be, particularly when it involves essentialized, reductionist conceptions of that group. But on the linguistic level, there are some interesting parallels to the kind of borrowing and/or appropriation we see among young adolescents in the UK who cross into Jamaican Creole, or Punjabi (Rampton 1995) youth in the Netherlands with the use of Moroccan-flavored Dutch (Nortier and Dorleijn 2008), youth in Germany who use Turkish (Auer and Dirim 2003), and Danish and Norwegian adolescents who use multiethnolects (Quist 2000; Opsahl and Røyneland 2008). In all of these situations, it seems that one code (or several codes in conjunction) has come to symbolize cultural otherness with respect to the dominant mainstream culture (Auer and Dirim 2003). Using elements from the relevant code(s) in each local context can signal an individual's orientation towards a particular ethnic group, a particular kind of street-oriented youth subculture, or simply an orientation towards a more generalized urban youth culture. It can also signal racial otherness or distance from certain groups.

The data from European immigrants in New York City point to the very interesting role that Hip Hop culture and HHNL/AAE-flavored speech play in the complicated processes of racialization and identity construction. Isko expresses an attraction to black American culture that goes back to his homeland and which extends to the experiences he has had with black and white families since coming to the US. He acknowledges that people see him as white, but doesn't passively accept this designation. Kin seems to be reacting against his parents' racism and coercive efforts by certain friends. He does not self-identify with blackness per se; rather he seeks to distance himself from whiteness because, for him, it's connected with racism. Dimebag is more oriented towards whiteness than either Kin or Isko and admits that his connection to Hip Hop comes through participation on a school basketball team where the team was mainly comprised of African American boys. He, like PJ, was also drawn to Hip Hop because of its ties to street culture and the gangster lifestyle. Finally, Ghetto Thug seemed deeply invested in the allure of projecting a Latino identity which aligned in interesting ways with how he was identified by others (as discussed in Chapter 4, this volume). Young immigrants who affiliate with Hip Hop are pulled in opposite directions by forces that would have them embrace whiteness. Hip Hop offers a range of symbolic resources that allows them to challenge and resist hegemonic social categories, processes of racialization, and perhaps even racism itself. In a multiethnic city like New York, different groups access and use Hip Hop's linguistic resources for their own purposes. Young European immigrants use HHNL/AAE-styled speech to express various identities, not necessarily black or white. The symbolic value of AAE is thus to offer Hip Hop-affiliated youth the possibility of expressing varying degrees of otherness, distinctiveness and/or distance from a mainstream white identity, as well as expressing degrees of affiliation with Hip Hop culture and an alignment with African Americans and Latinos.

Returning now to some of the questions raised earlier in this chapter, it is clear that HHNL/AAE provide a range of linguistic resources for young people to express a wide range of affiliations and alignments. HHNL speech markers have their origins in AAE and can symbolize a range of meanings. The examples shown above illustrate the complexities of positing a one-to-one connection between ethnic groups and ethnic speech styles or "ethnolects." Immigrant youth do not necessarily acquire or use standard forms of the target language, nor do they necessarily draw on the same ethnolects in their divergence from standard norms. Those who affiliate with Hip Hop use features of HHNL/AAE, but in ways that signal different meanings that may include rejection of racial categorization, distance from whiteness, identification with black or Latino youth, or simply Hip Hop contemporary urban youth lifestyle. The meanings attached to HHNL/AAE-styled speech however may be very different for young people outside of urban areas who have little contact with African American youth and who often de-racialize black urban youth culture so to claim it as a space for expressing coolness or toughness (cf. Bucholtz 1999; Perry 2002). Thus, although it is now possible to speak of an HHNL/AAE-flavored style spoken by young people in their teens and twenties across the United States, it does not appear to signal any form of unified, cohesive, or ethnic-oriented identity, making it difficult to argue that it constitutes an emerging ethnolect in its own right.

NOTES

1. DJ-ing is the art of mixing records, especially the practice of "scratching," or manually reversing the direction of the record on the turntable with the needle in place to achieve a rhythmic backdrop for the MC (master of ceremonies). The MC, in turn, performs his or her raps on top of the rhythm supplied by the DJ.
2. There were several *Shaft* films made in the early 1970s and in 2000. The 1971 film was directed by Gordon Parks and starred Richard Roundtree; it tells the story of a black private detective, John Shaft. Two sequels were made: *Shaft's Big Score* in 1972, and *Shaft in Africa* in 1973. These were followed by a short-lived 1973–1974 television series of the same name that aired on CBS. Many years later, in 2000, a new version was made with Samuel L. Jackson in the lead role.

6 MC Battles
Seeing Oneself through the Eyes of the Other

INTRODUCTION

Up to this point, we have been examining sociolinguistic interview data from a range of Hip Hop youth living in New York City. This chapter and the following one turn to televised media data, particularly the ways in which white youth are racialized within the cultural black "space" that is Hip Hop (Boyd 2002). George Lipsitz writes that whiteness, "as the unmarked category against which difference is constructed . . . never has to speak its name [or] acknowledge its role as an organizing principle in social and cultural relations" (1995: 369). On the flip side of this equation are people of color who are compelled to measure themselves up to a set of standards based on white American cultural norms. Referring to the mindset of African Americans, W.E.B. Du Bois called this "double consciousness," which he described as the compulsion to see oneself through the eyes of whites. Spears (1998) describes it as "the dual personality caused by the cohabitation of two consciousnesses or cultural systems within one mind, the white and the African-American" (248).

In pondering this idea, it struck me that double consciousness conceivably plays a role in Hip Hop culture, but in the opposite direction.[1] It would be overly reductionist to analyze Hip Hop culture as an exclusively black enterprise. Scholars have acknowledged the participation of Latinos and whites in the formative years of Hip Hop (Morgan 1998; Rivera 2003), and now, two decades in, Hip Hop is produced and consumed by young people all over the world. Yet in this country it seems that rap music, as Rose writes, "still largely prioritizes black voices" and "articulates the pleasures and problems of black urban life in contemporary America" (1994: 2; cf. Perry 2004). The reigning position of African Americans as the chief artistic creators and trendsetters is difficult to dispute. Back (1996) claims that although Hip Hop's following is multiracial and multicultural, the dominant culture is black. In fact the centrality of the black experience within American Hip Hop culture has led to an interesting role reversal such that blackness occupies the role of the dominant, unmarked social category and

"Whiteness is treated as the Other" (Boyd 2002: 23). In Hip Hop, it is whites who are forced to see themselves through the eyes of black people and try to measure up to the standards of authenticity, achievement, and knowledge established by the collective of individuals who make up the Hip Hop Nation.

The normativity of blackness in Hip Hop stems from a discourse that privileges the black body and the black urban street experience (Rebensdorf 1996), and despite the visibility and popularity of white American rappers such as Eminem, whiteness is still marked against the backdrop of normative blackness. This is particularly salient in public Hip Hop performances such as the MC battle analyzed here where every aspect of a performer's identity, is subject to scrutiny, including race. This chapter explores how ethnic boundaries get negotiated between a white contestant (Eyedea) and his African American opponents (R.K., E-Dub, and Shells) in an MC battle. The battle, sponsored by the now defunct *Blaze* Magazine, took place in New York in November 2000.[2] The analysis is based on three battles in which Eyedea and his competitors each performed and which I transcribed and analyzed in terms of linguistic features and content. A few research questions motivated this study: How do white rappers authenticate themselves in the black cultural space of an MC battle? Secondly, how do they signal linguistically and discursively to their competitors and the audience their acceptance of the normativity blackness in Hip Hop? Lastly, how do the competitors co-construct one another through the use of racial terms, racialized discourse, and the use of features that index white and black speech styles?

The chapter explores how Eyedea cooperates with his African American opponents in *marking* his own whiteness (cf. Mitchell Kernan 1974). *Marking* is normally thought of as a way to parody another person's or group's speech. Marking *white* is a sort of verbal performance that draws on commonly recognized white American linguistic features. In most analyses, marking white is done by African Americans in order to parody or mock white stereotyped ways of talking as well as white American attitudes and behaviors (Alim 2005). In the present study, white American MCs are drawing on stereotyped linguistic features such as hyper-rhotic /r/ to mark *themselves* as white. This might seem like a redundant gesture given the fact that the MC in question was, from all outwardly signs, unambiguously white. Yet whiteness seemed to occupy a unique position in the context of this MC battle that was reflective of its status in the broader Hip Hop culture: it was highly marked and its position vis-à-vis blackness was being challenged. Discursive and linguistic marking was a way for white and black competitors to challenge hegemonic whiteness. I argue that in this context *marking* plays a functional role in ratifying an alternative social reality in which blackness is normative and whiteness is rendered the "other."

THEORETICAL BACKGROUND

Stance

A useful tool in the attempt to provide a more subtle analysis of how speakers construct, resist, transform, and reject cultural differences is the interpretive framework of *stance*. Jaffe (2004) writes that "contemporary work on stance in linguistics, sociolinguistics, pragmatics and linguistic anthropology is related to a number of interpretive traditions, including Goffman's notion of "footing," (1981) and Gumperz' "contextualization cues" (1982, 1990) that focus on how speakers necessarily and simultaneously position themselves with respect to both the form and the content of their utterances and with respect to the social, cultural (including political) identities, values and relationships associated with that form and content."[3]

According to Irvine (2004), stance can take one of three forms: (a) *stance* as "footing," a position within a set of participant roles in an act of speaking; (b) *stance* as point of view, opinion, or ideological position; and (c) *stance* as social position in a larger sense, invoking broad categories of participation in social life such as class or ethnicity. Importantly, stance can index one or more social identities, liberating speakers from static interpretations of their utterances, their identities, and those of others. This makes stance a particularly productive way to look at how speakers manage multiple roles, points of view, and identities in intercultural interactions. In the performance data analyzed in this chapter, speakers adopt stances that invoke their respective positions within a Hip Hop community of practice (Eckert and McConnell-Ginet 1992) as well as social roles like race and class. This chapter will also show how stance reveals an alternative social order in which normative whiteness is challenged and ultimately subverted.

Outgroup Language Use within Hip Hop

One interesting question that arises in the study of white American participation in Hip Hop is the link between language and ethnicity. Hall (1995) writes that "the ideological link between language and ethnicity is so potent that the use of linguistic practices associated with a given ethnic group may be sufficient for an individual to pass as a group member" (cited in Bucholtz 1995: 355). Most white American MCs like Eminem, the Beastie Boys, and the one of the MCs we'll examine later in the chapter—"Eyedea"—employ a speech style that draws features of Hip Hop HHNL (Alim 2004a) and AAE. Lest they fall victim to the charge that they are wannabes because of the way they speak, white American rappers often adopt a stance that references their whiteness. They can achieve this by "outing" themselves discursively as the Beastie Boys do in their lyrics when they sing, "I'm a funky-ass Jew and I'm on my way" in "Right Here Right Now" or stylistically by playing up socially salient variables that index white American speech such as hyper-rhotic realizations of post-vocalic /r/. Taking a racial stance is part of a complex process of "keepin' it real"—a mantra in Hip Hop culture demanding individuals to be true to their roots, and not to "front" or pretend to be something they are not (Rickford and Rickford 2000). It is difficult not to underestimate the centrality of "realness" in Hip Hop and many controversies in Hip Hop surround accusations of "biting" or stealing someone's lyrics or selling out by making one's music palatable to mainstream audiences.

MC BATTLE DATA

The late 1990s and early 2000s witnessed a rise in the popularity and visibility of one aspect of Hip Hop culture—MC-ing and MC battles. Within Hip Hop, MC battles are one of the most visible and potentially humiliating ways for an MC to demonstrate his or her rhyming and freestyling skills. Two MCs face one another and each is given a fixed amount of time (usually 30 seconds to a minute) to generate a spontaneous ("freestyle"), rhyming litany of insults at his or her opponent. In most cases, MCs draw on a mix of spontaneous and pre-written rhymes, using hooks like "on the mic" and fillers like "yo" and "check it" to keep their rhymes flowing. A battle may also end in humiliation and defeat if the MC can't make his or her rhymes flow or if the rhymes are obviously written ahead of time rather than generated spontaneously. Ultimately the audience chooses the winner by applauding louder for one opponent than the other at the end of the battle. Crucially, each competitor tries not to take all of this criticism personally lest he or she lose face and the backing of audience. This chapter analyzes bouts between the white MC Eyedea and three African American competitors.

Whiteness and Inauthenticity

The first battle is between R.K. (a.k.a. Richard Kimble), a black MC from Miramar, Florida, and Eyedea (a.k.a. Mike Larsen), a white MC from Minneapolis-St. Paul, Minnesota (shown in examples (1) and (2) below).[4] R.K. is the first to perform and gets a minute to "spit" his rhymes. In the transcript, there are several overt references to Eyedea's whiteness. After a few rather light-hearted jabs at his appearance, R.K. refers to Eyedea as "Telly" in line 2, the polemical white rebel from the 1995 Larry Clark film *Kids*, implying that Eyedea, like the lead character Telly, is a wannabe—a white kid who wants to be black.[5] Then, in line 10, in a jab against MTV *and* Eyedea, R.K. alludes to a widespread sentiment among Hip Hop youth that MTV has no cachet for authentic Hip Hop youth when he says that Eyedea is "wacker than MTV's lyricist lounge." Finally, R.K. insinuates that Eyedea is so devoid of talent as an MC that a record deal with the major label Bad Boy still wouldn't help him get any "shine."[6]

(1) Round 2: R.K. vs. Eyedea, (R.K. and Eyedea are standing on the stage; R.K. has the microphone)

1	R.K.:	Son, you wanna spit? **Nigga**, I'mo split your wig.
2		Motherfucker, lookin' like **Telly** from "**Kids**."
3		R.K., nigga. Come in the game.
4		Understand everything that **I'mo** spit is flame.
5		I ((hide)) **niggas**. I'm glad that you try.
6		Your career's over like (( )) when Tupac died.
7		Yo son, I ((pillage)) **niggas** that spit.
8		Motherfuckers like me, yo, I'm a *real* lyricist.
9		I got more shit. I ain't feelin' you clown.
10		This **nigga** is wacker than MTV's lyricist lounge.
11		Yo, R.K., **nigga** don't (( )).
12		This **nigga** here, don't [-AGR] got nothin' to do.
13		So I can spit **shit**. Understand **nigga**, I rhyme.
14		If you signed to Bad Boy, you still wouldn't see no **shine**.

Hyper-Rhoticity as an Index of Whiteness

Although his competitor repeatedly indexes his whiteness, Eyedea also participates in the construction of himself as white. Whereas his competitors rely largely on discursive methods to do this, Eyedea collaborates in his ethnic self-marking phonologically. He possesses a high level of linguistic competence, employing many of the quintessential morphosyntactic patterns of HHNL/AAE such as verbal /s/ absence, copula absence, negative concord, and multiple negation, as well as a range of discourse genres like dissin' (criticizing) and freestyling (spontaneous rapping/rhyming). He also controls a range of phonological features found in Hip Hop on the East Coast such as /ay/ glide reduction, glottalized medial stops, and labialized intervocalic /r/ (Morgan 2002; Cutler 2002a). But he is careful to temper his displays of competence by deploying linguistic resources that mark him as white. One way he does this is via hyper-rhotic realizations of post-vocalic /r/—one of the features that typifies American English in Minnesota where Eyedea comes from. Crucially it also indexes white American speech.

   Clark (2002) has described "hyper-rhotic" /r/ as a strategy used by African American teenagers to mark white American speech in the classroom. This contrast relies on the interlocutors' access to linguistic stereotypes that contrast white rhoticity with black /r/-lessness.[7] Clark (2002) identifies three realizations of /r/ in the speech of his informants: vocalized /r/ (Ø); mildly pronounced (/r/); and strongly pronounced (/rr/). Using this three-way distinction, we can see how Eyedea performs and marks his own whiteness. When it comes to intervocalic /r/, Eyedea employs a labialized variant (/w/) that occurs frequently in New York City Hip Hop (Cutler 2002a). This variant is part of Eyedea's extensive repertoire of features that he uses to mark himself as part of the Hip Hop culture.

Eyedea's performance is shown in (2) below. Examples of hyper-rhotic post-vocalic /r/ are found in line 1, *murder,* and line 2, *heard,* and even more emphatically in the rhyming of *enhancer* and *dancer* in lines 29 and 31. There are also several instances where Eyedea omits post-vocalic /r/; in *motherfuckers* [mʌðəfʌkəz] in line 12 and again in lines 13, 21, 29, and 30. The fact that he retains post-vocalic /r/ at a high rate in his performance and that he chooses the hyper-rhotic variant to do this points to the role of /r/ as a marker of whiteness, signaling a racial stance. His puerile rhymes about dog manure and menstrual blood seem to further position him as a nerdy, white teenager. But in the final rhymes of the battle, Eyedea seizes upon an opportunity to take a stance as the stronger freestyler. R.K.'s attempt to mock Eyedea by dancing lethargically during his performance allows Eyedea to take the upper hand when he quips that R.K. wants to be "his fuckin' backup dancer" in line 31. The emasculating image of a backup dancer (a role often played by African American females) is played out in the final line when Eyedea tells R.K. that he should "sign a deal with little Janet Jackson." The audience roars with laughter and Eyedea wins the round hands down.

(2) Round 2: Eyedea vs. R.K. (Eyedea has the microphone).

1	Eyedea:	Hey yo, it's time to **murder** ['mʌrrdər] you.
2		From the crowd **yo**, all I [hʌrrd] was boos.
3		**Yo**, it's all good. On the mic, I just straight pound.
4		And I'll never ['nɛvərr] get beat by a cat that looks like Homey
5		the Clown.
6		So try to bring that back.
7		My **material's** [mə'tɪwiəlz] **ill.**
8		**Your** [jər] pants used to be white until your **period** [pɪwɪəd]
9		spilled.
10		What's it make you feel?
11		**Yo**, it's difficult. I'm battlin' **Mystikal** mixed with **Bizzy Bone.**
12		**Motherfuckers** [mʌðərfʌkəz] can't play me when I freestyle.
13		**Yo**, why you got **your** [jə] hand wrapped in that weak towel.
14		Comin' up dressed like a clown, **yo**, you talk a lot.
15		**Yo**, you just stepped in dog shit, **forgot** [fərrgɑt] to wash it
16		off. //R.K. lifts up his foot to check//
17		It's just like that. I'll grab the mic and straight ((tease me)).
18		Even if I come off wack, I'll win 'cause it's just easy.
19		//R.K. sits on the floor holding his knees and bobbing his head
20		to the rhythm//
21		**Yo**, sit down. Oh, that's right because **you're** [jə] nothin.'
22		And that's the same type like you like to dick suck man.
23		**Yo** man, **there** [ðɛw] it goes on the mic.
24		I'm oh so **terrible** [tɛwəbəl].
25		Look at him tryin' to mock me, knowin' that he jocks me.

25	You couldn't kick those lyrics with karate.
26	Come on, bring up the microphone and try to rock me.
27	//R.K. stand up and starts dancing lethargically in a mock Hip
28	Hop style//.
29	Yo, I'll grab the mic and try be **your** [jə] rap **enhancer**
30	[en'hænsərr].
31	This cat wants to be my fuckin' **backup dancer** ['dænsərr].
32	//audience roars in laughter//
33	Why Ø you doin' **that shit**? This man **ain't** rappin.'
34	He should go sign a fuckin' deal with **little Janet Jackson**. //
35	thunderous applause//

Indirect Indexing of Blackness

Eyedea's spit also contains several references to race. He alludes to blackness in line 11 when he says R.K. looks like a mixture of two famous black rappers—Mystikal and Bizzy Bone. But race is probably not the most important referent in this example. The mention of Bizzy Bone might have more to do with the fact that he, like R.K. has a big fluffy afro hairstyle. In line 31, Eyedea refers to and addresses R.K. as "this cat" which might also be interpreted as a racialized term, albeit an indirect one. Smitherman (2006) writes that it refers to a "male" rather than specifically a black man (25), but its status as an AAE lexical item appears to index the addressees' race in this context. Looking at all of the performances in which Eyedea participates, it is clear that whiteness is foregrounded in many more instances and in more overt ways than blackness. The paucity of references to blackness points to its unmarked status in Hip Hop. For obvious reasons, black MCs do not resort to race-referenced insults when they battle each other because blackness is normative in Hip Hop.[8] Nor do plausible references to blackness challenge a competitor's legitimacy in the way references to whiteness often seem to do.

In the next round of the battle, Eyedea faces "E-Dub," (a.k.a. Edward Dixon) an African American MC from Detroit. In Round 3 and Round 4 (the Final Round), there are two spits, so each MC must perform twice. E-Dub is older and quite a bit bigger than Eyedea. He has a fair complexion and has his hair braided against his head in corn rows. In the excerpt shown below, Eyedea draws on cultural references from *The Simpsons* and Hip Hop to create a ridiculous image of his opponent as a mixture between the underachieving son "Bart" from the long-running cartoon serial *The Simpsons* and the black MC, Mystikal.[9] Eyedea also compares E-Dub with Fred Durst, a white American MC who was popular in the late 1990s. Linking E-Dub to popular white American figures like Bart Simpson and Fred Durst seem to cast doubt on his authenticity as a black man. It also reinforces the connection between whiteness and inauthenticity.

(3) Round 3, Spit 1: Eyedea vs. E-Dub.

1	Eyedea:	Why Ø you walkin' around, pretendin' you ain't feelin' me?
2		That's just so funny when I **start** [stɑrrt] rippin' a diss on you.
3		You look like a mixture ['mɪkstjurr] between **Bart** [bɑrrt]
4		**Simpson** and **Mystikal.**
5		((thinkin' it)) just like when **your** [jər] mom made **pornos**
6		[pɔrrrnoz].
7		You look like fuckin' **Fred Durst** [dərst] with **corn** [kɔrrrn] rows.

Competitors can also adopt stances that index class. In the next excerpt from Round 3 (shown in (4)), Eyedea ridicules E-Dub's clothing when he suggests that his sweat suit came from the downscale K-Mart. The implication is that Eyedea is himself better off, i.e., middle class.

(4) Round 3, Spit 1: Eyedea vs. E-Dub.

1	Eyedea:	It's just that. You know I just straight talk.
2		I've won more battles than **your** [jər] bitch ass has watched.
3		So why Ø you walkin' around lookin' like that I wrecked you.
4		This **cat** straight got a K-**Mart** [mɑrt] sweat suit.
5		He think [-AGR] he Ø rockin' like that.
6		**Yo,** the late is night.
7		I'm about to show this **motherfucker** ['mʌðəfʌkə] how to
8		break the mic.

Practices Linked to Whiteness

Class is invoked again in E-Dub's rebuttal shown in (5) when E-Dub tells Eyedea that he shouldn't be "rappin'—he should be skateboardin' the X-games" in line 2—a sort of pseudo-Olympic athletic event featuring a gaggle of mainly post-adolescent white males performing daring stunts on boards and bikes. The rhyme frames Eyedea as a white, middle class suburban skater kid who shouldn't be rapping because he lacks the street credentials. There are additional instances where whiteness is highlighted in (5). In line 4 below, E-Dub calls Eyedea a "fake Eminem" with a "long nose." The rhetorical question about Eyedea's origins in line 9 conveys a sense of disbelief that any half decent MC could come from a place as inauthentic in the Hip Hop world as Minnesota. E-Dub once again casts doubt on his opponent's legitimacy by saying that he belongs on MTV in line 12 and that he couldn't sell a cassette on a Detroit street corner if it came with a bag of marijuana. This final line points to a longstanding practice among MCs in urban black neighborhoods who would attempt to generate a local following by selling homemade rap cassettes on the street.

(5) Round 3, Spit 2: E-Dub vs. Eyedea (E-Dub on the mic).

1	E-Dub:	Believe me. I'm the next to spit the flames.
2		You shouldn't be rappin'. You should be **skate boardin'** the
3		**X-Games.**
4		You Ø a **fake Eminem** with a fucked-up haircut. Long nose.
5		You remind me of my ex-ho. A bitch that don't really work
6		that hard.
7		A faggot rapper that can't rap that hard.
8		And on top of that I'mo have to float ya.
9		Where the fuck are you from? Minnesota?
10		Yo, the home of the Vikings and the ho-ass Timberwolves.
11		I bring shit to kill you.
12		Believe me, you belong on **MTV.**
13		You couldn't sell a cassette on 25th ((and McCane)) if it came
14		with a bag of (( )) weed.

Eyedea in his rebuttal (shown in (6)), attempts to seize the discursive space by tacitly acknowledging who he is and where he comes from discursively and phonologically via emphatic rhyming of word-final hyper-rhotic /r/ at the end of lines 4, 6, 7, and 9 (hat*er*, lat*er*, fad*er*, skat*er*). Remaining cool-headed in the face of these repeated references to race and embracing his whiteness are part of how Eyedea "keeps it real."

(6) Round 3, Spit 2: E-Dub vs. Eyedea (Eyedea on the mic).

1	Eyedea:	This cat's talkin' 'bout my clothes, he's rockin' an Eyedea
2		shirt.
3		**Nah,** I'm just playin'. Up on the mic, you **ain't** a **hater**
4		[heytərr].
5		Here's my backstage pass. Have **your** [jərr] momma meet me
6		back there **later** [leyrərr].
7		And if she really wanna a ((fader)) [feyrərr] . . .
8		**Yo,** I'm **doper** ['dopə] (r-Ø) than you even if I am a **skater**
9		[[skeyrərr]
10		So it's all good. Up on the mic you slobber ['slabə] (r-Ø) the
11		nut.
12		Come on, y'all. Who's gonna beat me. Want ((it to be)) **Jabba**
13		**the Hutt?**

In the last six lines of his spit, Eyedea brutally disparages E-Dub's looks, comparing him to the bloated overlord Jabba the Hutt from Star Wars, and again when he compares E-Dub to a gopher who couldn't get a girl to look at him if he were a D'Angelo poster (shown in (7)).[10]

(7) Round 3, Spit 2: E-Dub vs. Eyedea (Eyedea on the mic).

1	Eyedea:	This cat needs to **motherfuckin'** [mʌðəfʌkən] call the dogs
2		off.
3		**Yo,** you say you poor hoes. You look like a **gopher** [gowfərr].
4		Couldn't ((get a girl)) to stop and look at you if **you was**
5		[-AGR] a D'Angelo **poster** [powstərr].

In his second and final spit E-Dub counters by marking Eyedea's whiteness with a quotative (shown in (8)). In line 9, he ventriloquizes Eyedea asking, "What's happinin' *black*?" The use of the vocative "black" as a licensed outgroup alternative to the ingroup term "nigga" is discussed in greater detail in the next section. Here, it offers up a pragmatically appropriate lexical alternative to "nigga." Comparisons between Eyedea and white American rappers like Eminem and Vanilla Ice were also common ways to mark Eyedea as white. E-Dub's allegation that Eyedea is a "light-skinned Eminem" (line 15) points up Eminem's authentic status within the Hip Hop community. Eminem is actually quite pale and blond so this latter comparison appears to confer on him an honorary black status within Hip Hop. It also serves to distinguish some white MCs from others, the implication being that Eyedea is not among the white MCs who are accepted by the black Hip Hop community.

(8) Round 3, Spit 2: E-Dub vs. Eyedea (E-Dub on the mic).

1	E-Dub:	You Ø in trouble if you try to win.
2		You heard Aliyah? Try again.
3		Bill Gates couldn't buy your win.
4		You Ø hyDRO.
5		I'm hydroGEN.
6		Who's official. Studio gangstas talk about packin' gat.
7		E-Dub come through; you ain't clappin' gat. //Eyedea looks
8		quizzically at audience//
9		You Ø on the ground like, "What's happenin' *black*?"
10		I don't sell drugs. I ain't no thug. I'm just rappin' that.
11		Kind of like flashin' gat.
12		Last cat that flashed his gat, left with a bad flashback with my
13		gun in his ass crack
14		(( )) for publishin' your ass cap, or get your ass capped
15		You ain't fuckin' with me, light-skinned **Eminem.**
16		You're not from Detroit. Stop tryin' to be **Eminem.** //Eyedea
17		mouths the lyrics as if he's heard them before//.

All of Eyedea's opponents make frequent and overt references to his whiteness; often this is done in ways that appear to challenge his legitimacy as an MC and as a member of the Hip Hop community. A list of all references to Eyedea's whiteness made by Eyedea's opponents throughout the contest appears in Table 6.1.

The final two excerpts shown in Table 6.1 show how another white American MC participating in the same *Blaze* Battle named "See For" gets discursively *marked* as white in similar ways to Eyedea. In this encounter, See For's opponent K.T., a black MC from Boston, Massachusetts, makes an association between whiteness and bizarre acts like "blowing up post offices" and "playing records backwards." In the 1970s there were rumors that white rock and heavy metal bands like Queen, Led Zeppelin, and Judas Priest, recorded satanic messages on their records that could be understood subconsciously when a song is played normally to influence the listeners' behavior, or incite them to acts of violence. These kinds of stereotypes come out of a discourse in the black community about how all of the bizarre, inexplicable crimes and serial murders in the US seem to have white perpetrators.[11] K.T. also marks whiteness when he says that his opponent must be related to Ron Howard, the pale, redheaded star of the TV series *Happy Days*. As we can see from these examples, white American culture offers a goldmine of content for rhymes that simultaneously encode the addressee's whiteness and critique hegemonic white American culture more broadly.

Table 6.1　References to Whiteness by African American MCs Battling White MCs in the *Blaze* Battle

MC Battle Opponents	Excerpt
R.K. vs. Eyedea (Round 2)	Motherfucker lookin' like **Telly** from *Kids*. This nigga is wacker than **MTV's** lyricist lounge.
E-Dub vs. Eyedea (Round 3)	You shouldn't be rappin', you should be **skate boardin'** the **X-games.** You belong on **MTV.** You Ø a **fake Eminem** with a fucked up haircut. You ain't fuckin' with me, light-skinned **Eminem.** You're not from Detroit. Stop tryin' to be **Eminem.**
Shells vs. Eyedea (Round 4)	They got Shells battlin' **Lil' Chuck Norris.** I'll be damned to lose against **Vanilla Ice.** You look like **Buffy the mother fuckin' rhyme slayer.**
K.T. vs. See For (Round 2)	You'd be safer **blowing up post offices** and **playing records backwards.** I know you was a coward. I know somehow you was related to **Ron Howard.**

Lexical Avoidance as a Strategy for Marking Whiteness

An additional way that white American MCs like Eyedea "keep it real" and acknowledge racial boundaries in MC battles and elsewhere is by avoiding certain themes and terms of address. Black competitors commonly refer to each other as "nigga" throughout the battle. As an ingroup form of address, the term indexes a stance of cool solidarity for young black men (Smitherman 1994). But its use has expanded so that it is now used as a general, (usually) male gendered address term for young people of diverse ethnic backgrounds in homogenous groupings. Indeed it seems that "nigga" is developing into a discourse marker that more generally encodes the speaker's stance to his or her current addressee(s)—a stance that is cool, urban, usually male, and streetwise.

Although it's quite common for American white male teenagers to use this term to refer to or address their white friends (Cutler 2002a), the public use of this term by white people is still highly controversial in the US (Smitherman 1994; Kennedy 2002). Even the enormously popular white American rapper Eminem who grew up on the border of an economically deprived black part of Detroit and who is widely accepted among black Hip Hop youth has stated publicly that he would never use the term. In the *Blaze* Battle analyzed here, Eyedea *never* employs this term with any of his competitors, whereas R.K. uses the term eleven times when he battles Eyedea perhaps to taunt the white opponent and dare him to use the term back again (in (1) above). But in Round 2 of the battle, Eyedea's opponent E-Dub, who is African American, does not use the term to address him even once. It seems to imply that he doesn't take Eyedea seriously and refuses to confer on him the insider status that "nigga" might imply. The one other white competitor in this battle, See For, similarly avoids the term completely when up against his African American opponent K.T., although K.T. uses it with him on three occasions.

As we might predict based on these general observations, the use of "nigga" as a positive ingroup solidarity marker is complicated in biracial interactions; its use is unidirectional in the sense that black competitors can use it with one another and with whites, but whites cannot reciprocate. This allows black MCs the option of whether or not to ratify their competitor's legitimacy and to express solidarity in a way that is not reciprocal.

Eyedea prevails in Round 3 against E-Dub and passes on to Round 4, the final round, where he battles Shells, an MC from New York City (shown in (9) below). As in the previous round, *marking* emerges in oblique ways when Eyedea employs the vocative "black" to address Shells in line 10. It's the only such token in all of Eyedea's performances and it serves not only to racialize his opponent, but perhaps also indexes his own whiteness in that he is not licensed to use "nigga."

In line 1, Shells has begun to mouth Eyedea's lines, signaling to the audience that they are pre-written rather than spontaneous or freestyle (as they should be). Eyedea jumps on this and turns it around, implying that it is actually Shells who is "biting" or copying Eyedea's lines—a grave allegation within Hip Hop—and furthermore implies that this is the only way Shells will "ever sell a record." Eyedea takes a stance as an authority figure vis-à-vis Shells in lines 8–9 when he tells him that he and his crew need to "go back to school"—Eyedea being the "teacher" who will set him straight. He finishes off his spit with five rhyming hyper-rhotic realizations of /r/ in which he frames himself as the "grim reaper" who has just finished off his opponent.

(9) Round 4 (final round): Eyedea vs. Shells (Eyedea on the mic).

1	Eyedea:	Always **spittin'** [spɪʔn] my lines, thinkin' that he's **fresher**
2		['frɛʃərr]. //Shells mouths Eyedea's lines as if he's heard them
3		before//
4		**Spittin'** [spɪʔn] Eyedea lines Ø the only way you'll **ever** [ɛvə]
5		sell a **record** [rɛkərrd].
6		So why'd you do that?
7		You don't wanna be (( )).
8		You know what, you need to take **your** [jer] whole fuckin'
9		crew back to school.
10		**Black,** that's how it goes. Pull up a stool. I'm the **teacher**
11		['titʃərr].
12		I'm about to **wear** [wɛr] your **bitch ass** ((sounds like)) **your**
13		[jə] **sneakers** ['snikərrz].
14		**You** [POSS] MCs to me is just **geekers** ['gikərrz].
15		This cat stays close to my dick like a **beeper** ['bipərr].
16		He **ain't** even comin' with the **cheaper** ['tʃipərr].
17		You just lost your life by Eyedea the grim **reaper** ['ripərr].

In his rebuttal spit (shown in (10)), Shells indexes Eyedea's whiteness in line 3 when he calls him "lil' Chuck Norris," the white American martial arts actor.

(10) Round 4 (Final Round): Shells vs. Eyedea (Shells on the mic).

1	Shells:	Listen man, yo. Hey, yo, listen. Hey yo, hey yo.
2		I'mo spit hot bars even if this dude is borin'.
3		They got Shells battlin' lil **Chuck Norris**.
4		We get it goin' man; you don't really want that.

Shells marks Eyedea's whiteness later in the spit in line 17 when he says he'll be "damned to lose against Vanilla Ice," the universally reviled white American rapper from the early 1990s. Note Eyedea's physical response to this when he throws up his hands and looks to the audience for a bit of sympathy. It's at least the third time one of his competitors has called him Eminem or Vanilla Ice, and he seems to be saying, "Yes, I'm white. Can't you think of a better rhyme?" Finally, it's noteworthy that Shells—like Eyedea's previous opponent E-Dub—never uses "nigga" to address or refer to him even once. Indirectly, he refers to Eyedea as "this dude" at the outset of his spit. The cumulative effect of these acts seems to suggest that Shells does not accept Eyedea as a full-fledged competitor. As a native of New York City, performing for a home crowd, Shells may have assumed that a white skater from Minneapolis wouldn't have the skills or credibility to pull off a win.

(11) Round 4 (Final Round): Shells vs. Eyedea (Shells on the mic)

14 Shells: You don't know—I'mo let this go.
15   And you talk about my teeth, talk about my flow.
16   I'm a hot ((skimity)) cat. Me Ø mad nice.
17   I'll be damned to lose against **Vanilla Ice.**

CONCLUSION

There is one more spit in the final round between Eyedea and Shells in which Shells loses face when he starts stumbling on his rhymes, allowing Eyedea to prevail as the overall champion in the tournament. Part of why Eyedea is so successful throughout the battle is because he is careful to maintain racial boundaries and doesn't try to "front." His clean-cut style and absence of head coverings or gang symbols of any kind show that he is not trying to claim street credibility or indeed be anything more than a white suburban skater kid. His hyper-rhotic /r/ is a way for him to mark himself both ethnically and in terms of class. The fact that he can let his opponents' incessant references to his whiteness roll off his back, tacitly accepting that while his identity is marked in this context, it, along with his impressive skills as a freestyler, is a crucial part of his success.

This data shows that in MC battles, whiteness is a highly marked category that triggers overt and oblique references to the racialized identities of all participants. Black and white contestants cooperate to construct differences in ways that reflect a shared orientation about the markedness of whiteness within Hip Hop. The foregrounding of whiteness serves an important functional role in the MC battle as a way to ratify an alternative social order—an order that must be acknowledged and embraced by white competitors if they are to be accepted by their opponents and the audience as "real."

There are a number of interesting implications that come out of the reversal of hegemonic racial hierarchies within Hip Hop culture: young people who participate in Hip Hop can become aware of what it feels like to experience the other side of the black/white racial boundary; white American youth can experience a bit of what it feels like to see themselves through the eyes of black people; and black youth can experience the sense of entitlement and self-confidence that belonging to the dominant culture entails—even though they often recognize that this dominance is generally limited to the realms of sports and entertainment. As Michael Eric Dyson powerfully affirms in a recent interview, "America, and indeed the globe, sees itself through the prism of blackness" which has become a kind of home for people around the world seeking "self-definition in the midst of a global culture of flux" (Jones 2006: 792). Hip Hop's global reach extends this metaphorical home to a surging wave of culturally distinct young people who are grappling with its power to help them understand themselves.

NOTES

1. I am indebted to the Samy Alim and Awad Ibrahim for their important suggestions and comments on earlier drafts of this chapter when it was first published in 2009.
2. I would like to express my thanks to Renée Blake for generously providing me with a videotape of the *Blaze* Battle and for insights into the language of rap lyrics. The *Blaze* Battle Face-Off 2000 World Championship was broadcast on HBO on November 25th at 11:30 p.m. EST. The competing MCs were previous winners and runner-ups from the Face-Off 2000 Tour. It is important to point out that as a highly commercialized event, the *Blaze* Battle is qualitatively different from the spontaneous, informal battles that take place on street corners and local Hip Hop clubs. It is impossible to know to what extent the final edit was controlled and shaped by the producers.
3. Gumperz maintains that a given aspect of linguistic behavior (lexical, prosodic, phonological) can function as a cue for interpreting what is said by a speaker. Contextualization cues hint at relevant aspects of the social context (via particular codes, styles, and dialects), enabling participants in a discourse to reason about their respective communicative intentions and purposes (Gumperz 1982, 1990). Goffman's related notion of footing (1981) refers to a speaker and hearer's shifting alignments in relation to the events at hand.
4. Tragically, the rapper Eyedea (Michael Larsen) passed away in his sleep on October 16, 2010, at his home in St. Paul, Minnesota.
5. Most reviews of the film *Kids* focus on Telly's amoral sexual behavior—having unprotected sex with virgins. A less explored aspect of Telly's skater persona is his adoption of Hip Hop style both in his speech and his dress.
6. Smitherman (1994) defines "shine" as a derogatory reference to a black male, but one definition on the website Urban Dictionary (www.urbandictionary.com) is to "do big things" as in "to get one's shine on." It seems like this is the meaning that comes closest to what R.K. intends in his performance.
7. This is not meant to imply that post-vocalic /r/-lessness is a universal feature of HHNL. It is however commonly found in the speech of African American rappers in the Northeast as well as among many young whites who want to signal their affiliation with Hip Hop. In the interview data I collected in New York City among white Hip Hop youth, I found rates of postvocalic /r/-lessness that ranged from 0% to 82% (Cutler 2002a). Eyedea's rate based on all the performance data in this battle was 8% (N = 64), suggesting that he can control this feature stylistically. His choice to adopt a hyper-rhotic realization of /r/ appears to be a way for him to emphasize his local (Minnesota) whiteness.

8. Ibrahim (personal communication) notes that black MCs often make references to color, such as "light-skinned" or "dark-skinned," or "you blacker than a . . . ."

9. Presumably this comparison refers to Mystikal's braided hairstyle.

10. D'Angelo (Michael D'Angelo Archer) is a successful R & B singer whose career peaked in the mid-1990s.

11. Alim's (2004b) black teenage informants offer further ethnographic evidence for the existence of this mentality in their stereotyping of whites as "sick, insane, criminals."

7 "She's So Hood"
Ghetto Authenticity on Reality TV

INTRODUCTION

This chapter continues the exploration of media representations of language and identity, focusing specifically on some of the cultural and linguistic boundaries that white Hip Hop youth experience as participants on a television reality show.[1] Conceived of and created by a team of five male Hip Hop journalists of color who call themselves the "Ego Trip," *Ego Trip's (White) Rapper Show* consisted of 10 episodes that aired weekly across the US on the cable station VH1 in early 2007.[2] It was presented as a contest to discover "the next great white rapper." The promotional trailer for the show asks, "Who will step up to become Hip Hop's next great white hope?—'Cause lord knows, it's lonely at the top," while an image of white rapper Eminem in Jesus robes appears on the screen.[3] Audition tapes were solicited from interested rappers across the US and a select number of these were invited to audition in person on camera. In one of these auditions, a young white woman called 'Nomi' is asked by the host and former white rapper, MC Serch, what she got out of the experience growing up in the affluent, overwhelmingly white town of Waterford, Connecticut.

(1) Nomi: What did I get out of my neighborhood? **Raw**, real life experiences. My neighbors are—FIERCE! I see it **real**, I see it **raw**.

Nomi says that her wealthy neighbors are "fierce" and implies that they engage in some of the same kinds of vicious or violent behavior that is more commonly associated with "ghetto" types. MC Serch replies with a big smile, "Wow, I didn't know it was that hard in Connecticut. That's great!" Nomi does not make it past the audition stage, but this clip sets up a discourse in the show about where real Hip Hop (and by extension, real Hip Hop youth) comes from, pitting the contestants against one another in a prolonged competition to connect themselves to a received version of the core Hip Hop experience. The show's creators (the Ego Trip crew) and its white host (MC Serch) are all connected to a particular time and place in the history of Hip Hop (New York City and the 1980s) and feel it is their duty to instill in the audience a respect for this "Old School" style as well as who they consider the founding rappers of Hip Hop to be, and the specific locations in the Bronx that they consider to be pivotal in Hip Hop's genesis.[4]

The analysis focuses on the first episode, although many details and facts were gleaned from multiple viewings off all eight episodes and the numerous associated websites and video clips available on the website that accompanied the show. The research questions I set out to answer pertaining to this data were extensions of some of the questions raised in previous chapters, but in the context of a reality TV show: How do white rappers attempt to authenticate themselves linguistically and (meta)pragmatically as competitors and how do they interpret what it means to be authentic in Hip Hop? How do the producers attempt to make whiteness visible and marked within the context of the show, and what functions does the show have pertaining to the way white youth understand Hip Hop's origins and their own relationship to Hip Hop?

THEORETICAL BACKGROUND

The theme of authenticity runs throughout this book and the present chapter considers it again in the context of televised interactions between white rappers who are competing with one another to be the most "real." Authenticity is a common theme in many studies of language, identity, and Hip Hop culture across the disciplines (Alim 2004a; Armstrong 2004; Hall and Bucholtz 1995; Cutler 2003a; Gordon 2005; Hess 2005; McLeod 1999; White 2006). Bucholtz and Hall (2005) describe authenticity as "the ways in which identities are discursively verified," which is distinct from authentication, "a social process played out in discourse" (Bucholtz and Hall 2005: 601). In some instances, the term authenticity refers to the legitimacy of one's claim to a particular ethnic identity and the ability of individuals to pass as legitimate members of a particular ethnic group (Hall and Bucholtz 1995). It may also have a social dimension relating to the specific criteria set up by a community of practice or subculture. Indeed, various music scenes from rock to country to rap each seem to have their own definitions (Davison 2001: 263, cited in Armstrong 2004: 6).

As noted in Chapter 3, another way in which some white rappers and Hip Hop youth try to authenticate themselves is through foregrounding their status as poor whites (cf. Eminem), thus establishing a connection to blackness by referencing a common disempowerment (White 2006). The various semantic dimensions of authenticity discussed above are summarized in Table 7.1, adapted from McLeod (1999: 139). Not included in McLeod's original is the talent/skill dimension (author's addition), an arguably important part of any rap artist's self-presentation. Indeed, Hess (2005) notes that the ability to rap and freestyle "live" is "one of a set of cultural values by which the artist's authenticity is judged" (299).

Table 7.1   Claims of Authenticity

Semantic Dimensions	Real	Fake
Social-psychological	Staying true to yourself	"Selling out," i.e., following mass trends
Racial	Black	White
Political-economic	The underground	Commercial
Gender-sexual	Hard	Soft
Social locational	The street	The suburbs
Cultural	The old school	The mainstream
Talent/skill	Ability to write and perform clever rhymes; ability to freestyle and battle spontaneously	"bites" or steals lyrics from other rappers; inability to freestyle and battle.

Building on this work, the present chapter examines how *Ego Trip's (White) Rapper Show* fulfills a gate-keeping as well as an educational function for the viewers. It also explores processes of identity formation and the authenticating strategies that the contestants use to construct themselves as "real." Along these lines, this chapter examines the stances a female contestant on the show ("Persia") takes towards her rival John Brown and towards her own utterances during a particularly ribald scene during the first episode of the show. Stances encompass the methods (e.g., linguistic or other) that speakers employ to create and signal relationships with their utterances and interlocutors (Johnstone 2009). Another way to define stances is "the display of evaluative, affective, and epistemic orientations in discourse" (Bucholtz and Hall 2005: 595). Persia, as with the other contestants and creators of the show, is engaged in an identity project which emerges through her linguistic and discursive practices in interaction.

Following Bucholtz and Hall's (2005) framework, particularly the principles of Indexicality and Relationality, this chapter focuses on Persia's interactional use of particular syntactic and lexical markers, the content of her statements, and her challenge to John Brown to engage in a freestyle "battle," and how they work together to authenticate and construct her as socially real. The Indexicality Principle states that:

Identity relations emerge in interaction through several related indexical processes, including: (a) overt mention of identity categories and labels; (b) implicatures and presuppositions regarding one's own or others' identity position; (c) display of evaluative and epistemic orientations to ongoing talk, as well as interactional footings and participant roles [i.e., stances]; and (d) the use of linguistic structures and systems that are ideologically associated with specific personas and groups [i.e., styles] (Bucholtz and Hall 2005: 594).

The overt mention of identity categories and labels such as "white" or "black," the "circulation of such categories within ongoing discourse, their explicit or implicit juxtaposition with other categories, and the linguistic elaborations and qualifications they attract (predicates, modifiers, and so on) all provide important information about identity construction" (Bucholtz and Hall 2005: 594). Implicatures and presuppositions are indirect ways of establishing an identity, involving the use of coded or indirect language (e.g., words like "hood" or "ghetto") to convey ingroup cues to particular listeners. Stance involves the linguistic strategies speakers use to "position themselves and others as particular kinds of people," (e.g., "real," "white trash," etc.) and style refers to the "repertoire of linguistic forms associated with personas or identities" (Bucholtz and Hall 2005: 595).

A second principle, the Relationality Principle, is also at work in Persia's identity construction as well as in the motives behind the show's creation. It holds that identities are "intersubjectively constructed through several, often overlapping, complementary relations," including adequation/distinction, authentication/denaturalization, and authorization/delegitimation (Bucholtz and Hall 2005: 598–603), and stems from the idea that "identities are never autonomous or independent but always acquire social meaning in relation to other available identity positions and other social actors" (Bucholtz and Hall 2005: 598).

The term adequation is about positioning groups or individuals as alike (e.g., poor whites and poor blacks). It involves dismissing differences that may be "irrelevant or damaging" and foregrounding "similarities viewed as salient" (Bucholtz and Hall 2005: 599). The contrary of adequation is distinction which depends on "the suppression of similarities that might undermine the construction of difference" (Bucholtz and Hall 2005: 600). Authentication and denaturalization are the "processes by which speakers make claims to realness and artifice, respectively" (Bucholtz and Hall 2005: 601). The first focuses on how "identities are discursively verified" and what kinds of language and language speakers count as authentic for a given purpose (Bucholtz and Hall 2005: 601). The second is concerned with how "assumptions regarding the seamlessness of identity can be disrupted" (Bucholtz and Hall 2005: 601). Authorization entails the local or translocal "affirmation or imposition of an identity through structures of institutionalized power and ideology" whereas delegitimation speaks to the ways in which identities are "dismissed, censored, or simply ignored by these same structures" (Bucholtz and Hall 2005: 603). These terms provide useful constructs for analyzing Persia's discursive work in interaction. First, however we turn to a brief discussion of the emergence and social function of reality television in the 1990s and 2000s.

OVERVIEW OF THE SHOW

Reality TV

So-called "reality television" has been enormously popular in recent years, with well over 400 different shows airing since the 1990s ("List of Reality Television Programs," 2008). Sparks (2007) identifies a combination of factors that led to the rise of reality TV shows: they are relatively cheap to produce; there is no need to pay writers or actors, no rehearsals, and no need for elaborate sets. In a blistering Marxist critique of the genre, Sparks (2007) claims that people are drawn to reality TV by the enormous liberating potential associated with celebrity status (i.e., freedom from the drudgery of an ordinary job and the enormous attention heaped upon the individuality of celebrities as opposed to everyday individuals). Thanks to the numerous iterations of reality shows like *Big Brother* and *Survivor* and the minor celebrity status attained by particular participants, viewers are highly attuned to the possibility of leading a life of leisure and consumption as opposed to labor (Sparks 2007).

Critics say that the term "reality television" is somewhat of a misnomer because they frequently portray a modified and highly controlled form of reality (Johnson-Woods 2002). Participants are put in exotic locations or abnormal situations, sometimes coached to act in certain ways by off-screen handlers, and events on screen are often manipulated through editing and other post-production techniques. Furthermore, the shows are often highly scripted; contestants are chosen more for their looks and personalities than for their talent, and screenwriters cynically plot out scenarios that will pit contestants against one another for maximum shock value.

Nevertheless, some reality TV shows have aspects of a social experiment (Smith and Wood 2003) and may even get viewers to think critically about certain social issues, e.g., *Black. White,* (2006) on FX, *Frontier House* (2002) on PBS, or *Shalom in the Home,* (2006) on TLC, potentially offering a view into the lives of people in very different situations than those of the viewers. *Ego Trip's (White) Rapper Show* has some aspects of this more socially conscious subgenre and a close examination of outtake interviews with the creators (the "Ego Trip" crew) makes it clear that they had a social and political agenda in creating the show.[5]

The Setting

Ego Trip's (White) Rapper Show (henceforth WRS) is set in the South Bronx, the commonly recognized birthplace of Hip Hop in the 1970s (Chang 2005). The show was shot during the summer of 2006 and aired from January through March of 2007. Ten white male and female contestants from all over the country were selected from hundreds of aspiring MCs to demonstrate their lyrical talent and knowledge of Hip Hop culture for the chance to win $100,000. In Hip Hop, an MC (emcee) or "master of ceremonies" raps (performs rhymes) against the backdrop of a beat provided by the DJ or "disc jockey." The contestants were brought to a warehouse in the Bronx called "Tha White House" where they live communally; the house also serves as the primary set for the show where rap contests and meetings with the host and other invited guests take place and where the contestants can be filmed during their down time.

In each of the eight episodes, the host, MC Serch (a white MC from the interracial 1980s group "3rd Bass") comes by the house and introduces the white rappers to Hip Hop luminaries like Grandmaster Flash, and sites in the Bronx where Hip Hop emerged, e.g., the 1520 Sedgewick Avenue housing project, Cedar Park, and the Rucker playground.[6] Typically the contestants are divided into teams and presented with a challenge in which they have to demonstrate their rapping skills, or some aspect of their Hip Hop knowledge. The losing team is then faced with an elimination challenge and the weakest competitor among them is then kicked off the show.

The Contestants

The ten finalists chosen to be on the show include three white women and seven white men, all in their 20s, from diverse regions of the country as well as one from the UK. Each has a short bio on the VH1 website (Cast Bios) with a link to a personal MySpace page where they can promote their careers, sell merchandise, and correspond with fans. Table 7.2 provides basic biographical information about each contestant.

It appeared as if the contestants were chosen because they represent easily accessible white American ethnic stereotypes. Great care is taken to strengthen these associations in the first few episodes through carefully edited clips. The male rappers include a hard-drinking, small town, southern "good old boy" (100 Proof); a bespectacled, tie-wearing "nerd" from the Midwest (Dasit); an affluent, self-promoting entrepreneur (John Brown);[7] a clean-cut Christian rapper (Jon Boy); and a PhD student in ethnic studies (Jus Rhyme). The last two male rappers included Shamrock, a "jock" from Atlanta with a huge golden grill over his teeth, and Sullee, a working class Irish American from Boston whose father was allegedly a petty mob leader. The three female rappers are Misfit Dior, a telegenic blonde originally from London, her oversized, in-your-face counterpart Persia who grew up in a predominantly African American neighborhood in Queens, NY, and G-Child from Allentown, Pennsylvania, a working class girl who fits Eckert's (1989) definition of a "burnout" and who is also a devotee of the disgraced, has-been white rapper Vanilla Ice. G-Child ultimately gets framed as "white trash," an identity she eventually seems to accept. The extent to which any of these individuals has actual rapping skills or any involvement in a local Hip Hop scene seems less important than the entertainment value each of them can potentially provide.

Table 7.2   Ten Contestants Chosen to Be on *Ego Trip's (White) Rapper Show*

Stage Name (Legal Name)	Age	Gender	Origin
100 Proof (Chuck Baker)	28	Male	Blue Mound, Texas
Dasit (David Shinavar)	29	Male	Toledo, Ohio
G-Child (Gina Morganello)	21	Female	Allentown, Pennsylvania
John Brown (Greg Kaysen)	26	Male	Davis, California; Brooklyn, New York
Jon Boy (John Wertz)	25	Male	Reedville, Virginia
Jus Rhyme (Jeb Middlebrook)	27	Male	Austin, Minnesota; Los Angeles, California
Misfit Dior (Laeticia Guzman)	27	Female	London, UK; Brooklyn, New York
Persia (Rachel Mucerino)	25	Female	Far Rockaway, New York
Shamrock (Timothy Rasmussen)	23	Male	Atlanta, Georgia
Sullee (Bobby Sullivan)	21	Male	Boston, Massachusetts

The "jock" and "burnout" constructs are developed fully by Eckert (1989) and refer to oppositional social categories found in typical American high schools. Teenagers who orient towards the "jock" identity tend to be more middle class and embrace the institutions of the school (sports, school government, etc.), whereas "burnouts," generally working class, adopt an oppositional stance towards school and "jock" culture. "Nerds" on the other hand (studious, but socially awkward types) reject both "jock" and "burnout" orientations while asserting white or even "hyperwhite" identities (Bucholtz 1997, 2011).

The limited biographical information provided on the show makes it difficult to determine the extent to which any of the contestants actually identifies as a "jock," "burnout," "nerd" or any other category, or what their actual class and white ethnic origins are. The bios on the VH1 website give some hints in this regard (Cast Bios). Shamrock is described as a "high school athlete," but in an interview clip on the show he describes how he was homeschooled through fifth grade because he had a cleft lip and had to undergo multiple surgeries, only later finding his identity through "sports" and "music" (Shamrock on his Childhood). G-Child and Dasit may fit the "white trash" and "nerd" categories more neatly. In her rap about the theme "white trash" during the elimination round in Episode 3, G-Child describes how she and her friends engage in burnout-type activities like hanging out on rooftops and "smokin cigs to pass the time, cause we can't do shit right." Referencing a nerd identity, Dasit's bio describes him as "a dude who looks like an office worker gone postal" (Cast Bios). The reference to these widely recognizable "characterological types" (Johnstone 2011) on the show points to their ubiquity and longevity in the American psyche, but we are simply not given enough ethnographic detail to assume that any of the competitors actually conforms any particular social category.

The Ego Trip Crew

"Ego Trip" is the name given to the team of producers. The team consists of five young men of color with journalism backgrounds: Elliott Wilson, Jeff Mao, Sacha Jenkins, Brent Rollins and Gabriel Alvarez. From 1994–1998, the group published a magazine that dealt with issues of race while disguised as a magazine about Hip Hop (*Ego Trip* (magazine), 2008).[8] Describing the magazine, Kleinfeld (2000: 6) writes,

> They invented a white owner, one Theodore Aloysius Bawno, who offered a message in each issue, blurting his bigoted views and lust for Angie Dickinson. His son, Galen, was a Princeton-educated liberal who professed common cause with blacks. But in truth, he was an unaware bigot, as Mr. Wilson says he feels so many young whites are.

Exploring what the Ego Trip crew is about and its motives is crucial for understanding what the white rapper show is trying to accomplish. The VH1 website that accompanied the show included a large number of short interviews with the Ego Trip crew. It is evident from these outtakes that the Ego Trip intended for the show to be a forum for educating the mainly white audience about the received version of Hip Hop history, focusing on its African American roots in the Bronx and its some of its male founders (Grandmaster Flash, Kurtis Blow, Melle Mel, Fat Joe, and others), and about some of the contradictions arising when Whites' participate in Hip Hop. The Ego Trip have a stake in guarding the gates of the Hip Hop nation (Kleinfield 2000), and the show is a symbolic attempt to define who can gain entrance and what knowledge is required in order to be member. With an average of over one million viewers in the 18–34 age group so highly coveted by television marketers during the first three episodes, the show had the potential to get its message out to a large number of young people (Fitzgerald 2007).[9]

The creators of the show claim they want to dispel the myth that white rappers inherently lack credibility. In the preview outtakes (Preview Extras: "Tha [sic] Interrogation"), Sacha Jenkins, a member of Ego Trip, states that the whole Ego Trip crew had a certain fascination with white rappers because they appear to be trying to be "something that they're not." The title of the show certainly implies that the creators are trying to discover white rappers with real talent. In the preview that was aired to promote the WRS, MC Serch introduces the show as a chance for white rappers to demonstrate their "love and knowledge" of Hip Hop as well prove "their lyrical prowess" (White Rapper: New Series Preview). But the real motive is to establish a set of ground rules for whites who want to be part of Hip Hop. These include acknowledging that Hip Hop is part of the cultural heritage of black people, acknowledging the preeminent role of the Bronx in the birth of Hip Hop, and paying tribute to Hip Hop's founding rap artists as well as its places of origin. In the outtakes, Brent Rollins of the Ego Trip crew says that if Hip Hop is going to be "gentrified" by white youth, it is imperative that young white people "learn about its origins" (Roundtable: South Bronx). By acknowledging Hip Hop's rootedness in the Bronx and in the African American community, and by developing the requisite skill to write clever rhymes and perform them, white rappers, and by extension the mainly white audience, can learn better how they can "be real."

DATA AND ANALYSIS

Whiteness as a Marked Category

The WRS is an interesting site for analyzing questions of authenticity precisely because of the contested nature of white participation in Hip Hop culture and the conglomeration of artists and fans who produce and consume the products of Hip Hop culture: rapping, DJ-ing, graffiti art, and break dancing. In mainstream American culture, white people usually do not have to think about their skin color or worry about conforming to socially prescribed behaviors in the ways that people of color often do. Du Bois (1903), Spears (1998), and others have written extensively on the double consciousness that affects black Americans and which forces them to see themselves through the eyes of whites. But on the WRS, it is the white contestants who are continually reminded of their whiteness and are made to see themselves to some degree through the eyes of black Hip Hop authorities (embodied by guest judges like Prince Paul, Grandmaster Caz, Kwamé, and Little X). In the Episode 1 outtakes, (Roundtable: The N Word), Sacha Jenkins of the Ego Trip says that the show is a "conversation about race . . . in the hands of white people," implying that part of the goal is to get white viewers to understand what it is like to be racialized and objectified.

Often, overt references to whiteness are made via naming and labeling (Indexicality). The contestants are housed in an old warehouse complete with bunkbeds, a garbage can labeled "white trash," and other props chosen to give a sort of trashy urban loft vibe. The use of Hip Hop orthography with regards to the determiner "tha" in "Tha White House" indexes the cultural backdrop of the show and contrast it with the ethnicity of the contestants as well as create an ironic contrast between the real White House in Washington, D.C. where supreme power rests, and the powerless Bronx where "Tha White House" is located. Periodically the contestants receive a video message from the host, MC Serch, which is played on a television screen set into a human-sized jar of mayonnaise. They are alerted to the message with a voice that says, "You've got mayo," a play on America Online's ubiquitous email reminder "You've got mail," but also a reference to the Hip Hop expression "to have mayo" or to have skin the color of mayonnaise which refers to white or light-complected people who lack melanin in their skin.

In other instances, the contestants are forced to address whiteness more directly within the rapping contests. In Episode 3, during the elimination challenge, the contestants on the losing team must take a slice of white bread from a bag with themes like "white power," "white trash," "white wash," and "white guilt" and go into the "Ice Ice Chamber" (a sort of isolation tank and play on Vanilla Ice's 1989 hit song "Ice Ice Baby") and write a 16-line rap about their topic. Two competing interpretations of whiteness emerge in the Shamrock and Sullee rhymes. Shamrock whose theme is "white guilt" writes about how being white gets him off the hook for shoplifting and driving too fast whereas a young black man would face very different consequences. In response to the theme "white power," Sullee expresses indignation at the idea that whiteness confers any advantage on him, saying that it is not about race, but rather economic status. The overt and indirect references to "whiteness" in these multiple instances (Tha White House, "you've got mayo," the Ice Ice Chamber, white guilt, white trash, white wash, and white power) draw attention to whiteness as marked within the hermeneutics of Hip Hop, contrasting it with normative blackness (Boyd 2002).

Competing Forms of Authenticity in Interaction: Persia versus John Brown

The audition process for the WRS has already set up an interesting dialectic between competing ownership claims to Hip Hop authenticity: social-locational vs. gender/sexual and social psychological. Throughout the show, we learn that some of the rappers—with the exception of John Brown, the self-professed "King of the 'burbs"—claim to come from pretty rough circumstances. Persia says she was "homeless" at one time, Shamrock says he came from "nothin," Sullee says that his dad was in prison when he was young, and G-Child is self-professed "white trash." They use their putative class origins throughout the show in order to excuse or explain their behavior and as a way to try to authenticate themselves in a subculture that privileges blackness and urban "street" origins (Alim 2003). Highlighting social traits that connect whites and blacks can be classified as a form of adequation (Bucholtz and Hall 2005).

Asserting a connection to blackness through poverty also follows the tradition of the white rapper, Eminem, who proudly touts his "trailer trash" identity (White 2006). Indeed, this is a dimension that the creators seem eager to explore in the show. Brent Rollins confesses that he, like many other African Americans, grew up believing that all white people "had it easy" and only later came to believe that poor white people are just like poor black people (The White Rapper Show is Born).

Persia, a self-chosen moniker that indexes a non-white and somewhat exotic female identity, is a young white woman who distinguishes herself from the other white competitors as someone who was socialized among black people in a rough part of New York (Far Rockaway, Queens).[10] As we can see in her bio (below), Persia flouts her "hood" credentials as her ticket to legitimacy as a rapper.

> Rapping Far Rockaway, Queens to the fullest, the no-nonsense queen of tough talk bites her tongue for no one. As talented as she is confrontational, Rachel Mucerino,[11] otherwise known as Persia, takes pride in embodying the rough, gritty attitude of old school New York. This is in stark contrast to her smooth-as-hell singing ability that complements her sharp-as-razors raps. The product of a hectic life growing up, 25-year-old Persia has walked the line between right and wrong and has emerged as a rising star. (A rising star who prefers to call herself "That Bitch"; Cast Bios).

Persia's bio authenticates her by locating her in a black neighborhood (Social-Locational), connecting her to "Old School" New York (Cultural), and by referencing her talent as a rapper (Talent/Skill). Finally, the fact that she self-identifies as a "bitch" may be an attempt to lay claim to some of the more positive connotations it can have in Hip Hop. It also works via implicature to suggest black femaleness. Although scholars of Hip Hop have debated the widespread use of the word "bitch" and "ho" (from whore) in the lyrics of black male rappers and their misogynist connotations (Potter 1995; Perry 2004; Perkins 1996), Keyes (2004) writes that "bitch" can have positive, empowering meanings such as an "aggressive or assertive female who subverts the authority of men" (Keyes 2004: 200).

By the end of the first episode, Persia, the full-bodied woman with a large mop of hair and a flair for rapping, emerges as the show's principle protagonist. She has shown natural ability to relate to the local black community around the south Bronx in "meet and greet" occasions. She has also demonstrated her prowess at performing spontaneous "freestyle" raps in front of appreciative black audiences on the street, and has garnered the respect of some of her fellow contestants such as G-Child who remarks, "She's so hood! She's perfect for this Hip Hop game" (Rappin' in the hood).

Early in the first episode, Persia targets her main rival, John Brown. By openly acknowledging his affluent, suburban California origins, John Brown lays full claim to authenticity by trying to represent himself for what he is (McLeod 1999). He also fully embraces a kind of hyper-capitalism embodied in the Hip Hop expression "I'ma get mine" and characteristic of entrepreneurial rappers who came up in the late 1990s such as Sean "Puffy" Combs (Gaunt et al. 2008: 13). He is the leader of a movement and brand called "Ghetto Revival," of which he constantly reminds the audience throughout the series by punctuating the end of every utterance with "Ghetto revival, baby! Hallelujah, holla back!" Brown also refers to himself as the "King of the 'Burbs" (Cast Bios), which he defines as being all about "SATs, SUVs, and keg parties"—metonyms of American upper middle class suburbia, and the college experience.[12] Persia is the utter contrast, having grown up in Far Rockaway, a lower working class part of Queens—and makes it no secret that she thinks John Brown is a fraud and cannot be a credible rapper.

These two characters emerge in the first episode as chief protagonists of competing versions of the authentic white rapper. They are repeatedly chosen to head up opposing teams and have had verbal run-ins from early on. Towards the end of Episode 1, the contestants are sitting around "Tha White House" having drinks. Persia challenges John Brown to a freestyle battle—something that every MC is supposed to be able to do. She hounds him around the house trying to provoke him into battle, finally waving a dildo (which is censored out of the image via pixilation) in his face. Persia hurls insults at Brown and questions his integrity and his masculinity by calling him a fake and a "bitch," but he refuses to engage her. The increasing use of "bitch" to refer to men was noted in a recent New York Times article (Heffernan 2005). Calling a male "bitch" is particularly insulting because it implies not only weakness and femininity, but also possible sexual domination by another man (as commonly occurs in male prisons), contrasting with the positive connotations it can have when used in Hip Hop by women to describe themselves (Keyes 2004).

Persia's Challenge to John Brown

Persia's challenge to John Brown is to engage in a "battle," a Hip Hop performance genre in which two people agree to a verbal duel instead of a physical fight. The opponents each get a chance to "diss" one another using spontaneous rhymes for a fixed length of time, and the surrounding spectators then judge whose rhymes were better, thus diffusing the conflict. In Hip Hop culture, MCs are supposed to be able to freestyle and battle spontaneously, and Brown's unwillingness suggests that he either lacks the skills or that he does not take Persia seriously. By challenging him, Persia is trying to expose him as a "fake" MC, as well as authenticate herself by demonstrating her own freestyling skills. Sullee's threat to fight John Brown in order to defend Persia's honor during the confrontation is wholly inappropriate in the context of an MC battle, and points to the likelihood that he was not socialized among urban African American Hip Hop youth. In (2), we see a transcript of the interaction.[13] Brown has just uttered something inaudible, but presumably insulting at Persia and Sullee jumps up from the table and threatens Brown with physical violence. Shamrock tries to hold Sullee back and Persia shoves him away, pointing her finger at John Brown.

(2) Persia challenges Brown to a battle; Episode 1, Ch. 6: 26:38.

1	Persia:	This Ø how I'mo show ((you))—This Ø how I'mo show
2		the ((motherfuckin')) world he Ø a bitch!
3	Sullee:	Exactly! //louder// Exactly!
4	//camera cuts to post hoc interview with Shamrock//	
5	Shamrock:	That's when like she disrespected him straight up.
6	//camera cuts to Persia waving dildo in John Brown's face//	
7	//Persia walking towards John Brown; John Brown retreating//	
8	//camera cuts to Sullee running at John Brown//	
9	Sullee:	Exactly!
10	Persia:	Ø you gonna battle? You got a dick in your face. Ø you
11		gonna battle?
12	//camera cuts to post hoc interview with Shamrock//	
13	Shamrock:	//smiling guiltily// <u>Persia brings out a dildo and put it on</u>
14		<u>that man's mouth! Like</u> //shrugs// <u>that's—that's' it!</u>
15	//camera cuts back to Persia waving dildo in John Brown's face//	
16	John Brown:	//protecting face; retreating// All right. All right.
17	Persia:	Ø you gonna battle? Ø you a real **nigga**? You got a
18		((dick)) in your face. Ø you gonna battle?
19	//camera cuts to Persia's post hoc interview//	
20	Persia:	//speech stylized in a more standard direction// <u>I</u> [ɑ:]
21		<u>honestly wanted to push him by any means possible to</u>
22		<u>battle me.</u>
23	//camera cuts back to Persia waving dildo in John Brown's face//	
24	Persia:	Are you gonna battle?
25	John Brown:	Girl!
26	Persia:	You Ø a dude right? Any dude that have [-AGR] a dick
27		in his face will man up.
28	//camera cuts to Persia's post hoc interview//	
29	Persia:	//speech stylized in a more standard direction// <u>I</u> [ɑ:] was
30		thinkin', this is how I'm [ɑ:m] gonna test him 'cause
31		everybody I [ɑ:] know would just crack me.
32	//camera cuts back to Persia and John Brown//	

We can analyze this scene using Bucholtz and Hall's (2005) Indexicality and Relationality Principles to show how Persia works to construct herself as an authentic Hip Hop persona. From the beginning of the confrontation, she invokes a knowledgeable, epistemic stance (Bucholtz and Hall 2005) as a Hip Hop insider with the authority to show the "motherfuckin' world" that John Brown is a "bitch." Persia's attempt to battle John Brown is juxtaposed to post hoc interviews about the event with some of the other contestants (e.g., Shamrock) as well as herself, in addition to interview outtakes with the show's creators. Shamrock's comments and facial gestures signal his orientation towards the encounter as a bemused spectator and sympathizer with Persia.

In Bauman's terms (1986), these carefully edited excerpts function as metanarratives, contextualizing the event to the perceived objective of the show as well as to the personal agendas of each competitor. Persia explains that she attacked John Brown in order to frame him as a fake MC and a wimp. In terms of participant roles, Persia positions herself as a representative and protector of the other contestants and of Hip Hop itself, and she is determined to expose "posers" and "wannabes." She tells us that any of the "real" men she knows would have smacked her for waving a dildo in their faces, implying that John Brown lacks the requisite masculinity to be a "real" man. Boyd (2002) writes that there is a "strong sense of physicality and sensuality that informs society's definition of black masculinity" (122), and a "detached, nonchalant sense of being" that is the "antithesis of what would be described as white masculinity" (Boyd 2002: 118). In Persia's mind, John Brown's failure to respond to her taunting in a physical way or to step up to the challenge of a freestyle battle is evidence that he fails to live up to the standards of black masculinity and is therefore not an adequate representative of Hip Hop. She, in contrast, positions herself as someone who is ready and willing to battle, making her a legitimate Hip Hop MC.

When John Brown responds, he addresses not Persia, but rather the wider audience—the TV viewers, and especially the record company representatives. He warns them not to sign up any of his competitors (especially Persia) because they would be a financial "liability," once again indexing his stance as a modern day capitalist rapper with an eye to the market. In his interview, he objectifies Persia's outburst from the perspective of someone with commercial interests who wants to promote a "good look" in order to sell a product. Here, he becomes that product, and he essentially is trying to sell himself and his Ghetto Revival brand as marketable to potential customers. He contrasts his image as a clean cut, business savvy frat boy with that of Persia as a big, mouthy woman, as someone who will scare away marketers and potential consumers.

Linguistic Competence

In terms of her speech style, Persia demonstrates a degree of linguistic and verbal competence that sets her apart from any of the other participants. In addition to copula absence, a lack of subject-verb agreement, and third person verbal /s/ absence, Persia stylizes her speech by using some of the characteristic phonological, intonational, and morphosyntactic features of HHNL/AAE.

Some of the other competitors demonstrate copula absence as part of their linguistic repertoires, but use it only in performing raps: Shamrock omits the copula when quoting a black friend in his rap about "white guilt" in Episode 3,[14] and in Episode 4, John Brown, Jon Boy, and Sullee write a song called "She Ø a stunner" (She's a stunner). Persia, on the other hand, uses copula absence throughout her confrontation with John Brown and also on a few isolated occasions in conversation. Referring to the losing team during a dinner with black rapper Juelz Santana, Persia says, "That four lost the competition so they Ø over there, doin' our laundry." An analysis of her speech in the scene transcribed in (2) and (3) indicates that her performance style contains frequencies of copula absence that are similar to the performance style of African American female rap artists such as Eve (Alim 2002).

Alim (2002) looks at copula variation in the lyrics and interview data he collected with two rappers, Eve and Juvenile. As we might expect, both artists had higher rates of absence in their lyrics than in their interviews.[15] The data from the emotionally charged scene in (2) and (3) illustrate that, at least with respect to copula absence, Persia's performance in verbal confrontation approaches the frequencies found in the lyrics of an African American female rapper (60.9% deletion of "is" and 93.2% deletion of "are"; Alim 2002: 296) (see Table 7.3).

Indeed, Persia's social experience resembles that of the white woman documented in the work of Sweetland (2002) who was socialized in a black community in Cincinnati, Ohio and who demonstrates both the linguistic competence and the social license to use AAE syntax in ways that native speakers inherently possess. Persia's speech is also notable for its lack of subject-verb agreement and for its AAE intonational features, wide pitch range, and raspy falsetto voice, all of which make it conceivable for her to pass linguistically as an African American woman. To borrow Sweetland's expression, Persia appears to be an "authentic speaker" of AAE both in terms of her ability to pass linguistically, but also in terms of the lexical choices she makes and the stance she takes towards her use of these choices.

Table 7.3 Persia's Use of AAE Syntactic Features (Battle Style)

Feature	Frequency	No. of tokens
Copula absence (is) (D/C+D)	60%	N = 5
Copula absence (are) (D/C+D)	77%	N = 13
Ø agreement	36%	N = 11

Taken together, Persia's phonological, morphosyntactic, lexical, and intonational style markers serve to demarcate the interaction as a performance and differentiate it from the way she styles her speech in more formal settings where she restricts her speech to monophthongal realizations of /ay/, and post-vocalic /r/-lessness.

Persia's use of AAE morphosyntax, her claims to ghetto identity, and her challenges to John Brown's masculinity as a rapper also constitute stance-taking moves. Effectively, she is claiming the Racial (blackness), Gender-Sexual (hard), Social-Locational (the street), Cultural (old school), and Talent/Skill (ability to freestyle/battle) dimensions of authenticity listed in Table 7.1. By taking an epistemic stance as an insider and a judge of who is "real," she is setting herself apart not only from John Brown, but from all of the other contestants, none of whom can lay claim to the range of authenticating dimensions which she possesses. As shown below, she also achieves this in her choice of lexis.

Lexical Usage: Who Can Use the N-Word?

At the lexical level, Persia makes use of Hip Hop expressions like "bitch," "peoples," "they" in place of "their," "stupid ass," and "nigga." There have been enormous debates in Hip Hop about the use of the last of these—the so-called "N-word," its various meanings, and who is allowed to say it. Smitherman (2000) writes that while it is true that among blacks, the word has a unique /r/-less pronunciation (nigga), and a variety of meanings, only one of which is negative, and that it has become more acceptable for black people to use it in the public arena since the advent of Hip Hop culture, it is still unacceptable for a white person to use the term. This generalization may be extended to any non-African American person, judging from the controversy that erupted when the pop singer Jennifer Lopez who is of Puerto Rican descent used the N-word in her song "I'm Real" (even though the song was written by the African American rapper Ja Rule). Among the most vocal critics were African American radio hosts Star and Buc Wild (from New York's Hot 97 Star and Buc Wild Morning Show), who vehemently oppose non-African Americans using the term (Alonso 2003). The white rapper Eminem has also stated publicly that he would never use the N-word.

Persia's use of the N-word and the comments she makes in her own defense (shown in (3) below) index her insider status and acceptance in the black community. In an interview clip, she reported that she uses the term "among her black friends," who presumably accept her as part of their peer group as well as their speech community. Elliott Wilson of the Ego Trip observes that she is using it in an "N-I-G-G-A" way—not an "N-I-G-G-E-R" way, meaning that she is pronouncing it the r-less way that African Americans do and that she is using it in a positive or neutral sense, rather than as a racial epithet with its requisite rhotic pronunciation (Roundtable: The N-Word). He also notes that although Persia feels licensed to use the N-word around her black friends, she fails to recognize that it may be offensive to other African Americans (Roundtable: The N-Word).

The next excerpt, which follows directly on the heels of (2), shows how Persia's rampant use of the N-word in her attack against John Brown is addressed by the show's most politically-aware contestant, Jus Rhyme.

(3) Persia challenges John Brown to a battle; Episode 1, Ch. 6: 26:38.

```
 1  Persia:      //walking down the hallway in pursuit of John Brown// You's
 2               [-AGR] a ((fuckin')) bitch, yo. Niggas is [-AGR] ready to
 3               knock you out =
 4  //cut to John Brown chewing lip; cut back to Persia//
 5  Persia:      = and lose they [POSS] whole chance—because you's
 6               [-AGR] a bitch.
 7  //camera cuts to John Brown//
 8  John Brown:  Let's get it poppin'!
 9  Persia:      //cynical tone// Oh, now we Ø about to get it poppin',
10               right? You want to fight but you don't want to battle.
11  //camera pans to Persia//
12  Persia:      Only because you want the **nigga** //referring to Sullee//
13               to hit you first and go home, right? But you know, this is
14               ((some rap shit)). You don't want to battle. You just want
15               the **nigga** to hit you first.
16  Jus Rhyme:   |Persia. Persia.
17  Persia:      |You Ø a bitch!
18  //camera cuts to Jus Rhyme lying on bunkbed//
19  Jus Rhyme:   Would you mind please not using the N-word, 'cause it
20               bothers me.
21  //cut to Jus Rhyme's post hoc interview//
22  Jus Rhyme:   The N-word is not appropriate for people to use—it can
23               be ((a)) hurtful word.
24  //cut to Persia and Jus Rhyme//
25  Persia:      Yeah, well life sucks and there ain't no doors on this
26               room.
27  Jus Rhyme:   I know, I'm just sayin', would you . . .
28  Persia:      //louder//      |Yeah, well life sucks and ((they)) ain't no
29               doors on this room!
30  //camera pans to Persia//
31  Jus Rhyme:   All right.
32  Persia:      It ain't personal. How Ø you takin' it?
33  //cut to Jus Rhyme's post hoc interview//
34  Jus Rhyme:   My friends are predominantly black and Latino and I'm
35               offended—at her saying the word.
36  //cut to Persia and Jus Rhyme//
37  Jus Rhyme:   I know, I'm just saying, the use—your use of the N-word =
```

38		//Subtitles appear on screen: I KNOW, I'M JUST SAYING
39		YOUR USE OF THE N-WORD BOTHERS ME.//
40	Persia:	//angrily/Yeah, well I grew up in the **hood** =
41	Jus Rhyme:	= bothers me.
42	Persia:	= and we ain't—no color. Everybody's my **nigga**, right
43		there!
44	Jus Rhyme:	O.K.
45	Persia:	So whoever the fuck takes disrespect, it's **they** [POSS]
46		((fuckin')) problem. Wherever they Ø from, they can't say
47		it in front of they [POSS] peoples, that's they [POSS] prob-
48		lem. Everybody's my **nigga**, and I'm somebody's **nigga**
49		right now.

Within the black community, the N-word can have a variety of meanings, some of which are positive or neutral (Major 1994; Smitherman 2000). Smitherman writes that it can express personal affection ("He Ø my main nigga"), describe someone who is culturally black ("Niggas is beautiful, baby"), refer to any black person as a stand-in noun ("Niggas was runnin' all over the place"), or express disapproval of a person's actions ("The nigga ain't shit"; Smitherman 2000: 362–3). As we see in Table 7.4, Persia has access to the different meanings of the word and uses it in a variety of ways, none of which are negative. All of the tokens occur in the scene transcribed above in (2) and (3).

Persia initially uses the expression "real nigga" in a positive sense, refer-ring to someone who is authentic and who stands for something—all quali-ties that she feels John Brown lacks. She then uses the term in a neutral sense in referring to the other white contestants on the show (*Niggas* is [-AGR] ready to knock you out . . .) and then in referring to Sullee (Only because you want the *nigga* to hit you first . . .). The last three tokens, delivered in a defiant, huffing voice (Everybody's *my nigga*, right there; Everybody's *my nigga*; and I'm somebody's *nigga* right now) are used in a highly positive, inclusive ingroup way that indexes her ingroup identity.

When Jus Rhyme, a doctoral student in ethnic studies, asks her not to use the "N-word" because he feels that "it's not appropriate," Persia retorts, "There ain't no doors on this room. How Ø you takin' it?," meaning that she thinks it is acceptable to use the N-word if there are not any black people around to hear it and/or when it is not meant to be a racial epithet. In another short interview clip following the incident, Persia says that she never uses the N-word in a malicious manner, but because she uses it around her friends, "it's bound to happen" (Serch lays down the law). She's clearly aware of the different meanings that it can have based on who says it and how it is meant (cf. Smitherman 2000), but asserts her right to use this word as shown in (4). In this particular instance, we see Persia emphatically tak-ing the stance of an insider and aligning herself with blackness through the implicature of the statement "we ain't no color." We also see adequation

Table 7.4   Persia's Use of the N-Word during Attack on John Brown

Token	Connotation
Ø you a real **nigga**?	Positive; someone who is true to themselves and doesn't "front" or pretend to be something they're not.
Niggas is [-AGR] ready to knock you out and lose they whole chance.	Neutral; any (presumably) male person, but could refer to an unspecified female person as well.
Only because you want the **nigga** to hit you first and go home, right?	Neutral: referring to the white contestant Sullee
You just want the **nigga** to hit you first.	Neutral: referring to the white contestant Sullee
Yeah, well I grew up in the hood and we ain't—no color. Everybody's my **nigga**, right there!	Positive: meaning something like friend or partner.
Everybody's my **nigga**, and I'm somebody's **nigga** right now.	Positive: By saying that everyone is a nigga, including her, Persia is trying to show that she's not using the word in its restricted negative sense, but rather a positive one.

(suppression of social difference) at work in her use of the inclusive deictic pronoun "we" which groups her with other, presumably black, people in the "hood" and implies that there is no difference (in terms of skin color) between them (Bucholtz and Hall 2005).

(4) Yeah, well **I** grew up in the **hood** and **we ain't**—no color. Everybody's my **nigga**, right there!

The utterance is delivered with an emphatic raspy voice and AAE phonology (the monophthongization of "I" and "my," /r/-lessness in "color," and "there," and particularly the fricated realization of /h/ in "hood" as [x]. Although this last item may not derive from any previously documented feature of AAE, it does seem be a way for Persia to place special emphasis on the word "hood," making it especially salient for anyone listening.

The Ego Trip have anticipated this moment and were prepared to deal with it. In the outtakes (Roundtable: The N-Word), Gabriel Alvarez explains that "you can't do a show like 'Ego Trip's (White) rapper show' without thinking about white people using the N-Word" (Roundtable: The N-Word). MC Serch then explains that the position of the Ego Trip was that any use of the N-word on the show "would not be tolerated." By highlighting the problem, and asserting their right not to tolerate it, as well as referring to their "Old School" roots, the Ego Trip establish themselves as arbiters and authorities of Hip Hop. The next day, the host MC Serch, gathers the rappers for a special meeting. Because of her repeated use of the word "nigga" during the previous confrontation, MC Serch obliges Persia to wear a special "bling" (flashy, ostentatious accessory)—in this case an enormous metal placard hanging on an oversized metal chain around her neck with "N-Word" stamped on it—for the rest of the day, while the whole cast goes to play miniature golf. He addresses her use of the N-word in terms of the national audience, saying that the word does not "flow around the country" in places like Mississippi, Tallahassee, and Birmingham (Roundtable: The N-Word). Elliott Wilson allows that while it may be possible for someone like to Persia to use the N-word in "her environment," she (and by extension the white Hip Hop youth in the audience) need to recognize that using it anywhere else is offensive to black people (Roundtable: The N-Word). The scene cuts to Jus Rhyme who explains that "There was a time in history when those chains were real and they were on black people, so what are you really doing if you use that word and you claim to represent Hip Hop?" Persia accepts her guilt and after the golf game she breaks down in tears, admitting that she may have hurt people by her use of the N-word. It is interesting to note here that Persia's use of the word "bitch" during the confrontations with John Brown in contrast to the N-word receives no attention whatsoever, despite the sexist and misogynist connotations it has in the context of the interaction. Nor is either word censored in the audio, in contrast to "motherfucker" and "fuckin'" which are "bleeped out" and appear as subtitles rendered partially with symbols on the screen (e.g., motherf*****; f*****).

DISCUSSION AND CONCLUSION

Persia seems on course to win the show, but is eliminated unexpectedly in Episode 6, much to the chagrin of the host, MC Serch, who breaks down in tears. The episode starts off by having the remaining rappers (Jus Rhyme, Persia, John Brown, and Shamrock) complete the "thug challenge" obstacle course which involves stealing three bags of groceries in a shopping cart, smashing a piñata, collecting two dollars' worth of dimes, running to a store and exchanging the dimes for lock cutters, stealing a bike, and returning back to "Tha White House." Jus Rhyme wins that challenge, while Persia collapses and is hospitalized briefly for dehydration.

The rappers are then required to write a "thug" version of an old nursery rhyme. Persia stumbles on her rhyme halfway through, and when MC Serch urges her to get back up and try again, she declines. The judges concur that even though her rhymes are better than many of the others, her failure to finish and refusal to try again mean that she must go. The enormous symbolic potential of a white female rapper winning out over a group of white male rappers is ultimately derailed by a contest and who can write the most "thuggish" rhyme and a trying physical contest (which inherently favored the males) about who can act most "thuggish."

The scenes described above can help to address some of the questions raised throughout the book, in particular how authenticities are produced and reproduced through semiotic forms of expression, how the application of notions of authenticity legitimates some individuals, and not others, and whose interests are served by the assessment of others' authenticity.

Persia constructs herself as an authentic Hip Hop persona by establishing a cultural affiliation with blackness via implicature and adequation. She talks about coming from the "hood," calls herself "bitch," refers to herself as a "nigga" in (3), and uses the inclusive pronoun "we" in (4) "Yeah, well I grew up in the hood and we ain't—no color." She further authenticates herself by adopting a knowledgeable insider stance through her attacks on John Brown by calling him a "bitch," and questioning his integrity and manhood (Ø you a real nigga?). Finally, in terms of style, she employs syntactic features of HHNL/AAE such as Ø copula, and lack of subject-verb agreement, in addition to a range of phonological features and lexical items that directly and emphatically index her connection to the "hood."

We can also see adequation and distinction at work in the discursive strategies Persia employs to liken herself to an urban, outspoken black female and to distinguish herself from the other white contestants on the show. Authentication and denaturalization are evident in her discursive and stylistic efforts to construct herself as a "real" MC and John Brown as a "fake." Authorization and delegitimation are visible in the workings of the show itself, the motives of its creators (the Ego Trip crew), the rules they lay down about who is licensed to use particular words, and in the messages being directed at the audience (presumably mostly white) about who can be "real" in Hip Hop. It is through the analysis of identity work at these multiple indexical levels that we can arrive at a fuller understanding of identity formation on the show and the individual identity projects of contestants on the show, particularly that of Persia.

There is also an identity project at work in the show itself. The Ego Trip and the host, MC Serch, use their "Old School" status as a way to assert their authority and license to judge who is "real" and what the received history of Hip Hop should be. The foregrounding of whiteness in the title of the show, and its frequent mention throughout the show in overt and indirect ways all constitute a strategy of distinction, making the audience aware of the fact that whiteness is marked and problematic in the Hip Hop worldview. Hegemonic whiteness and its privileged position as the unmarked, unnamed, normative category are challenged by the show's insistence on naming it, making fun of it, and challenging white rappers to rap about it.

Previous studies on *Ego Trip's (White) Rapper Show* have accused it of promulgating essentialized representations of blackness. During a roundtable discussion about the WRS among a group of musicologists that took place in 2007 in Boston, Miles White equates the representations of blackness on the show with minstrelsy, implying that the white rappers on are performing blackness in ways that reproduce and promulgate white stereotypes about how black people behave (White 2008; cf. Gaunt et al. 2008; Lott 1993). Shohat reminds us that while dominant groups need not worry too much about being adequately represented, "representation of under-represented groups is, within the hermeneutics of domination, overcharged with allegorical significance" (Shohat 1995: 170). This is certainly another way to examine Persia's identity project and it raises interesting questions about how much control the Ego Trip were given over the content of the show and the degree to which commercial interests may have thwarted efforts to challenge whiteness while failing to problematize damaging stereotypes about black people.

NOTES

1. I would like to thank Jacquelyn Rahman for the invitation to speak at Miami University and Marina Terkourafi for organizing the "Language and Hip Hop Culture in a Globalizing World" workshop where I was able to present earlier versions of this research. I am also very grateful to Marina Terkourafi for the insightful comments she and others have given me on earlier versions of this research. Finally, I would like to thank Jeff Mao for granting me permission to quote from *Ego Trip's (White) Rapper Show* and for his helpful corrections of my transcript.
2. According to Purcell (2007), the parentheses around *white* in the title of the show (*Ego Trip's (White) Rapper Show*) suggest that the message of the show is not only directed at aspiring white rappers, but the larger audience of rap fans.
3. Eminem emerged in 1999 under the tutelage of the black rapper and producer Dr. Dre and was the first white rapper to achieve a level of success and fame comparable to contemporary black rappers such as Nas and Jay-Z.
4. Bogdanov et al. (2003) writes that for rappers who emerged in the 1980s, 'Old School' usually refers to artists who came from the late 1970s and early 1980s such as Kurtis Blow, Grandmaster Flash and the Furious Five, the Sugar Hill Gang, the Treacherous Three, Afrika Bambaataa, and Kook DJ Herc. During the Old School period, lyrics tended to be light-hearted and frivolous, contrasting notably with violent and/or misogynist lyrics associated with the "gangsta rap" period of the 1990s.
5. An outtake is a portion of a work (usually a DVD version of a film) that is not included in the work's final, publicly released version. The outtake interviews with members of the Ego Trip crew were not aired on VH1, but were available on the VH1 website while the show was being aired.
6. According to Gonzalez (2007), the housing project at 1520 Sedgewick Avenue was one of the places where Hip Hop was created. DJ Kool Herc held parties in the common room starting in 1973, using sound system and turntable technology that rapidly spread to the surrounding streets and playgrounds.
7. John Brown, the MC, may have named himself for the white, southern abolitionist by the same name (1800–1859) who was hanged for inciting a slave insurrection and for the murder of five white pro-slavery Southerners. If indeed this was his intention, it suggests that he sees himself as some kind of modern day liberator. (http://en.wikipedia.org/wiki/John_Brown_(abolitionist)).

8. Ego Trip has also collectively published two books (*Ego Trip's Book of Rap Lists* 1999; *Ego Trip's Big Book of Racism!* 2002).
9. Television ratings are tracked by the age of the viewers. Viewers aged 18–34 constitute the most sought-after age group for the marketers who pay for advertising on television programs because they are thought to be forming their lifelong purchasing habits.
10. According to the *New York Times*, Far Rockaway is 47.3% black (Far Rockaway Queens: Data Report, Downloaded Dec. 1, 2008: http://realestate. nytimes.com/community/far-rockaway-queens-ny-usa/demographics).
11. Persia's surname suggests that she may have Italian American heritage, although that is not stated in her bio.
12. The SAT or Scholastic Aptitude Test is a standardized test for college admissions in the US. One's score on the SAT (based on 1600 points) is one way that college admissions boards rate potential applicants. SUVs, or Sport Utility Vehicles, are large, four-wheel drive vehicles, the largest of which (Hummers, Cadillac Escalades, etc.) became status symbols due to their enormous size and luxury features in the late 1990s and early 2000s. Keg parties are very common events in the fraternities (young men's clubs) found on American college and university campuses. They involve the consumption of large quantities of beer from a "keg," or half barrel of beer.
13. Part of this interaction can be viewed online on the VH1 website: www.vh1. com/video/play.jhtml?id=1549458andvid=127122
14. In his rap about "white guilt," Shamrock distinguishes himself morphosyntactically when he drops the copula in voicing his black friend in the last line: "Got caught shopliftin' man, Ain't fuckin' funny. I was stressin' like hell, would I be all right. My black friend said, 'Yeah, Shamrock, you Ø white!' " Shamrock chooses to demonstrate his knowledge of copula absence only when quoting his black friend. It is through this subtle, linguistic cue that Shamrock asserts his linguistic competence as well as his respect for an unspoken ethnolinguistic boundary.
15. Copula absence can be tallied in a number of ways. This analysis employs Labov Deletion (Labov 1969), which is calculated by tallying the deleted and the contracted forms of "is" and/or "are," putting the total number of deleted forms in the numerator (D), and dividing it by the sum of the deleted (D) plus the contracted forms (C), i.e., $D/(C + D)$.

8   Conclusion
Implications for Theories of Style, Identity Formation, and the Status of African American English in the Hip Hop Age

IMPLICATIONS FOR SOCIOLINGUISTIC THEORY

Language and Identity

Despite its focused scope and context (styled HHNL/AAE used among white adolescent Hip Hop youth in the US), the research presented here has some important implications for the field of sociolinguistics with respect to language and identity, theoretical constructs like "style," and the status of African American English in the US. Sociolinguists have increasingly turned their attention towards questions of identity and how this is manifested in terms of the linguistic features speakers use dynamically and variably to signal different aspects of their identities: ethnicity, gender, sexual orientation, membership in various communities of practice, etc. More recently, scholars have begun to describe identity as fluid, hybrid, and differentiated even at the level of micro-interaction. The research presented here displays this pattern by showing how white adolescent Hip Hop youth use HHNL/AAE in ways that obscure their ethnic/racial origins and challenge conceptions of who uses these varieties. The ability of people to reinvent themselves and break free of their class, ethnic, gender, and sexual identities is said to be a distinctive fixture of our "post-modern" age. White Hip Hop youth are part of this long-standing trend in adopting speech patterns that index African American identity, and although they generally use HHNL/AAE in emblematic and non-systematic ways that do not signal full identification with AAE speakers, it can still be argued that this practice has symbolic value as a form of resistance vis-à-vis the racial and ethnic categories ascribed to them and as an agentive declaration of personal choice in the projection of identity.

Although most of my informants were aware that some of their speech patterns derive from AAE, their intent was usually to signal a stance and an orientation towards Hip Hop rather than to make ethnic identity claims about membership in the AAE speech community. Indeed, some white Hip Hop youth had little appreciation for the African American origins of Hip Hop and no particular sympathy or interest in African American culture (e.g., some participants on *Ego Trip's (White) Rapper Show*), while others, like Mike (discussed in Ch. 2), expressed resentment towards African Americans when he felt that his identification with Hip Hop culture and African American youth was rebuffed.

Yet, it was clear that for other individuals, Hip Hop and HHNL were doing some weighty identity work, giving them a space to experiment and try on identities other that those ascribed to them by teachers and adults. Each young person had different motivations for getting involved in Hip Hop; sometimes it was very much about identity, but in other cases it was about some type of civic or political activism. This was true for Ivy who, after moving from Ann Arbor, Michigan to Harlem in New York City at age 18 (discussed in Chs. 3, 4, and 5), returned to the Midwest in her 20s and became heavily involved in community activism in Detroit. This was also the case for Jus Rhyme who finished his doctorate and is now an Assistant Professor of Sociology at California State University, Dominguez Hills, where he teaches social justice and activism (discussed in Ch. 6). Others, like Kin (Ch. 3), experienced it as a rejection of racism within their own families and communities. Although they were all from relatively affluent backgrounds and lived in white neighborhoods, some individuals identified with African American and/or Latino boys. Mike (Ch. 1) initially aligned himself with African Americans, but later felt that his attempts were rebuffed and eventually expressed resentment about it. Ghetto Thug flirted with passing as Latino, Clay says that his "mind patterns" were more African American than white, Benny said that he felt "black on the inside," and PJ described himself as "blackinese." Finally, there were some individuals who had more than just a passing relationship with black and Latino youth. Young people like Isko, a refugee from Bosnia (Ch. 3), and Persia (Ch. 7), appeared to have established lasting bonds of friendship with African Americans. In Persia's case, it was because she lived in an urban, largely African American neighborhood in Queens, New York (Far Rockaway), whereas Isko befriended African Americans and was welcomed in their homes.

Hip Hop held special resonance for young people from immigrant or ethnic minority backgrounds who were grappling with how to become American and how to choose which group(s) they wanted to align themselves with (e.g., Bobo, Ivy, Trix, Kin, PJ, Ghetto Thug). PJ, Ivy, Benny, and Bobo are also Jewish, and although this is not something I have analyzed or written about, it seems to me that they might have had a more fluid idea of what it means to be white than others. Ghetto Thug, the son of ethnic Armenian immigrants, identified with Latinos in part because of his appearance, because many people thought he was Hispanic (Chs. 3, 4, and 5). For him, urban Puerto Rican and African American youth stood out as exemplars of coolness in terms of style, music, and attitudes towards the mainstream. For virtually all of the informants interviewed in the book, African American culture was imbued with great cultural capital and the position of African Americans in the US historical and cultural landscape helped them make sense of their relationship to whiteness and to themselves. However, the "othering" of African Americans or Latinos as cooler, more masculine, sexual, or real than other groups is its own form of essentialization that perpetuates the sense that these groups are irreconcilably different from other Americans (cf. Morgan 1994).

Most recently, in July 2012, the murder of Trayvon Martin, an African American teenager who was confronted and shot for walking through a predominantly white gated community in Florida, prompted many Americans to confront the fact that black and brown bodies are watched, policed, and sentenced differently that white bodies. News reports at the time quoted white Americans saying that wearing a hooded sweatshirt as Trayvon Martin did the day he was shot isn't a problem for them, but for young male African Americans, it often singles them out as a criminal to police officers and to white Americans (Samuels 2012). Similarly, using AAE or styling one's speech with AAE features doesn't carry the same consequences for white youth as it does for African Americans. For the former, it may be regarded as an aberration or short-lived dalliance from "normal" behavior, but for African American youth, failure to use mainstream US English (Lippi-Green 2010) may be interpreted as a sign of willful ignorance and a refusal to conform to the rules of mainstream society.

Theories of Style

The second area in which I believe this research has an impact is in terms of theories of style. The biggest theoretical challenge for me has been to figure how to integrate this data into existing theories of style and the nature of the relationship between a speaker's voice and the self. Perhaps constructs such as "style shifting" and shifts in "register" according to the demands of the particular social setting, topic, or interlocutors, can be differentiated from "crossing," "stylization," and "double-voicing" in which speakers adopt the voices of *others* and signal various relationships to those voices.

One way to conceive of this relationship theoretically is to think in terms of a series of concentric circles from the center to the periphery; one's "natural" or unmarked voice (*in propia persona,* as Coupland 2001, describes it) occupies the center (See Figure 8.1). Slightly removed from the center are the various registers or styles that speakers employ during their daily interactions with others, but which are still clearly straightforward projections of the self and are part of a speaker's individual repertoire. Moving away from the center where the distance between the self and the voice becomes greater, we can use terms like "affected speech," implying a somewhat inauthentic departure from "natural" speech, but still a projection of the self. "Ethnic styling" is similar in that others perceive it as belonging to another group and thus also somewhat contrived. "Passing" linguistically as a member of another group might reside somewhere in this realm as well, because it involves outgroup language use, but as a way of projecting the self. As we move farther out from the center, the voices speakers adopt are more clearly not their own as in captured by terms like "crossing" (Rampton 1995), "stylization" (Coupland 2001), "marking" (Mitchell-Kernan 1972), and "double-voicing" (Bakhtin 1984), each of which involves various degrees of alignment between the individual and his or her speech. Generally, crossing and stylization imply that one is performing or putting on a voice, "as if this is me," or "as if I owned this voice," or "as if I endorsed what this voice says" (Coupland 2001: 349), whereas in the case of marking and vari-directional double-voicing, the self and the voice are more clearly demarcated and opposed (Bakhtin 1984: 193). The greatest distance between the self and the voice is captured by terms like mockery or "pejorative" outgroup talk (e.g., Mock Spanish in Hill 1993) which describe the most extreme forms of separation between the voice and the self.

This model conceptualizes the relationship between the various types of stylistic variation that have been identified in the literature as differing degrees of distance between the self and one's utterances.

Although there were cases (e.g., Ghetto Thug) in which young people seemed more actively engaged in trying to pass as a member of another ethnic group (i.e., as Latino), the speech of white Hip Hop youth generally seems to reside somewhere in between styling and ethnic styling; in most cases, the ethnic speech markers they employ are mainly meant to project a Hip Hop identity and traits associated with African American Hip Hop youth (masculinity, urban street-smarts, toughness, coolness, etc.) rather than an African American ethnic identity. Parallels can be made to the speech of urban Hip Hop affiliated youth in many European countries

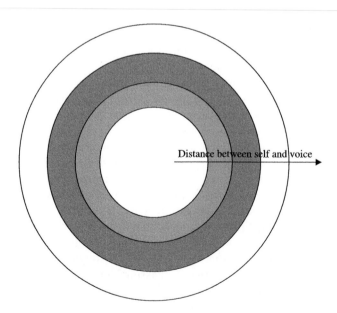

Figure 8.1   A Model of Style as Distance between the Self and One's Voice

who use multiethnolectal speech patterns to signal feelings of otherness or an alignment with ethnic "others" (Auer and Dirim 2003; Nortier 2001; Opsahl and Røyneland 2008; Quist 2000).

Understanding the linguistic practices of the white adolescents discussed in this book would not have been possible without some investigation of Hip Hop culture. Thus another implication of this research pertains to the typical scope of analysis in sociolinguistics which rarely goes beyond a handful of "external" factors like age, ethnicity, and gender. Analyses of style can benefit enormously from an elaborated approach that would encompass "forms of comportment" that extend beyond the linguistic system itself (cf. Irvine 2001) to include practices such as adornment, makeup, hairstyle, sexual orientation, participation in social, political, and sporting activities, and choices in terms of lifestyle and employment. A more socially comprehensive, ethnographically informed approach has the added benefit of making this kind of work more meaningful and accessible to a wider audience.

Attitudes Toward African American English

One pressing question that emerges from this research is what effect the language practices of white Hip Hop youth and the globalization of Hip Hop may have on societal attitudes towards AAE. The Ebonics controversy in early 1997 and the election of Barack Obama in 2008 constitute rough bookends for this research, marking significant points in public discourse regarding race and AAE. The spread of rap music and Hip Hop culture within the US starting in the mid-1980s may have raised people's awareness about the existence of AAE, but ultimately did little to change longstanding prejudice among many white and black Americans about its legitimacy. The Ebonics controversy in early 1997 only seemed to further cement associations between AAE and deviant behavior, and the rise of gangster rap in the late 1990s certainly made the public recognition of the legitimacy of AAE even less likely as many Americans came to view rap music as associated primarily with the glorification of gang violence, drug culture, and misogyny.

These kinds of attitudes are even evident among African Americans themselves. The Reverend Jesse Jackson, poet Maya Angelou, and former Secretary of Education William Bennett all condemned the Oakland School Board Resolution to recognize Ebonics as a legitimate dialect. In 2004, Bill Cosby, an African American comedian and actor known for his role on "The Electric Company" in the 1970s and his portrayal of an upper middle class physician, Dr. Huxtable, on *The Cosby Show*, leveled scathing criticism at vernacular AAE speakers. In his remarks at a Constitution Hall event commemorating the 50th anniversary of the *Brown v. Board of Education* decision,[1] Cosby was quoted in the Washington Post, saying:

> "They're standing on the corner and they can't speak English," he exclaimed. "I can't even talk the way these people talk: 'Why you ain't,'

'Where you is.'. . . . And I blamed the kid until I heard the mother talk. And then I heard the father talk. . . . Everybody knows it's important to speak English except these knuckleheads. . . . You can't be a doctor with that kind of crap coming out of your mouth" (Leiby 2004: C03).

That Cosby would heap such scorn on the speech of disadvantaged African Americans was regarded as highly illiberal by some on the left. On the other hand it's understandable why successful, educated African Americans like Cosby would view attempts to legitimize the speech and behavior of their lower status counterparts as misguided: they may view their own success as partly based on the acquisition of standard English; legitimizing a language they have "left behind" belittles their own hard-won status and reflects the "soft bigotry of low expectations."

His comments are also reminiscent of the response of middle class Whites toward their underclass "white trash" counterparts in the early 20th century (Hartigan 2005; Wray 2006). According to Wray (2006), the invention of terms like "poor white trash" is exemplary of a certain kind of symbolic boundary which he calls a "stigmatype"—a term that both denotes and enacts cultural and cognitive divides between ingroups and outgroups, between acceptable and unacceptable identities, between proper and improper behaviors.[2] The African American speakers Cosby animates in his speech are racialized as "others" whose objectionable behavior and speech he constructs as socially self-crippling. These events point to the fact that sociolinguists have still not achieved mainstream recognition of AAE as a legitimate dialect in the US.

The data presented in this book suggest that there is a growing social recognition of AAE as a distinct variety of English among young people. The popular web-based "Urban Dictionary," which leans towards expressions that often relate to Hip Hop, has 7 million entries to data and an enormous following among adolescents and college-age web users. Since the election of President Barack Obama, newspapers have begun printing stories about his ability to shift between various registers of mainstream US English and colloquial styles of AAE. Indeed, the term "code-switching" seems to have entered the national dialog, sparking debates about whether this kind of behavior is somehow dishonest. Alim and Smitherman (2012) review these issues at length, noting that some white Americans (including politicians like former President George W. Bush and current Vice President Joseph R. Biden Jr.) seemed surprised that an African American man like Mr. Obama could be so "articulate." The authors conclude that Obama's speech style, particularly his ability to draw on a black preacher style that was familiar to white Americans, was a vitally important part of his electoral success. These events may signal the beginning of a shift in the way that many Americans view AAE, allowing them to associate it with someone as highly educated and accomplished as the president of the United States, as well as a broader understanding of the ability of African Americans to code-switch between

AAE and mainstream varieties of English. Finally, it may also make AAE speakers more aware of how code-switching can benefit them in their interactions with other mainstream English speakers.

Global Hip Hop and Hip Hop Nation Language

One final topic in which this research may have an impact is in understanding the global impact of Hip Hop in terms of language change. Recent work on language in Hip Hop has illustrated the centrality of popular culture and music in language contact and in language variation and change (Alim 2009; Morgan 2004; Pennycook 2007). Alim's term "translocal style communities" or sets of styles, aesthetics, knowledge, and ideologies that transcend localities seems to be an apt way to show how disparate Hip Hop communities around the world see themselves as connected (Alim 2009). The white American youth analyzed in this book are part of this globalizing process, both as fans and consumers of rap music and participants in global Hip Hop culture. Like their Hip Hop counterparts in other parts of the world, they are involved in transforming and "theorizing" language and identity by blurring the boundaries between individual language varieties and ethnic and racial categories, and legitimizing marginal, low-status language varieties. Granted, this is not always a neutral, progressive, or necessarily "anti-racist" project and it's important to scrutinize what kinds of essentialized images and stereotypes are animated in the linguistic styling and identity projection we observe among white Hip Hop youth in the US context. Yet, in the final analysis, it is clear that Hip Hop is a unique site for finding evidence of linguistic and other forms of cultural change.

NOTES

1. *Brown v. Board of Education* was a 1954 Supreme Court case that effectively ended the educational practice of allowing schools to be racially segregated (known as "separate but equal") and paved the road for racial integration of the public schools.
2. Originally interchangeable with comparable epithets like "mean whites," "poor whites," "clayeaters," and "crackers," Hartigan (2005) claims that the term "white trash" ultimately prevailed because it more precisely symbolized and encapsulated what was at stake in early 20th century intra-racial efforts to maintain white racial identity (99)—namely fears about pollution and contamination which figure prominently in discourses of cultural identity.

Bibliography

CITED MUSICAL RECORDINGS

Beastie Boys. (2004) "Right here right now." On To the 5 boroughs [LP]. New York: Capitol.

CITED RADIO AND TELEVISION BROADCASTS

Radio Broadcasts

Blair, E. (2007) "Is hip hop dying or has it moved underground?" All Things Considered. March 11 (2007). National Public Radio. Retrieved May 10, (2011) from: www.npr.org/templates/story/story.php?storyId=7834732
Ludden, J. (1998) "French rap music popularity grows." Morning Edition. September 23 (1998). National Public Radio. Retrieved July 10, (2013) from: www.npr.org/templates/story/story.php?storyId=1024288
Purcell, R. (2007) "Rapping about guilty pleasures." News and Notes. March 23, (2007). National Public Radio. Retrieved May 3, (2009) from: www.npr.org/templates/story/story.php?storyId=9097615

FILMS

Bigel, D., Mailer, M., and Rotholz, R. (Producers) and Toback, J. (Director). (1999) *Black and White*. Bigel and Mailer Films/Palm Pictures.
Hoch, D. (Director). (1999) *Whiteboys*. Bac Films, Canal+, Fox Searchlight Pictures.
Lee, S. (Producer and Director). (2000) *Bamboozled*. New Line Cinema.
Lucas, G. (Producer and Director). (1977) *Star Wars*. Twentieth Century Fox.
Panzarella, P. (Producer) and Clark, L. (Director). (1995) *Kids*. Shining Excalibur Films.
Parks, G. (Director). (1971) *Shaft*. Metro-Goldwyn-Mayer.
Parks, G. (Director). (1972) *Shaft's Big Score*. Metro-Goldwyn-Mayer.
Parks, G. (Director). (1973) *Shaft in Africa*. Metro-Goldwyn-Mayer.
Singleton, J. (Director). (2000) *Shaft*. Munich Film Partners & Company (MFP) Shaft Productions, New Deal Productions, Paramount Pictures.

TELEVISION BROADCASTS

Big Brother. (2000–present) CBS.
Black. White. (2006) FX.
Blaze Battle World Championship. (2000) HBO.
Ego Trip's (White) Rapper Show. (2007) VH-1.
Frontier House. (2002) PBS.
Happy Days. (1974–84) Henderson Productions.
Shaft. (1973–74) CBS.
Shalom in the Home. (2006) TLC.
Survivor. (2000–present) CBS.
The Cosby Show. (1984–92) NBC.
The Simpsons. (1989–present) Gracie Films (in association with) 20th Century Fox Television; Curiosity Company.

Television Episodes

From Ego Trip's (White) Rapper Show:

Preview Extras: "Tha Interrogation." (2007) Retrieved August 15, (2013) from *Ego Trip's (White) Rapper Show* Official Website: www.vh1.com/video/shows/ego-trips-white-rapper-show/126388/tha-interrogation.jhtml
Rappin' in the Hood. (2007) Retrieved January 1, (2009) from *Ego Trip's (White) Rapper Show* Official Website: www.vh1.com/video/play.jhtml?id=1549458andvid=127120
Roundtable: The N-Word. (2007) Retrieved August 15, (2013) from *Ego Trip's (White) Rapper Show* Official Website: www.vh1.com/video/shows/ego-trips-white-rapper-show/127086/white-rapper-episode-1-roundtable-the-n-word.jhtml
Roundtable: South Bronx. (2007) Retrieved August 15, (2013) from *Ego Trip's (White) Rapper Show* Official Website: www.vh1.com/video/shows/ego-trips-white-rapper-show/127088/white-rapper-episode-1-roundtable-south-bronx.jhtml
Serch Lays Down the Law. (2007) Retrieved January 1, (2009) from *Ego Trip's (White) Rapper Show* Official Website: www.vh1.com/video/play.jhtml?id=1549458andvid=127123
Shamrock on His Childhood. (2007) Retrieved January 1, (2009) from *Ego Trip's (White) Rapper Show* Official Website: www.vh1.com/video/play.jhtml?id=1549361andvid=126935
The (White) Rapper Show Is Born. (2007) Retrieved August 15, (2013) from *Ego Trip's (White) Rapper Show* Official Website: www.vh1.com/video/shows/ego-trips-white-rapper-show/125712/white-rapper-new-series-preview.jhtml
(White) Rapper: New Series Preview. (2007) Retrieved August 15, (2013) from *Ego Trip's (White) Rapper Show* Official Website: www.vh1.com/video/shows/ego-trips-white-rapper-show/125712/white-rapper-new-series-preview.jhtml

REFERENCES AND OTHER WORKS CONSULTED

Agha, A. (2007) *Language and social relations.* Cambridge: Cambridge University Press.
Ahearn, L. (2001) "Language and agency." *Annual Review of Anthropology* 30: 109–37.

Alim, H. S. (2001) "I be the truth: Divergence, recreolization, and the 'new' equative copula in African American language," paper presented at NWAV 30, Raleigh, North Carolina, October 2001.

Alim, H. S. (2002) "Street conscious copula variation in the Hip Hop Nation." *American Speech* 77(3): 288–304.

Alim, H. S. (2003) "We are the streets: African American language and the strategic construction of a street conscious identity." *Black Linguistics*. S. Makoni, G. Smitherman, and A. Ball, eds. New York: Routledge. 40–59.

Alim, H. S. (2004a) "Hip Hop Nation language." *Language in the USA*. E. Finegan and J. Rickford, eds. New York: Cambridge University Press. 387–409.

Alim, H. S. (2004b) *You know my steez an ethnographic and sociolinguistic study of styleshifting in a Black American speech community*. Durham, NC: Duke University Press.

Alim, H. S. (2005) 'The whitey voice: Linguistic variation, agency, and the discursive construction of Whiteness in a Black American barbershop,' paper presented at New Ways of Analyzing Variation 34 Conference, New York University, New York, October 2004.

Alim, H. S. (2009) "Translocal style communities: Hip hop youth as cultural theorists of style, language, and globalization." *Pragmatics* 19(1): 103–28.

Alim, H. S. and Smitherman, G. (2012) *Articulate while black: Barack Obama, language, and race in the U.S.* Oxford: Oxford University Press.

Alonso, A. (2003) "Won't you please be my nigga: Double standards with a taboo word." *Streetgangs Magazine*. Retrieved May 29, (2009) from: www.streetgangs.com/magazine/053003niggas.php

Anderson, B. (1983) *Imagined communities: Reflections on the origin and spread of nationalism*. London: Verso.

Androutsopoulos, J. (2010) "Multilingualism, ethnicity and genre in Germany's migrant hip hop." *Languages of global hip hop*. M. Terkourafi, ed. New York: Continuum. 19–44.

Androutsopoulos, J. and Georgakopoulou, A. (2003) "Discourse constructions of youth identities: Introduction." *Discourse constructions of youth identities*. J. Androutsopoulos and A. Georgakopoulou, eds. Amsterdam: Benjamins. 1–25.

Androutsopoulos, J. and Scholz, A. (eds.). (1998) "Jugendsprache—langue des jeunes—youth language." *Soziolinguistische und linguistische Perspektiven*. Frankfurt: Lang (VarioLingua 7).

Androutsopoulos J. and Scholz, A. (2003) " 'Spaghetti funk': Appropriations of hip-hop culture and rap music in Europe." *Popular Music and Society* 26(4): 489–505.

Anisman, P. (1975) "Some aspects of code-switching in New York Puerto Rican English." *Bilingual Review* 2(1–2): 56–85.

Armstrong, E. G. (2004) "Eminem's construction of authenticity." *Popular Music and Society* 27(3): 335–55.

Ash, S. and Myhill, J. (1986) "Linguistic correlates of inter-ethnic contact." *Diversity and Diachrony*. D. Sankoff, ed. Philadelphia: Benjamins. 33–44.

Auer, P. and Dirim, I. (2003) "Socio-cultural orientation, urban youth styles and the spontaneous acquisition of Turkish by non-Turkish adolescents in Germany." J. Androutsopoulos and A. Georgakopoulou, eds. *Discourse constructions of youth identities*. Amsterdam/ Philadelphia: John Benjamins. 223–46.

Auer, P. and Hinskens, F. (2005) "The role of interpersonal accommodation in a theory of language change." *Dialect change: Convergence and divergence in European language*. P. Auer, F. Hinskens, and P. Kerswill, eds. Cambridge: Cambridge University Press. 335–57.

Back, L. (1996) *New ethnicities and urban culture: Racisms and multiculture in young lives*. London: Routledge.

Bailey, B. (2000a) "The language of multiple identities among Dominican Americans." *Journal of Linguistic Anthropology,* 10(2): 190–223.

Bailey, B. (2000b) "Language and negotiation of ethnic/racial identity among Dominican Americans." *Language in Society,* 29, 555–82.

Bailey, G. and Thomas, E. (1998) "Some aspects of African American vernacular English phonology." *African American English.* S. Mufwene, J. R. Rickford, G. Bailey, and J. Baugh, eds. New York: Routledge. 85–109.

Bakhtin, M. (1984) *Problems of Dostoevsky's Poetics.* Edited and translated by C. Emerson. Minneapolis: University of Michigan Press.

Baugh, J. (1992) "Hypocorrection: Mistakes in production of vernacular African American English as a second dialect." *Language & Communication* 12 (3–4): 317–26.

Bauman, R. (1986) *Story, Performance and event: contextual studies of narrative.* Cambridge: Cambridge University Press.

Bauman, Z. (1991) *Modernity and ambivalence.* Cambridge: Polity Press.

Bazin, H. (1995) *La culture hip-hop.* Paris: Desclée de Brouwer.

Becker, K. (2009) "/r/ and the construction of place identity on New York City's Lower East Side." *Journal of Sociolinguistics* 13(5): 634–58.

Bell, A. (1984) "Language style as audience design." *Language in Society* 14(2): 145–204.

Bell, A. (1999) "Styling the other to define the self: A study in New Zealand identity making." *Journal of Sociolinguistics* 4(3): 523–41.

Bennett, A. (1999) "Rappin' on the Tyne: White Hip Hop culture in northeast England—An ethnographic study." *Sociological Review* 47(1): 1–24.

Bigham, D. S. (2010) "Mechanisms of accommodation among emerging adults in a university setting" *Journal of English Linguistics* 38(3): 193–210.

Blake, R. (1993) "Search of genres. A sociologically informed linguistic analysis of the positive subgenre in rap music." Unpublished term paper, Stanford University.

Blake, R. and Shousterman, C. (2010) "Diachrony and AAE: St. Louis, hip-hop, and sound change outside of the mainstream." *Journal of English Linguistics* 38(3): 230–47.

Bjürstrom, E. (1997) "The struggle for ethnicity: Swedish youth styles and the construction of ethnic identities." *Nordic Journal of Youth Research* 5(3): 44–58.

Bogdanov, V., Woodstra, C., Erlewine, S.T., and Bush, J. (2003) *All Music guide to hip-hop: The definitive guide to rap and hip-hop.* San Francisco: Backbeat Books.

Boucher, M. (1998) *Rap: Expression des Lascars. Significations et enjeux du Rap dans la société française.* Paris: L'Harmattan.

Bourdieu, P. (1991) *Language and symbolic power.* Cambridge: Harvard University Press.

Boyd, T. (2002) *The new H.N.I.C. (Head Nigga in Charge): The death of civil rights and the reign of hip hop.* New York: New York University Press.

Brodkin, K. (1999) *How Jews became White Folks and what that says about race in America.* Rutgers: Rutgers University Press.

Bucholtz, M. (1995) "From Mulatta to Mestiza." *Gender articulated: Language and the socially constructed self.* K. Hall and M. Bucholtz, eds. New York: Routledge. 351–74.

Bucholtz, M. (1999) "You Da Man: Narrating the racial other in the production of white masculinity." Theme issue, "Styling the other," *Journal of Sociolinguistics* 3(4): 443–60.

Bucholtz, M. (2001) "The whiteness of nerds: Superstandard english and racial markedness." *Journal of Linguistic Anthropology* 11(1): 84–100.

Bucholtz, M. (2011). *White Kids: Language, race and styles of youth identity.* New York: Cambridge University Press.

Bucholtz, M. and Hall, K. (2005) "Identity and interaction: A sociocultural linguistic approach." *Discourse Studies* 7(4–5): 585–614.

Butters, R.R. (1984) "When is English Black English vernacular?" *Journal of English Linguistics* 17(1): 29–36.

Cast Bios. (2007) Retrieved January 1, (2009) from the (White) Rapper Show Official Website: www.vh1.com/shows/dyn/white_rapper/series_characters.j html

Chang, J. (2005) *Can't stop won't stop*. New York: St. Martin's Press.

CityTownInfo. New York University. Retrieved December 14, (2009) from www.citytowninfo.com/school-profiles/new-york-university

CityTownInfo. Stony Brook University. Retrieved December 14, (2009) from www.citytowninfo.com/school-profiles/stony-brook-university

CityTownInfo. University of North Carolina, Chapel Hill. Retrieved December 14, (2009) from www.citytowninfo.com/school-profiles/university-of-north-carolina-at-chapel-hill

Clark, J.C. (2002) "Maintaining class and ethnic borders in a North American high school." *Proceedings of II Simposio Internacional Bilingüismo*. 1525–1536. Retrieved May 1, (2006) from www.webs.uvigo.es/ssl/actas(2002)/08/01.%20J.%20T.%20Clark.pdf

Coggshall, E. and Becker, K. (2010) "The vowel phonologies of African American and White New York City residents." *AAE speakers and their participation in local sound changes: A comparative study*. M. Yeager-Dror and E. Thomas, eds. Publication of the American Dialect Society, 94. Durham: Duke University Press. 101–128.

Condry, I. (1999) "Japanese rap music: An ethnography of globalization in popular culture." Ph.D. Dissertation, Yale University.

Cornips, L. (2000) "The use of gaan + infinitive in narratives of older bilingual children of older bilingual children of Moroccan and Turkish descent." *Linguistics in the Netherlands* 17: 57–67.

Cornyetz, N. (1994) "Hip-hop and racial desire in contemporary Japan." *Social Text* 4: 113–39.

Coupland, N. (2001) "Dialect stylization in radio talk." *Language in Society* 30: 345–75.

Coupland, N. (2007) *Style: Language variation and identity*. Cambridge: Cambridge University Press.

Cutler, C. (1997) "Yorkville Crossing: The influence of hip hop on the speech of a white middle class teenager in New York City." *University of Pennsylvania Working Papers in Linguistics* 4(1): 371–97.

Cutler, C. (1998) 'Crossing and the reproduction of language ideologies through white adolescent use of AAVE,' paper presented to the 6th International Pragmatics Conference, Reims, France, July 1998.

Cutler, C. (1999) "Yorkville Crossing: A case study of hip-hop and the language of a white middle class teenager in New York City." *Journal of Sociolinguistics* 3(4): 428–42.

Cutler, C. (2002a) "Crossing over: White teenagers, AAVE and hip-hop." Ph.D. Dissertation, New York University.

Cutler, C. (2002b) 'The authentic speaker revisited: a look at ethnic perception data from white hip hoppers,' paper presented at New Ways of Analyzing Variation in English Conference, Stanford, University, October 2002.

Cutler, C. (2003a) "Keepin' it real: White hip-hoppers discourse on language, race, and authenticity." *Journal of Linguistic Anthropology* 13(2): 211–33.

Cutler, C. (2003b) "Chanter en yaourt: Pop music and language choice in France." *Global pop, local language*. H. Berger and M. Carroll, eds. Jackson: University of Mississippi Press. 329–48.

Cutler, C. (2005) 'Interculturality and Stance in an MC Battle,' paper presented at the Association of International Applied Linguistics, Madison, Wisconsin, July 2005.

Cutler, C. (2008a) "Brooklyn style: Hip-hop markers and racial affiliation among European immigrants." *International Journal of Bilingualism* 12(1–2): 7–24.

Cutler, C. (2008b) "'You shouldn't be rappin', you should be skate boardin' the X-games: The co-construction of whiteness in an MC Battle." *Global linguistic flows: Hip hop cultures, youth identities, and the politics of language.* A. Alim, A. Ibrahim, and A. Pennycook, eds. New York: Routledge. 79–94.

Cutler, C. (2010) "She's so hood: Ghetto authenticity on the (White) Rapper Show." *The language(s) of global hip-hop.* M. Terkourafi, ed. New York: Continuum. 300–28.

Cutler, C. and Royneland, U. (In Press). "Where the fuck am I from?: Hip Hop youth and the (re)negotiation of language and identity in Norway and the US." *Adolescents in multilingual contexts in Europe and beyond.* B. Svendsen & J. Nortier, eds. Cambridge: Cambridge University Press.

Dalzall, T. (1996) *Flappers 2 Rappers. American youth slang.* Springfield: Merriam-Webster.

Davison, A. (2001) "Critical musicology study day on 'authenticity.'" *Popular Music* 20(2): 263–64.

Du Bois, W.E.B. (1903) *The souls of black folk.* Retrieved July 27, (2007) from Bartleby.com: Great Books Online, www.bartleby.com/114/

Dubois, S. and Horvath, B. (2003) "Verbal morphology in Cajun vernacular English." *Journal of English Linguistics* 31(1): 34–59.

Dunstan, S. (2010) "Identities in transition: The use of AAVE grammatical features by Hispanic adolescents in two North Carolina communities." *American Speech* 85(2): 185–204.

Eberhardt, M. (2010) "African American and White vowel systems in Pittsburgh." *AAE speakers and their participation in local sound changes: A comparative study.* M. Yeager-Dror and E. Thomas, eds. Publication of the American Dialect Society, 94. Durham: Duke University Press. 129–57.

Eckert, P. (1989) *Jocks and burnouts: Social categories and identity in the high school.* New York: Teachers College Press.

Eckert, P. (2003) "Language and adolescent peer groups." *Journal of Language and Social Psychology* 22(1): 112–18.

Eckert, P. (2008) "Variation and the indexical field." *Journal of Sociolinguistics* 12(4): 453–76.

Eckert, P. and McConnell-Ginet, S. (1992) "Think practically and look locally: Language and gender as community-based practice." *Annual Review of Anthropology* 21: 461–90.

Eckert, P. and McConnell-Ginet, S. (1995) "Constructing meaning, constructing selves: snapshots of language, gender, and class from Belten High." *Gender articulated: language and the socially constructed self.* K. Hall and M. Bucholtz, eds. New York: Rutgers. 469–507.

Ego Trip (magazine). (2008) Wikipedia, the free encylopedia. Retrieved December 1, (2008) from http://en.wikipedia.org/wiki/Ego_trip_(magazine)

Fagyal, Z. (2005) "Prosodic consequences of being a Beur: French in contact with immigrant languages in Paris." *Working Papers in Linguistics* 10(2): 91–104.

Fasold, R. (1972) *Tense marking in Black English.* Arlington: Center for Applied Linguistics.

Fasold, R.W., Labov, W., Vaughn-Cooke, F.B., and Bailey, G. (1987) "Are Black and White vernaculars diverging? Papers from the NWAVE panel discussion" *American Speech* 62: 1–80.

Ferguson, C. (1994) "Dialect, register, and genre: Working assumptions about conventionalization." *Sociolinguistic Perspectives on Register*. D. Biber and E. Finegan eds. Oxford: Oxford University Press. 15–30.

Fitzgerald, T. (2007) "VH1's (White) Rapper, the new sitcom: Kids living in a house and playing the fool." Jan 31. Retrieved June 1, (2009) from: www.media lifemagazine.com/cgibin/artman/exec/view.cgi?archive=483andnum=9857

Fix, S. (2009) 'Representations of blackness by white women: Linguistic practice in the community versus the Media,' poster presented at New Ways of Analyzing Variation 38, Ottawa, Canada, October 2009.

Fordham, S. and Ogbu, J.U. (1986) "Black students' school success: Coping with the burden of 'acting White.'" *The Urban Review*, 18(3): 134–64.

Fought, C. (2003) *Chicano English in context*. New York: Palgrave Macmillan.

Foulkes, P. and Barron, A. (2000) "Telephone speaker recognition amongst members of close social network." *Forensic Linguistics* 7: 180–98.

Fowler, J. (1986) "The social stratification of (r) in New York City department stores, 24 years after Labov." Unpublished manuscript, New York University.

Gal, S. (1988) "The political economy of code choice." *Codeswitching: Anthropological and sociolinguistic perspectives*. M. Heller, ed. The Hague: Mouton de Gruyter. 245–64.

Gal, S. and Irvine, J. (1995) "The Boundaries of language and disciplines: How ideologies construct difference." *Social Research* 62: 967–1001.

Gaunt, K., Keyes, C.L., Mangin, T.R., Marshall, W., and Schloss, J. (2008) "Roundtable: VH1's (White) Rapper Show: Intrusions, sightlines, and authority." *Journal of Popular Music Studies* 20(1): 44–78.

Giles, H., Coupland, J., and Coupland, N. (eds.). (1991) *Contexts of accommodation: Developments in applied sociolinguistics*. Cambridge: Cambridge University Press.

Gilroy, P. (1993) *The Black Atlantic: Modernity and double consciousness*. Cambridge: Harvard University Press

Giroux, H. (1996) *Fugitive Cultures: Race, violence and youth*. Routledge: New York.

Goffman, E. (1981) *Forms of talk*. Philadelphia: University of Pennsylvania Press.

Goldstein, L. (1987) "Standard English: The only target for nonnative speakers of English?" *TESOL Quarterly*, 21(3): 417–438.

Gonzalez, D. (2007) "Will gentrification spoil the birthplace of hip-hop?" *New York Times*. May 21. Retrieved June 1, (2009) from www.nytimes.com/(2007)/05/21/ nyregion/21citywide.html

Gordon, L.R. (2005) "The problem of maturity in hip hop." *The Review of Education, Pedagogy, and Cultural Studies* 27(4): 367–89.

Gumperz, J. (1982) *Discourse strategies*. Cambridge: Cambridge University Press.

Gumperz, J. (1990) *Language and social reality*. Cambridge: Cambridge University Press.

Guy, G.R. (1991) "Explanation in variable phonology: An exponential model of morphological constraints." *Language Variation and Change* 3(1): 1–22.

Guy, G.R. and Cutler, C. (2011) "Speech style and authenticity: Quantitative evidence for the performance of identity." *Language Variation and Change* 23(1): 139–62.

Hall, K. (1995) "Lip service on the fantasy lines." *Gender articulated: Language and the socially constructed self*. K. Hall and M. Bucholtz, eds. London: Routledge. 183–216.

Hall, K. and Bucholtz, M., (eds.). (1995) *Gender articulated: Language and the socially constructed self*. London: Routledge.

Hall, S. (1988) "New ethnicities." *Stuart Hall: Critical dialogues in cultural studies.* D. Morley and D. H. Chen, eds. London: Routledge. 441–49.

Hartigan, J. Jr. (2005). *Odd tribes: Toward a cultural analysis of White people.* Durham: Duke University Press.

Hassa, S. (2010). "'Kiff my zikmu': Symbolic dimensions of Arabic, English and Verlan in French rap texts." *Languages of global hip hop.* M. Terkourafi, ed. New York: Continuum. 44–67.

Hatala, E. (1976) "Environmental effects on white students in black schools." Unpublished M.A. thesis, University of Pennsylvania.

Heffernan, V. (2005) "Epithet morphs from Bad Girl to Weak Boy." *New York Times.* March 22. New York: E8. Retrieved October 1, 2013 from: www.nytimes.com/2005/03/22/arts/television/22chie.html.

Hess, M. (2005) "Hip-hop realness and the White performer." *Critical Studies in Media Communication* 22(5): 372–89.

Hewitt, R. (1986) *White talk Black talk: Inter-racial friendship and communication amongst adolescents.* Cambridge: Cambridge University Press.

Hill, J. H. (1993) "Is it really 'No Problemo?': Junk Spanish and Anglo racism." *Texas Linguistics Forum* 33(1): 1–12.

hooks, b. (1994) *Outlaw culture.* New York: Routledge.

Ibrahim, A. (1998) "'Hey, whassup homeboy?' Becoming Black: Race, language, culture, and the politics of identity." Ph.D. dissertation, Department of Curriculum, Teaching and Learning, University of Toronto.

Ibrahim, A. (2003) "Marking the unmarked: Hip-hop, the gaze and the African body in North America." *Critical Arts: A Journal of South-North Cultural and Media Studies* 17(1–2): 52–70.

Ignatiev, N. (1995) *How the Irish became white.* New York: Routledge.

Irvine, J. (2001) "Style as distinctiveness: the culture and ideology of linguistic differentiation." *Style and sociolinguistic variation.* P. Eckert, and J. Rickford, eds. Cambridge: Cambridge University Press. 21–43.

Irvine, J. (2004) "Losing one's footing: Stance in a colonial encounter." *Stance: Sociolinguistic perspectives.* A. Jaffe, ed. Oxford: Oxford University Press. 53–71.

Irvine, J. and Gal, S. (2000) "Language ideology and linguistic differentiation." *Regimes of Language.* P. V. Kroskrity, ed. Santa Fe: School of American Research Press. 35–83.

Irwin, P. and Nagy, N. (2007) "Bostonians' /r/ speaking: A quantitative look at (R) in Boston." *University of Pennsylvania Working Papers in Linguistics* 13: 135–47.

Jacobs-Huey, L. (1997) "Is there an authentic African American speech community: Carla revisited." *University of Pennsylvania Working Papers in Linguistics* 4(1): 331–70.

Jaffe, A. (2004) 'Stance in social and cultural context,' paper presented at the Sociolinguistics Symposium 15, Newcastle upon Tyne, UK, April 2004.

Jaspers, J. (2008) "Problematizing ethnolects: Naming linguistic practices in an Antwerp secondary school." *International Journal of Bilingualism* 12(1–2): 85–103.

Jenkins, S., Wilson, E., Mao, C. M., Alvarez, G., and Rollins, B. (1999) *Ego trip's book of rap lists.* New York: St. Martin's Press.

Jenkins, S., Wilson, E., Mao, C. M., Alvarez, G., and Rollins, B. (2002) *Ego trip's big book of racism!* Los Angeles: Regan Books.

John Brown (abolitionist). Retrieved December. 1, (2008) from http://en.wikipedia.org/wiki/John_Brown_(abolitionist)

Johnson-Woods, T. (2002) *Big bother: Why did that reality-TV show become such a phenomenon?* St. Lucia: University of Queensland Press.

Johnstone, B. (2009) "Stance, style, and the linguistic individual." *Stance: Sociolinguistic perspectives.* A. Jaffe, ed. Oxford: Oxford University Press. 29–52.

Johnstone, B. (2011) '"Making Pittsburghese: Communication technology, expertise, and the discursive construction of a regional dialect." *Language & Communication* 31: 3–15.

Jones, J. (2003) "African Americans in Lansing and the northern cities vowel shift: Language contact and accommodation." Ph.D. Dissertation, Michigan State University.

Jones, M.D. (2006) "An interview with Michael Eric Dyson." *Callaloo* 29(3): 786–802.

Kennedy, R. (2002) *Nigger: The strange career of a troublesome word.* New York: Pantheon.

Keyes, C.L. (1991). *Rappin to the beat: Rap music as street culture among African Americans.* Ph.D. Dissertation, Indiana University.

Keyes, C.L. (2004) *Rap music and street consciousness.* Urbana: University of Illinois Press.

Kitwana, B. (1994) *The rap on gangsta rap.* Chicago: Third World Press.

Kleinfeld, N.R. (2000) "Guarding the borders of the Hip Hop Nation." *New York Times.* July 6. Retrieved December. 1, (2008) from: www.nytimes.com/(2000)/07/06/us/guarding-the-borders-of-the-hip-hop-nation.html?sec=andspon=andpagewanted=6

Kochman, T. (ed.). (1972) *Rappin' and stylin' out: Communication in urban Black America.* Urbana: University of Illinois Press.

Labov, W. (1966) *The social stratification of English in New York City.* Washington, DC: Center for Applied Linguistics.

Labov, W. (1969) "Contraction, deletion, and inherent variability of the English copula." *Language* 45: 715–62.

Labov, W. (1972) *Language in the inner city: Studies in the Black English vernacular.* Philadelphia: University of Pennsylvania Press.

Labov, W. (1980) "Is there a creole speech community?" *Theoretical orientations in Creole studies.* A. Valdman and A. Highfield, eds. New York: Academic Press. 369–88.

Labov, W., Ash, S., and Boberg, C. (2006) *Atlas of North American English: Phonology and sound change.* Berlin: Mouton/de Gruyter.

Labov, W., Cohen, P., Robins, C., and Lewis, J. (1968) "A study of the non-standard English of Negro and Puerto Rican speakers in New York City." Final Report, Cooperative Research Project. #3288, Washington D.C.: Office of Education.

Labov, W. and Harris, W.A. (1983) "De facto segregation of black and white vernaculars." *Diversity and diachrony.* D. Sankoff, ed. Philadelphia: Benjamins. 1–24.

Leiby, R. (2004). "Publicists with a Cannes-Do attitude." *Washington Post.* May 19, C03.

Leland, J. and Mabry, M. (1996) "France: Street culture." *The International Newsweek*, February 26, 36–45.

LePage, R.B. and Tabouret-Keller, A. (1985) *Acts of identity: Creole-based approaches to language and ethnicity.* New York: Cambridge University Press.

Lippi-Green, R. (2010) *English with an accent: Language, ideology and discrimination in the U.S.* New York: Routledge

Lipsitz, G. (1995) "The possessive investment in Whiteness: Racialized social democracy and the 'white' problem in American Studies." *American Quarterly* 47(3): 369–87.

List of Reality Television Programs. (2008) Wikipedia, the free encyclopedia. Retrieved December 1, (2008) from http://en.wikipedia.org/wiki/List_of_reality_television_programs

Lott, E. (1993) *Love and theft: Blackface minstrelsy and the American working class.* Oxford: Oxford University Press.

Macklemore. Retrieved June 1, 2013 from http://en.wikipedia.org/wiki/Macklemore—cite_note-billboard1–3.

Madsen, L. (2009) "Interactional renegotiations of educational discourses in recreational learning contexts." *Linguistics and Education* 22: 53–67.

Mailer, N. (1959) *Advertisements for myself*. New York: Signet.

Maira, S. (1999) "Identity dub: The paradoxes of an Indian American youth subculture (New York mix)." *Cultural Anthropology* 14(1): 29–60.

Maira, S. (2000) "Henna and hip hop: The politics of cultural production and the work of cultural studies." *Journal of Asian American Studies* 3(3): 329–69.

Major, C. (1994) *Juba to Jive: A dictionary of African-American slang*. New York: Viking.

McCrum, R., Cran, W., and MacNeil, R. (1986) *The story of English*. New York: Viking.

McLeod, K. (1999) "Authenticity within hip-hop and other cultures threatened with assimilation." *The Journal of Communication* 49(4): 134–50.

McRobbie, A. (1996) "Different, youthful, subjectivities." *The post-colonial question*. I. Chambers and L. Curti, eds. London: Routledge. 30–46.

Mendoza-Denton, N. (1997) "Chicana/Mexicana identity and linguistic variation: An ethnographic and sociolinguistic study of gang affiliation in an urban high school." Ph.D. Dissertation, Stanford University.

Mitchell, T. (1996) *Popular music and local identity: Rock, pop and rap in Europe and Oceania*. Leicester: Leicester University Press.

Mitchell-Kernan, C. (1972) "Signifying and marking: Two Afro-American speech acts." *Directions in sociolinguistics: The ethnography of communication*. J. Gumperz and D. Hymes, eds. New York: Holt, Rinehart and Winston. 161–79.

Mitchell-Kernan, C. (1974) *Language behavior in a Black urban community*. Volume 2. Berkeley: University of California Press.

Mobilization to Free Mumia Abu-Jamal. Retrieved August 1 (2003) from: www.free-mumia.org/

Morgan, M. (1993) 'Hip-hop hooray! The linguistic production of identity,' paper presented at Annual Meeting of the American Anthropological Association, Washington, DC, November 1993.

Morgan, M. (1994) "Theories and politics in African American English." *Annual Review of Anthropology* 23: 325–45.

Morgan, M. (1996) "Redefining 'Language in the Inner City': Adolescents, media and urban space." *Proceedings of SALSA Conference* 4: 13–25.

Morgan, M. (1998) "More than a mood or an attitude: Discourse and verbal genres in African American English." *African American English*. S. Mufwene, J. R. Rickford, G. Bailey, and J. Baugh, eds. New York: Routledge. 251–81.

Morgan, M. (2001) "Nuthin" but a G Thang: Grammar and language ideology in hip-hop identity." *Sociocultural and historical contexts of African American English*. S. L. Lanehart, ed. Athens: University of Georgia Press. 187–210.

Morgan, M. (2002) *Reading between the lines: language, discourse and power in African American culture*. Cambridge: Cambridge University Press.

New York Times. Borough Park, Brooklyn, NY: Data Report. Retrieved December 14, (2009) from http://realestate.nytimes.com/community/borough-park-brooklyn-ny-usa/demographics

New York Times. Brighton Beach, Brooklyn, NY: Data Report. Retrieved December 14, (2009) from http://realestate.nytimes.com/community/brighton-beach-brooklyn-ny-usa/demographics

New York Times. Harlem, NY: Data Report. Retrieved December 14, (2009) from http://realestate.nytimes.com/community/harlem-ny-usa/demographics

Newman, M. (2001) "I represent me: Identity construction in a teenage rap crew." *Texas Linguistic Forum* 44(2): 388–400.

Newman, M. (2004) "Rap as literacy: A genre analysis of hip-hop ciphers." *Text* 25(3): 399–436.

Nguyen, J. (2006) *The changing social and linguistic orientation of the African American middle class*. Ph.D. Dissertation, University of Michigan.

Nortier, J. (2001) *Murks en straattaal. Vriendschap en taalgebruik onder jongeren*. Amsterdam: Prometheus.

Nortier, J. (2008) "Ethnolects? The emergence of new varieties among adolescents." *International Journal of Bilingualism* 12(1–2): 1–5.

Nortier, J. and Dorleijn, M. (2008) "A Moroccan accent in Dutch: A sociocultural style restricted to the Moroccan community?" *International Journal of Bilingualism* 12(1–2): 125–42.

Ochs, E. (1991) "Indexing gender." *Rethinking context: Language as an interactive phenomenon*. Alessandro Duranti and Charles Goodwin, eds. Cambridge: Cambridge Univ. Press. 335–58.

Olivo, W. (2001) "Phat lines: Spelling conventions in rap music." *Written Language and Literacy* 4(1): 67–85.

Omi, M. and Winant, H. (1994) *Racial formations in the United States: From the 1960s to the 1990s*. (2nd ed.) New York: Routledge.

Opsahl, T. and Røyneland, U. (2008) 'Hip hop and the formation of a Norwegian multiethnolectal speech style,' paper presented at Jugendsprache, The Fifth International Conference on Youth Language, Copenhagen, March 2008.

Pennycook, A. (2007) *Global Englishes and transcultural flows*. London: Routledge.

Perkins, W. (1996) *Droppin'science: Critical essays on rap music and hip hop culture*. Philadelphia: Temple University Press.

Perry, I. (2004) *Prophets of the hood: Politics and poetics in hip hop*. Durham: Duke University Press.

Perry, P. (2002) *Shades of white: White kids and racial identities in high school*. Durham: Duke University Press.

Potter, R. (1995) *Spectacular vernaculars: Hip-hop and the politics of postmodernism*. Albany: State University of New York Press.

Purnell, T. (2010) "The vowel phonology of urban southeastern Wisconsin." *AAE speakers and their participation in local sound changes: A comparative study*. M. Yeager-Dror and E. Thomas, eds. Publication of the American Dialect Society, 94. Durham: Duke University Press. 191–217.

Purnell, T., Idsardi, W., and Baugh, J. (1999) "Perceptual and phonetic experiments on American English dialect identification." *Journal of Language and Social Psychology* 18(1): 10–30.

Purnell, T. and Yaeger-Dror, M. (2010) "Accommodative tendencies in multidialect communication." *Journal of English Linguistics* 38(3): 187–92.

Queen, R. (2006) "Phrase-final intonation in narratives told by Turkish-German bilinguals." *International Journal of Bilingualism* 10(2): 153–78.

Queens: Data Report. Retrieved December 1, 2008: http://realestate.nytimes.com/community/far-rockaway-queens-ny-usa/demographics).

Quist, P. (2000) "New Copenhagen 'Multi-ethnolect.' Language use among adolescents in linguistic and culturally heterogeneous settings." *Danske Talesprog 1*. Institut for Dansk Dialektforskning. Copenhagen: C.A. Reitzels Forlag. 143–212.

Quist, P. (2008). "Sociolinguistic approaches to multiethnolect: Language variety and stylistic practice." *International Journal of Bilingualism* 12(1–2): 43–61.

Rampton, B. (1995) *Crossing: Language and ethnicity among adolescents*. New York: Longman.

Rampton, B. (1996) 'Language crossing and ethnicity in sociolinguistics,' paper presented to the NWAV XXV conference, Las Vegas, Nevada, October 1996.

Rampton, B. (2006) *Language in late modernity: Interaction in an urban school.* Cambridge: Cambridge University Press.

Rampton, B. (2010) "Social class and sociolinguistics." *Applied Linguistics Review* 1: 1–22.

Rebensdorf, A. (1996) "Representing the real: Exploring appropriations of hip-hop culture in the internet and Nairobi." Senior undergraduate thesis, Lewis and Clark University. Retrieved May 1, (2006) from www.lclark.edu/~soan/alicia/reB.sdorf.101.html

Rickford, J. (1999) *African American Vernacular English.* Oxford: Blackwell.

Rickford, J. and Rickford, A. (1999) [1973] "Cut-eye and suck-teeth: African words and gestures in New World guise." *African American Vernacular English.* J. Rickford, ed. Oxford: Blackwell. 157–73.

Rickford, J. and Rickford, R. (2000) *Spoken soul. The story of Black English.* New York: J. Wiley and Sons.

Rivera, R. (2003). *New York Ricans from the hip hop zone.* New York: MacMillan.

Roediger, D. (2006) *How Jews became White Folks and what that says about race in America.* New York: Basic Books.

Root, D. (1997) " 'White Indians': Appropriation and the politics of display." *Borrowed power: Essays on cultural appropriation.* B. Ziff and P. Rao, eds. New Brunswick: Rutgers University Press. 225–33.

Rose, T. (1994) *Black noise: Rap music and black culture in contemporary America.* Hanover: Wesleyan University Press.

Roth-Gordon, J. (2008) "Conversational sampling, race trafficking, and the invocation of the Gueto in Brazilian hip hop." *Global linguistic flows: Hip hop cultures, youth identities, and the politics of language.* H. S. Alim, A. Ibrahim, and A. Pennycook, eds. New York: Routledge. 63–77.

Rubin, M. (2000) "The sins and sorrows of Marshall Mathers." *Spin.* August. 90–8.

Sales, N. J. (1996) "Teenage gangland." *New York Magazine.* December 16. 32–9.

Samuel, A., Croal, N. and Gates, D. (2000) "Battle for the soul of hiphop." *Newsweek*, October 9. 58–65.

Samuels, D. (1991) "The rap on rap: The 'Black music' that isn't either." *Rap on rap: straight up talk on hip-hop culture.* A. Sexton, ed. New York: Delta. 241–52.

Samuels, R. (2012). "In the wake of Trayvon Martin's death, the hoodie takes on a greater meaning." March 29. *The Washington Post.* Retrieved from www.washingtonpost.com/blogs/therootdc/post/in-the-wake-of-trayvon-martins-death-the-hoodie-takes-on-a-greater-meaning/2012/03/29/gIQA44hHjS_blog.html

Scanlon, M. and Wassink, A. B. (2010) "African American English in urban Seattle: Accommodation and intra-speaker variation in the Pacific Northwest." *American Speech* 25(10): 205–24.

Seabrook, J. (2000) *Nobrow: The culture of marketing. The marketing of culture.* New York: Knopf.

Shohat, E. (1995) "Performing in the postcolony: The plays of Mustapha Matura." *Late imperial culture.* R. De La Campa, E. A. Kaplan, and M. Sprinker, eds. London: Verso. 166–78.

Slomanson, P. and Newman, M. (2004) "Peer group identification and variation in New York Latino English laterals." *English World-Wide* 25(2): 199–216.

Simeziane. S. (2010) "Roma rap and the Black train: Minority voices in Hungarian hip hop." *Languages of global hip hop.* M. Terkourafi, ed. New York: Continuum. 96–119.

Smith, M. J. and Wood, A. F. (eds.). (2003) *Survivor lessons: Essays on communication and reality television.* Jefferson: McFarland and Company.

Smitherman, G. (1994) *Black talk: Words and phrases from the Hood to the Amen Corner*. Boston: Houghton Mifflin.

Smitherman, G. (1997) "The Chain remain the same: Communicative practices in the Hip Hop Nation." *Journal of Black Studies* 28(1): 3–25.

Smitherman, G. (2000) *Talkin that talk: Language, culture, and education in African America*. New York: Routledge.

Smitherman, G. (2006) *Word from the mother: Language and African Americans*. New York: Routledge.

Spady, J., Lee, C., and Alim, H. S. (1999) *Street conscious rap*. Philadelphia: Black History Museum/Umum Loh Publishers.

Sparks, C. (2007) "Reality TV: the *Big Brother* phenomenon." *International Socialism* 114. Retrieved December 1, (2008) from www.isj.org.uk/index.php4?id=314 andissue=114

Spears, A. (1998) "African-American language use: Ideology and so-called obscenity." *African American English*. W. Mufwene, J. Rickford, G. Bailey, and J. Baugh, eds. New York: Routledge. 226–50.

Staples, B. (1995) "The politics of gangster rap." *Rap on rap: Straight up talk on hip-hop culture*. A. Sexton, ed. New York: Delta. 78–80.

Strand, T., Wroblewski, M., and Good, M. K. (2010) "Words, woods, woyds: Variation and accommodation in Schwar realization among African American, White, and Houma men in southern Louisiana." *Journal of English Linguistics* 38(3): 211–29.

Strauss, N. (1999) "A land with rhythm and beats for all." *New York Times*. August 22. Retrieved July 11, (2013) from www.nytimes.com/1999/08/22/arts/music-the-hip-hop-nation-whose-is-it-a-land-with-rhythm-and-beats-for-all.html?pagewanted=all&src=pm

Sweetland, J. (1998) 'Beyond crossing: AAVE in informal interaction between white and black friends,' paper presented at the annual meeting of the New Ways of Analyzing Variation conference, University of Georgia, Athens. October 1998.

Sweetland, J. (2002) "Unexpected but authentic use of an ethnically marked dialect." *Journal of Sociolinguistics* 6(4): 514–36.

Touré. (1999) "In the end, Black men must lead." *New York Times*. August 22. 2: 1, 28.

Trechter, S. and Bucholtz, M. (2001) "Introduction: White noise." *Journal of Linguistic Anthropology* 11(1): 3–21.

Trudgill, P. (1983) "Acts of conflicting identity. The sociolinguistics of British pop-song pronunciation." *On dialect. Social and geographical perspectives*. P. Trudgill, ed. Oxford: Blackwell. 141–60.

Tupuola, A. (2000) 'To be ethnic is to be cool—the Pasifika Flavour in New Zealand: A cultural renaissance of passing trend?' paper presented at the Symposium on Asian/Pacific American Youth Culture, New York University, April 2000.

Universal Zulu Nation. Retrieved August 1, (2002) from www.zulunation.com/

Urban Dictionary. (n.d.) Retrieved May 1, (2006) from www.urbandictionary.com

Urciuoli, B. (1991) "The political topography of Spanish and English: The view from a New York Puerto Rican community." *American Ethnologist* 18: 295–310.

U.S. Census. (2000) State and county Quickfacts: New York City, N.Y. Retrieved December 14, (2009) from http://quickfacts.census.gov

Wacquant, L. (1993) "Banlieues françaises et ghetto noir américain. Eléments de comparaison sociologique." *Racisme et modernité*. M. Wieviorka, ed. Paris: La Découverte.

Walcott. R. 1995. *Performing the postmodern: Black Atlantic rap and identity in North America*. Ph.D. dissertation. The Ontario Institute for Studies in Education, University of Toronto.

Watt, D., Llamas, C., Johnson, D. E. (2010) "Levels of linguistic accommodation across a national border." *Journal of English Linguistics*, 38(3): 270–89.

Weldon, T. (2004) 'African American English and the middle classes: Exploring the other end of the continuum,' paper presented at New Ways of Analyzing Variation, Ann Arbor, Michigan, September-October 2004.

White, M. (2008) "The (Black) boy shuffle: Internalizing, externalizing, and naturalizing the Black male body double." *Journal of Popular Music Studies* 20(1): 44–78.

White, R. (2006) "Behind the mask: Eminem and postindustrial minstrelsy." *Journal of American Culture* 25(1): 65–97.

Wimsatt, U. (1994) *Bomb the suburbs*. Chicago: The Subway and Elevated Press Company.

Wolfe, T. (1970) *Radical Chic and Mau-Mauing the flak catchers*. New York: Farrar, Straus and Giroux.

Wolfram, W. (1969) *A sociolinguistic description of Detroit Negro speech*. Arlington: Center for Applied Linguistics.

Wolfram, W. (1974) *Sociolinguistic aspects of assimilation: Puerto Rican English in New York City*. Washington, DC: Center for Applied Linguistics.

Wolfram, W. and Fasold, R. W. (1974). *The study of social dialects in American English*. Englewood Cliffs: Prentice Hall.

Wray, M. (2006). *Not quite white: White trash and the boundaries of whiteness*. Durham: Duke University Press.

Yaeger-Dror, M. (ed.). (1992a) "Communicative accommodation: A new perspective on 'hypercorrect' speech." Special double issue editor for *Language and Communication* 12(3–4): 181–358.

Yaeger-Dror, M. (1992b) "Introduction to communicative accommodation: A new perspective on 'hypercorrect' speech." *Language and Communication* 12(3–4): 181–92.

Zentella, A. (1999) *Growing up bilingual*. Oxford: Blackwell.

Ziff, B. and Rao, P. (1997) *Borrowed power: Essays on cultural appropriation*. New Brunswick: Rutgers University Press.

Index

Page numbers in italics refer to topics in tables.